ECONOMY, CULTURE AND SOCIETY

THEORIZING **SOCIETY**

Series editor: Larry Ray

Published titles:
Mary Evans: *Gender and Social Theory*
Barry Smart: *Economy, Culture and Society*

ECONOMY, CULTURE AND SOCIETY
A sociological critique of neo-liberalism

Barry Smart

Open University Press
Buckingham · Philadelphia

Open University Press
Celtic Court
22 Ballmoor
Buckingham
MK18 1XW

email: enquiries@openup.co.uk
world wide web: www.openup.co.uk

and
325 Chestnut Street
Philadelphia, PA 19106, USA

First Published 2003

A catalogue record of this book is available from the British Library

ISBN   0 335 20910 6 (pbk)   0 335 20911 4 (hbk)

Library of Congress Cataloging-in-Publication Data
Smart, Barry.
  Economy, culture, and society : a sociological critique of neo-liberalism /
Barry Smart.
      p. cm. – (Theorizing society)
  Includes bibliographical references and index.
  ISBN 0-335-20911-4 – ISBN 0-335-20910-6 (pbk.)
    1. Economics–Sociological aspects. I. Title. II. Series.
HM548 .S585 2003
306.3–dc21
                                                                    2002074953

Typeset by Graphicraft Limited, Hong Kong
Printed in Great Britain by Biddles Limited, Guildford and King's Lynn

CONTENTS

SERIES EDITOR'S FOREWORD

Sociology is reflexively engaged with the object of its study, society. In the wake of the rapid and profound social changes of the later twentieth century, it is important to question whether our theoretical frames of reference are appropriate for these novel configurations of culture, economy and society. Sociologists further need to ask whether recent theoretical preoccupations – for example with the 'cultural turn', post-modernism, deconstruction, globalization and identity adequately grasp social processes in the Millennium. One central issue here is the relationship between contemporary social problems and theories on the one hand and the classical heritage of Marx, Durkheim, Weber and Simmel on the other. Sociology is still reluctant to forget its founders and the relevance of the classical tradition is both powerful and problematic. It is powerful because the classics constitute a rich source of insights, concepts and analyses that can be deployed and reinterpreted to grasp current problems. But it is problematic because the social world of the classics is largely that of industrial, imperial and high bourgeois European societies prior to the First World War. How do we begin to relate the concepts formed in this milieu to the concerns of the globalized social world that is post-colonial, post-industrial and has seen the rise and collapse of Soviet socialism? Moreover, while it would not be true to say that classical theories ignored issues of gender, they did presuppose a social world in which relations were highly gendered and to some extent at least inscribed within 'nature'. How does sociology reconfigure the relations between gender, identity and 'nature' in ways that disrupt attempts to naturalize social difference, yet avoid simplistic polarization? These are some of the major challenges for sociology that this series, Theorizing Society, aims to address.

This series intends to map out the ways in which social theory is being transformed and how contemporary issues have emerged. Each book in the series offers a concise and up-to-date overview of the principle ideas, innovations and theoretical concepts in relation to its topic. The series is designed to provide a review of recent developments in social theory, offering a comprehensive collection of introductions to major theoretical issues. The focus of individual books is organized around topics which reflect the major areas of teaching and research in contemporary social theory, including modernity, post-modernism, structuralism and post-structuralism; cultural theory; globalization; feminism and sexuality; memory, identity and social solidarity. While being accessible to undergraduates these books allow authors to develop personal and programmatic statements about the state and future development of theoretically defined fields.

Barry Smart's *Economy, Culture and Society* addresses the key issues identified in this series. Smart's central focus is the contribution classical and contemporary social analysts have made to an understanding of significant features of economic life as well as the respects in which relations between economic, cultural and social processes have been transformed. Prior to the separation between sociology and political economy early in the twentieth century, sociological theory addressed the limitations of narrowly economic approaches, especially those that envisaged the market abstracted from other social relations. In contrast to these abstractions, classical sociology theorized economic life as embedded within a broader framework of institutions and social relations. Thus Comte thought economics was too abstract; Durkheim wrote of the non-contractual bases of contract; Marx regarded the apparent autonomy of the market as a fetishistic illusion; Simmel regarded money as an expression of the stylization of culture. Weber shared this broad and historical view of the integration of economic and social analysis, reflecting the influential German Historical School. One of the intentions of his Protestant Ethic study was to show that rational economic calculation was a historically specific form of behaviour that emerged from a particular conjunction of economic and cultural circumstances.

Smart begins his analysis with discussion of the classical relationship between sociology and economics tracing their separation during the first three decades of the twentieth century. Noting, however, that during the closing decades of the last century a new economic sociology began to emerge, he proceeds to elaborate on the relations between economic, cultural and social processes. He proceeds through a discussion of Polanyi to analyse more recent economic thought, notably the emergence of neo-liberalism and the transition from Fordism to post-Fordism and globalized capitalism. Multinational capital has brought a further shift though, to bring to dominance cultures of consumption and with this, attention to the impact of culture on the market. Developing this analysis, Smart undertakes an extensive theorization of the relations between culture and economy showing that while consumption is vital to economic and cultural capitalism, it can be properly understood only in the context of productive forces. This has implications for the sociological understanding of the market and neo-liberal claims for its autonomy from broader social and institutional processes. Developing a sociological critique of neo-liberalism Smart shows that with the development a neo-liberal global capitalism there has been a marked acceleration in affluence in private goods which has been paralleled by a rapid deterioration in public services and protection against the market. The uneven effects of global capitalism have created growing disparities both between and within countries along with new exclusions and social imbalances. Not only this, but the dominance of neo-liberal ideology has forgotten one of the central insights of sociological theory; namely that economic practices and institutions are themselves embedded in wider social, cultural and institutional relations. A crucial conclusion to be drawn from this is that the alleged 'inevitability' of the 'laws' of the market is a myth that needs to be challenged.

Economy, Culture and Society aims to nurture a return to the analysis of economic life in sociology. It demonstrates that economic logic is a dominant feature of modern social life and that an analytic readjustment in social and cultural analysis is overdue. One of the more important tasks of social theory is to expose the fragile foundations of 'freeing the market' and the social consequences of its implication. In order to properly address contemporary social and political issues we need to readdress neglect of economy in the recent 'cultural turn' in the social sciences. While being sensitive to the cultural dynamics of capitalism and indeed the importance of representation in social life, we should not fall into the trap of neglecting the economy as a major form of structuration in contemporary society. Throughout his discussion Smart maintains a dialogue between contemporary theories and the classical tradition, showing the continuing relevance of the latter for the former. Smart brings fresh insight to this central issue in sociology and for this reason *Economy, Culture and Society* will make an important contribution not only to the sociology of economic life but also to understanding the core theoretical challenges to sociology in the early twenty-first century.

Larry Ray
Professor of Sociology
University of Kent

ACKNOWLEDGEMENTS

I would like to thank Larry Ray, Bryan Turner and Doug Kellner for their constructive comments on the manuscript. The text has undoubtedly benefited from their advice and suggestions. I would also like to acknowledge the contribution of the reviewers of the original proposal, William Outhwaite, Andrew Sayer and John Scott, who drew my attention to a number of important issues and encouraged me to add an additional chapter.

I would like to thank Justin Vaughan and Miriam Selwyn of Open University Press for the efficient way in which they have dealt with the production of the book.

CHAPTER 1

SOCIOLOGICAL REASON AND ECONOMIC LIFE

Introduction: on sociology and the economic ordering of things

Sociology developed in substantial part through a critical engagement with political economy, demonstrating that government or state rests upon 'an institutional infrastructure of civil society' and that economic life and market relations are embedded in 'a broad institutional and normative framework' (Giddens 1987: 37). The relationship between economy and society is particularly prominent in the works of those thinkers accorded the status 'classical sociologists'. One important early legacy of this aspect of the development of sociology was the constitution of a 'tradition of economic sociology' (Martinelli and Smelser 1990). This tradition of inquiry has been identified as a part of economics, a part of sociology, and finally as lying somewhere between the two (Zafirovski 1999).

Sociology emerged within the developing modern field of knowledge through a complex, dual process of differentiation. A potential field of study emerged in the aftermath of the French Revolution and with the development of industrial society and an associated process of differentiation of economic and social structures and practices (Foucault 1973; Martinelli and Smelser 1990). The transformations in social and political life occasioned by these historic events undoubtedly gave rise to practical problems and requirements to which modern social sciences, including both economics and sociology, would claim to be able to provide answers. However, if the emergence of the social sciences was in good part occasioned by the consequences of pervasive transformations in social and economic life, an adequate explanation of their development has also to consider transformations in the order of knowledge that constituted their conditions of possibility. Addressing the question of the emergence of human sciences in the course of the nineteenth century, Michel Foucault argues that it is necessary to recognize the way in which 'the epistemological field became fragmented' (1973: 346). In a sense, Foucault might be regarded as revisiting and reaffirming, albeit with very different concepts and aims, Emile Durkheim's (1984) earlier analysis of the problem of anomie associated with the modern division of labour within knowledge.

Durkheim noted how the unity of science fragmented as specialization increased. Analysts in different fields became increasingly isolated from one another and little if any attention was devoted to the issue of the relationship between distinctive fields and associated studies. In consequence, 'carved up into a host of detailed studies that have no link with one another' (Durkheim 1984: 294), knowledge separated into segments became inadequate to the objects of study. This is particularly evident in what Durkheim (1984: 304) terms the field of the moral and social sciences where 'the jurist, the psychologist, the anthropologist, the economist, the statistician, the linguist, the historian – all these go about their investigations as if the various orders of facts they are studying formed so many independent worlds'. Durkheim adds that in reality the orders of facts studied are closely interrelated and that the same should hold for the corresponding scientific fields. A close interlocking relationship between the moral and social sciences has tended not to emerge as the example of the rather disconnected relationship between economics and sociology serves to confirm.

In his account, Foucault offers a detailed discussion of the respects in which the modern epistemological field differs from its predecessor ('the Classical period') and remarks that the modern form of knowledge cannot be 'ordered in accordance with the ideal of a perfect mathematicization' (1973: 346). Rather, the modern configuration of knowledge is represented, through a spatial analogy, as an epistemological trihedron. Along the three dimensions of this spatial figure lie the mathematical and physical sciences ('order is always a deductive and linear linking together of evident or verified propositions'); the sciences of linguistics, biology and economics ('that proceed by relating discontinuous but analogous elements in such a way that they are then able to establish causal relations and structural constants between them'); and finally philosophical reflection (Foucault 1973: 347). It is within the volume of space defined by these three dimensions that Foucault suggests that human sciences like sociology belong, loosely situated in relation to all the other forms of knowledge. It is this location that explains their precariousness and uncertainty as sciences.

A number of significant differences between sociology and economics are implicit in Foucault's discussion. For example, he argues that the first two dimensions identified above define a common plane, 'a field of application of mathematics to these empirical sciences, or as the domain of the mathematicizable in linguistics, biology and economics' (1973: 347). These sciences also form a common plane with philosophical reflection. It is here that issues which have arisen in the particular empirical domains of language, life and labour are 'transposed into the philosophical dimension' and ultimately into 'regional ontologies which attempt to define what life, labour and language are in their own being' (1973: 347). Lastly, the combination of the mathematical disciplines and philosophy defines another common plane – that of the formalization of thought.

Drawing on Foucault's spatial model of the modern epistemological configuration it can be argued that the development of modern economics has primarily taken place on the first and third planes – that is, in and through a process of mathematization and formalization. As numerous analysts have noted, modern economics is inclined to present mathematical model-building as the objective, the aim being to make economics a universal science just like physics (Bell 1990; Solow 1990). This preoccupation with 'theoretically oriented mathematical models of rational individual maximization' (Davern and Eitzen 1995: 79) has had considerable consequences, for economists (but importantly not only economists) have tended to regard their model(s) as the world. As Daniel Bell (1990: 219) cogently observes:

> economics detaches itself from institutions. What's involved is a shift from 'moral economy' to 'political economy' to 'economics'. And by detaching itself from institutions, economics follows the model of classical mechanics in the sense that you don't deal with concrete bodies but with abstract properties ... Now, in detaching itself from institutions in this way, neo-classical economics becomes a very powerful body of concepts. The real problem is the way back. How do you get back from the model, with its self-contained system of premises, and apply it to the real world?

Instead of treating the economic model as a basis against which to compare practices and processes taking place in the world, the model is taken to be the world; it is assumed to be how people actually behave (Akerlof 1990: 70).

In an earlier comparable discussion, Schumpeter attempted to draw a distinction between the fields of economics and what was depicted as an emerging economic oriented sociology. However, the description of economic analysis as dealing with 'questions [of] how people behave at any time and what the economic effects are they produce by so behaving' (Schumpeter 1954b: 21) avoids an important issue: specifically, the way in which particular 'unrealistic assumptions' (Smelser 1990) about conduct are deployed in analysis. Ideas about 'constant preferences ... maximizing behaviour [and] market coordination of social participants' (Davern and Eitzen 1995: 80) are deployed within models of behaviour that subsequently come to be regarded within the discipline, (but not only within the discipline) as the way people actually do, or perhaps worse, should behave. While Schumpeter is too generous towards economics, his remarks on economic sociology do not do sufficient justice to the range of concerns that may be addressed in that particular field of inquiry. Economic sociology does not only deal with the issue of how people 'came to behave as they do' (Schumpeter 1954b: 21). Fortunately, given the tendency to conflate model and world in economics, it also studies how people actually behave, how people conduct themselves in different institutional settings. And, in addition, how understandings of situations not only inform and shape conduct, and thereby, to a degree, the consequences of conduct, but also contribute to the constitution of the very realities they claim to represent.

Sociology, economics and the question of representation

Elaborating further on the issue of differences between the science of economics and the science of sociology, Foucault remarks that even though economics has 'recourse to human behaviour patterns . . . [it itself] is . . . not a human science' (1973: 352). The crucial difference between the two forms of analysis rests with the different significance to be accorded to the notion of representation. In the case of economics, if there is a recourse to representations – 'interest, the search for maximum profit, the tendency to accumulate savings' – Foucault comments that they are utilized as the 'requisite of a function . . . within human activity' (1973: 352). In contrast, within a *human* science such as sociology, the issue of representation is central, for the object of analysis is not

> that man who since the dawn of the world . . . is doomed to work; it is that being who, from within the forms of production by which his whole existence is governed, forms the representation of those needs, of the society by which, with which, or against which he satisfies them, so that upon that basis he can finally provide himself with a representation of economics itself.
>
> (Foucault 1973: 353)

In the human sciences the issue of representation is pivotal. The human sciences provide an analysis that extends from, and encompasses us as, living, working, speaking beings, to what makes it possible for us to know, and indeed what we consider we know, about life, labour and its laws, and language. As such the human sciences are 'in a position of duplication', they are 'in a "meta-epistemological" position' (Foucault 1973: 354, 355). What this means is that the conduct, behaviour, attitudes, gestures and comments of subjects studied in work, production, consumption and exchange are already informed and guided by, if they do not actually constitute, representations of economic life. In sum, for Foucault the 'sociological region' of the human sciences is

> situated where the labouring, producing, and consuming individual offers himself a representation of the society in which this activity occurs, of the groups and individuals among which it is divided, of the imperatives, sanctions, rites, festivities, and beliefs by which it is upheld or regulated.
>
> (1973: 355)

In so far as representation is not simply an object but the very basis on which the human sciences are possible, Foucault argues that two significant consequences follow. First, there is no way around representation and second, rather than following the attempts of the empirical sciences to enhance precision and the effectiveness of generalizations, the human sciences are constantly involved in 'demystifying themselves' (Foucault 1973: 364). They are also involved in demystifying other domains of inquiry and this is particularly evident in relation to sociologically informed reflections on economic life.

It follows that, significant as the criticisms of economics outlined above by Bell and Akerlof might seem, they are in need of substantial qualification because the relationship between 'representation' and 'reality' is more complicated than is recognized. It is not so much that the criticisms of economics for detaching itself from institutions, or for operating with an inadequate conception of how people behave, are inappropriate or incorrect. But rather, that in so far as particular representations of economic life enshrined in economic discourse are considered, to effectively represent the way things are they are likely to have real effects, or perhaps more appropriately, effects on and in the realities they claim to be about. If economic representations are regarded as 'reality', as telling it like it is, then relevant actions of convinced agents, whether governments, corporations and/or individuals, will be (in)formed and guided by the assumptions, values, ideas and expectations intrinsic to and inscribed within that discourse. In short, in so far as economic discourse defines itself, and is defined, as real, as providing a scientific description of reality, it has real consequences, indeed very significant consequences in, on and for the social and economic order(ing)s of everyday life.

However, there is more to say about the issue of the articulation of representation(s) and reality. It is not simply that social, economic and political discourses have consequences in and on everyday life – rather, they contribute to the constitution of reality. They help make the world. In other words, what is known and experienced as social reality is 'to a great extent representation or the product of representation' (Bourdieu 1990: 53). The accounts, explanations and theories of the social or economic analyst contribute to our sense of the world, to what the world is for us. The knowledge derived from the social sciences circulates in and out of the very domains of social life that are the focus of analysis, constructing and reconstructing both our sense of and the reality of those domains in the process (Giddens 1990: 15–16, 38–9, 177). Economics as a discipline and the economy as a form of life are closely articulated and it is 'meaningless to distinguish between an existing reality (economy) and the analytical discourse explaining it. Social science . . . actively participates in shaping the thing it describes' (Callon 1998: 28).

Two relatively brief examples will help to clarify this particular feature. Focusing specifically on economic discourse, Giddens notes that notions like

> 'capital', 'investment', 'markets', 'industry' and many others, in their modern senses, were elaborated as part of the early development of economics as a distinct discipline in the eighteenth and early nineteenth centuries. These concepts, and empirical conclusions linked to them, were formulated in order to analyse changes involved in the emergence of modern institutions. But they could not, and did not, remain separated from the activities and events to which they related. They have become integral to what 'modern economic life' actually is and inseparable from it.
> (1990: 41; see also 1987: 198)

Such concepts are not simply tools for understanding; rather they actively constitute conduct and contribute to its rationales. In short, there is 'continual mutual involvement between economic discourse and the activities to which it refers' (Giddens 1990: 41). Or, in the terms preferred by Callon, 'economics, in the broad sense of the term, performs, shapes and formats the economy' (1998: 2).

The second example also concerns the discourse of economics and begins to address the respects in which neo-liberalism is 'reflexively tied to what it is about' (Giddens 1987: 198). In the course of a series of critical reflections on neo-liberalism, the French sociologist Pierre Bourdieu provides an argument that reveals how a particularly dominant economic discourse contributes to the creation of conditions that effectively serve as 'the means of making itself true' (1998: 95). Critically questioning the status of neo-liberal free-market economic discourse as simply a 'scientific description of reality', Bourdieu remarks that it is more appropriate to regard it as a 'political programme' predicated on a process of abstraction that has at its centre an assumption of 'individual rationality'. Crucially omitted from this particular process of abstraction is any consideration of the

> economic and social conditions of rational dispositions (and in particular those of the calculating disposition applied to economic matters which is the basis of the neo-liberal view) and of

the economic and social structures which are the condition of their exercise, or, more precisely, of the production and reproduction of those dispositions and those structures.

(Bourdieu 1998: 95)

Elaborating on the respects in which neo-liberal economic discourse has the means of making itself true, Bourdieu describes the force of power relations with and through which it is articulated. Presented as a scientific discourse it has been adopted and 'converted into a political programme of action', the objective of which is the realization of the conditions necessary for the effective operation of the 'pure market' (Bourdieu 1998: 95–6). The neo-liberal programme influences and shapes the economic decisions of key players within the economy, particularly those whose interests it upholds. As a programme it 'tends overall to favour the separation between the economy and social realities and so to construct, in reality, an economic system corresponding to the theoretical description ... a kind of logical machine, which presents itself as a chain of constraints impelling the economic agents' (Bourdieu 1998: 96). What happens if those with economic and political influence – 'shareholders, financial operators, industrialists, conservative politicians or social democrats converted to the cosy capitulations of laissez-faire' (1998: 96) – take neo-liberal economic discourse to be an expression of the reality of economic life? Bourdieu's answer is that related programmes of political action effectively serve to contribute to forms of social and economic transformation that tend to give reality to what is scathingly described as the neo-liberal 'utopia'. In short, as another French analyst has noted in a discussion of wide-ranging transformations in the processes of legitimation of forms of knowledge, context control ' "reinforces" reality, and one's chances of being just and right increase accordingly' (Lyotard 1986: 47). The potential for powerful interests to produce proof through 'performativity' led Bourdieu to take issue with what he termed the 'new myths of our time' and Andre Gorz (1989) to develop a critique of economic reason.

In so far as an economic logic is now a dominant feature of modern social life, an analytic readjustment in the field of social and cultural analysis is overdue. An analytic reorientation is required that simultaneously recognizes the significance of culture, but redresses the relative neglect of economy that has accompanied the 'cultural turn' in social inquiry (Ray and Sayer 1999). Few, if any, would dispute that we 'live in a highly economized culture' (Sayer 1999: 53), a culture in which economic forms of life and an associated economic logic are prominent, if not paramount. Our way of life is one in which emphasis is placed on the calculating, rational, self-interested subject and a commercialized competitive individualism that is increasingly constitutive of thought and conduct in private and public life. *Homo economicus* is not a fiction, but 'exists in the form of many species' (Callon 1998: 51). The extent to which our culture has become economized is exemplified by the degree to which existence has 'accommodated to division of labour, class, commodification and instrumental rationality' (Sayer 1999: 53) and *homo capitalisticus* has become universal (Bourdieu 1993: 18).

An analytical concern with economic processes, with the broad issue of the relationship between economy and society, has had a substantial presence in the development of modern social theory. The articulation of economy, culture and society is at the centre of the work of those classical analysts like Marx, Simmel, Weber and Durkheim who contributed to the development of social theory. In many respects it is their early representations of the key features and powerful impact of the modern capitalist economy on social and cultural life that have continued to inform academic discussion and debate. Their analyses have constituted a benchmark against which to determine the significance of subsequent processes of social and economic transformation.

Classical analysts: Marx, Simmel, Durkheim and Weber

The writings of figures accorded prominence within the discourse of sociology, in particular such key thinkers as Max Weber, Emile Durkheim, Georg Simmel and Karl Marx, reveal analytic orientations and commitments ranging across a number of disciplines and substantive concerns. These thinkers had a common primary concern with achieving an understanding of the distinctive features of a new emerging form of life: modernity. They were also concerned with the impact of capitalist economic conditions on the organization and experience of forms of social and cultural life. In addition, their intellectual orientations and affinities varied considerably and extended well beyond the disciplinary field of sociology.

Karl Marx and capitalist economic life

In the case of Karl Marx, a thinker who does not directly address sociology, apart from a brief condemnation of Comte's 'trashy positivism' (Marx and Engels 1953: 210), the primary intellectual affinity is clearly with economics, although as has been widely acknowledged there is much of sociological relevance in Marx's writings (Bottomore 1979). The subsequent development of a tradition of Marxist informed sociology led to a plethora of analyses that ultimately subscribed, in one form or another, to the idea of the significant impact, if not the paramount influence, of economic factors on social life. Marx would probably not have approved of former American

President Bill Clinton but he would surely have agreed with the latter's public comment in the course of an electoral campaign in 1992 that the issue that matters most is the economy – 'It's the economy, stupid' (Elliott and Atkinson 1999: 143).

The continuing significance of Marx's contribution to our understanding of modern life is to be found in aspects of his analysis of the distinctive features of the capitalist mode of production and the impact of the associated process of modernization on other aspects of everyday life. Marx carefully identified the economic and social dimensions of capitalism, in particular the way in which the commodity form and commodity production, and the associated notion of exchange value, began to shape all other social relations. In a society in which exchange through the market has achieved dominance, social relations between people are increasingly likely to assume the form of economic transactions. For Marx, capitalism is a system that is based on the production and exchange of commodities in and through the market, a mode of production that has as its primary objective not the satisfaction of human need but the realization of profit or capital accumulation. What is produced, and how and when things are produced, are determined by market forces to which human subjects and activities are ultimately subordinated. It is the potential exchange value of goods and services, their values as commodities in the market, over and above any use value they may have for satisfying the needs or wants of people, that determines whether or not they are produced.

Subsequently, in the context of a more highly developed consumer orientated late capitalism, where the basic living needs and wants of a substantial majority may be readily satisfied, pursuit of the objective of increasing capital accumulation has led to the constitution of new markets. This has meant, among other things, that the process of production of goods and services has had to include the simultaneous production or creation of new wants and desires for the same. From this perspective individuals, social relationships and values are considered to have become increasingly subject to the exchange form, to have been reduced to the status of commodities, and thus to be available, on the market, for a price, to be bought and sold.

The bulk of Marx's work is concerned with identifying the structure and dynamic of modern capitalism, and the consequences that flow from the '[c]onstant revolutionizing of production, uninterrupted disturbance of all social conditions [and] everlasting uncertainty and agitation' (Marx and Engels [1848] 1968: 83) unleashed by it. There are profound passages on the development of the capitalist mode of production, specifically in relation to the increasing importance of science and technology as forces of production (Marx 1973: 704–6). In addition there are controversial observations on the subject of capitalism's probable development and possible fate. A distillation of many, if not all, of the key sociologically relevant themes in Marx's work may be found in the short text co-authored with Friedrich Engels under the title *The Communist Manifesto* (1968) to which I have already made an oblique reference. In a discussion of this historic text Joseph Schumpeter (1949) comments that the 'economic sociology of the *Manifesto* . . . is far more important than its economics proper' (1949: 204).

Schumpeter retrieves three particular sociologically relevant contributions from the text. These are the economic interpretation of history, the theory of social classes and the theory of the state – very familiar themes within Marxist sociology. The idea that significant aspects of transformations in social structure and cultural forms and practices may, in the final instance, be accounted for largely in terms of economic factors, processes and developments has been regarded as a distinctive feature of Marx's approach. The notion that economic processes and developments should be at the forefront of analysis has been vulnerable, ever since Marx first outlined his ideas, to the criticism that it risked diminishing the significance of social, cultural, political and legal structures and practices (Smart 1983). From the 1980s, concerns on this score contributed to analysts turning away from a focus on economy and towards questions of culture and discourse (Ray and Sayer 1999).

The 'cultural turn' in analysis constitutes more than a reaction against Marxist forms of analysis. It represents a response to the perceived transformed place and status of cultural forms and practices in modern society. To an extent, the cultural turn represents a long overdue analytic adjustment to the neglect of the significance of discourse and discursive practices in social life. It may also reflect the fact that 'material production is becoming secondary to a more strongly culturally inflected service economy' (Ray and Sayer 1999: 8), itself an important manifestation of a more widely transformed relationship between culture and economy. Paradoxically, the analytic 'turn away from economy to culture' (Ray and Sayer 1999: 21) coincided with increasing evidence of the growing significance of economic problems and practices in politics and everyday life. It is necessary and important to give due analytic consideration to the increasing significance of cultural forms and processes. But it is also vital not to neglect the economic dimension, particularly as it is in relation to the informational economy, consumption, marketing and branding that the growing significance of cultural forms and dynamics has become apparent (Lash and Urry 1994; Castells 1996; Klein 2001).

The second sociologically relevant theme identified is that of social class 'defined exclusively in economic terms' (Schumpeter 1949: 206), a conception of the social process that has been central to a Marxist analysis of social life. The notion that 'The history of all hitherto existing society is the history of class struggle' (Marx and Engels 1968: 79) constituted a novel formulation, one that effectively confirmed the specificity of a Marxist perspective. But it has also proven to be a problematic notion. Analysing the transformation of social life from the perspective of social class struggle has proven to be insightful, however it represents *a* history rather than *the* history. There are other significant social divisions and identities that are not readily subordinated to social class forms – for example, non-class social divisions deriving from differences of age, gender, ethnicity and sexuality. Relative neglect of these forms lent further weight to the argument for a cultural turn in social analysis and contributed to a 'shift from the "politics of distribution" to a new "politics of recognition" which is more cultural in character' (Ray and Sayer 1999: 18).

Alienton in liberal used form.

It has been suggested that an analytic preoccupation with class is no longer appropriate for understanding the nature and dynamic of contemporary social life, for individuals are no longer primarily engaged as producers or workers in contemporary society, but as consumers. Rather than continue to regard contemporary society as a 'producer society' ruled by a work ethic, Bauman has suggested that there has been a significant shift of emphasis towards consumption. The increasing engagement of individuals in society, 'primarily in their capacity as consumers' (1998b: 24), justifies the use of the term 'consumer society' to designate the 'deep and ubiquitous' differences that distinguish present-day society from earlier modern industrial capitalist forms of life. However, while individuals may now be engaged primarily as consumers rather than as producers, forms of inequality and poverty continue to have an impact on people's experiences as the welfare state is undermined and eroded by what Bauman describes as 'the pressure of consumer mentality' (1998b: 59). The status and condition of the public sector, of public provision and welfare within a neo-liberal capitalist consumer society is a key issue to which further consideration will be given in due course.

Postmodern impact.

The third sociologically relevant theme in Marx's work identified by Schumpeter is that of the state, in respect of which he remarks that 'Marx . . . hauled down this state from the clouds and into the sphere of realistic analysis' (1949: 209). However, a qualification is once again in order. While Marx might be credited with being 'the founder of modern political science', in so far as his analyses of the state conceptualize politics primarily in class terms, these same analyses have been described, in turn, as 'completely unrealistic and perfectly inadequate to account for the facts' (Schumpeter 1949: 209). Marx may have brought the state into focus as an object of inquiry, but Schumpeter argues that it remains for others to deliver realistic analyses. Schumpeter ([1918] 1954a) sought to outline some of the issues a realistic analysis ought to consider in a paper on the problems confronting the modern democratic state facing a capitalist economy and a culture of individualism. The historical context in which the paper was written (the close of the First World War) is one in which there existed competing diagnoses of the disorderly condition of economic life. On one side there were those advocating more economic freedom, and on the other were those calling for more protectionism and an administered economy. It was a setting in which the role of the state in the economic life of a developing modern capitalist society was quite clearly in question, a setting that led Schumpeter to reflect on the fiscal needs and policy of the state. More detailed consideration of Schumpeter's conception of the tax state is offered in Chapter 5.

Marx's broad critical analytical legacy is still present in contemporary social inquiry. In a wide-ranging analysis of the respects in which modern industrial capitalism was transformed in the latter part of the twentieth century, Scott Lash and John Urry ask, 'Who now reads Marx?' (1994: 1). In some respects the analysis that Marx provided of a developing nineteenth-century industrial capitalism might seem to be of questionable relevance for understanding present conditions. However, Lash and Urry provide a timely reminder to their readers that there is much more to Marx. In particular, Marx's critical reflections on modernity and his analysis of the process of capital circulation continue to inform understandings of the transformations associated with contemporary capitalism. To make sense of new forms of social and cultural life it is necessary to consider the impact of transformations in contemporary capitalism following the development of new 'economies of signs and space' and an increasing inter-penetration of culture and economy (Lash and Urry 1994: 64).

Marx's critical reflections on capitalist economic life continue to provide important resources for sociological analyses of contemporary conditions. What Jacques Derrida has hailed as the 'Marxist "spirit"' continues to be a source of inspiration for critical analysts, an inspiration for 'radical critique', for 'the critical idea or the questioning stance', if not 'a certain emancipatory ... affirmation' (1994: 85, 88, 89). The inspiration of the Marxist critique makes possible the problematizing of 'the State, of the nation-State, of national sovereignty' as well as 'the critique of the market, of the multiple logics of capital, and of that which links the State and international law to this market' (Derrida 1994: 94).

Georg Simmel on the modern economy and commodity culture

In the respective writings of Max Weber, Emile Durkheim and Georg Simmel the question of sociology – its subject matter, method and relationship to cognate fields of investigation – is explicitly addressed. In the case of Simmel, sociology represents merely one of a number of fields of intellectual interest, significant others including philosophy, social psychology and cultural criticism. Indeed it has been argued that for Simmel it was philosophy that constituted his life's task, with sociology representing merely a 'subsidiary discipline' (Frisby 1984: 25).

Notwithstanding the fact that Simmel regarded himself primarily as a philosopher, his sociological writings on processes of social differentiation and the development of forms of individuality, and his reflections on modern culture have led to him being accorded the status of a key sociologist. However, it is *The Philosophy of Money* (1990), a work that attempts to determine the impact of money and the modern money economy on social and cultural life, that has been identified as Simmel's most systematic analysis – a work that, until recently, has been relatively neglected within sociology (Frisby 1990: xxix). With the belated (re)generation of sociological interest in our 'highly economized culture' (Sayer 1999: 53) the value of Simmel's writings on the modern money economy and commodity culture for achieving an understanding of social life under conditions of capitalist modernity has begun to be more widely recognized (Frisby 1990, 1997; Turner 1999).

Simmel's study of money constitutes an analysis of one of the most important institutions of the modern economy. It is an analysis that explores the effect of the modern economy on social and cultural life and to that extent there are potentially interesting parallels to be drawn with the works of other classical figures like Marx (Simmel 1990: 56) and Weber (Frisby 1987; Turner 2000). Although in the Preface to *The Philosophy of Money* Simmel comments 'Not a single line of these investigations is meant to be a statement about economics (1990: 54), there is a great deal in his work that enhances our understanding of economic phenomena. The passages that follow the statement cited above make it clear that Simmel is approaching the subject of money and related 'economic' phenomena (value, purchase, exchange, production) from another perspective than economics. Simmel presents a philosophical study which acknowledges the multi-faceted character of phenomena, their complex preconditions in 'non-economic concepts and facts' and indeed their consequences for 'non-economic values and relationships' (p. 55). It is made clear that money serves as a convenient topic or means for exploring the relations that exist between 'economic affairs' and the more profound orders of human existence and history – 'ultimate values and things of importance in all that is human' (p. 55).

A broadly comparable recognition of the multi-faceted character of such phenomena is implied in the analyses of the forms of social suffering characteristic of late twentieth-century neo-liberal capitalist society provided by Pierre Bourdieu and his colleagues. At the forefront of their narrative is a critical consideration of the difficulties men and women have encountered as the economy of neo-liberalism ('belief in a free market, *laissez-faire* economics') has precipitated a retreat of the state. In the course of a discussion of the impact of the neo-liberal programme on state intervention, Bourdieu notes that the conventional 'division among disciplines – ethnology, sociology, history and economics – translates itself back into separated segments that are totally inadequate to the objects of study' (Bourdieu *et al.* 1999: 181, Note 1).

What emerges from Simmel's work is confirmation that it is necessary to retain the explanatory value of an analytic approach that reveals the extent to which economic life shapes and influences culture, but that it is also necessary to recognize that economic structures and practices emerge from, and are bound up with, cultural preconditions and values. In short, while it is necessary 'to construct a new storey beneath historical materialism', it is important to remember that in the analysis of economic, cultural and social forms of life the 'practice of cognition . . . must develop in infinite reciprocity' (1990: 56). In a sense, Simmel's caution concerning reciprocity can, in the current analytic context, be invoked in support of the call to redress the relative marginalization of economic matters in social analysis following the cultural turn (Ray and Sayer 1999).

Emile Durkheim and the social conditioning of economic life

While for Marx and Simmel it is economic analysis and philosophy that are the more prominent analytic preoccupations in their respective writings, for Durkheim the discipline of sociology is accorded far greater significance and is located at the centre of his work. In his attempt to establish a distinctive place for sociology, Durkheim draws distinctions between psychology and sociology in terms of both subject matter and method. However, while a distinction between social and psychological facts represents an important focus of Durkheim's methodological observations, there is in his work recognition of the affinity between sociology and anthropology, and in addition a critical contrast is drawn between the competing claims of classical economics and an emerging sociological science. The method of the economists was criticized by Durkheim for the way in which its abstractions distorted reality. He remarks that 'Classical economics fashioned a world that does not exist . . . a world in isolation, everywhere uniform, in which the clash of purely individual forces would be resolved according to ineluctable economic laws' (1982: 197). In contrast, he argues that the reality of economic activity is that it is shaped by the characteristics of the particular society in which it is located – for example, by the policies and reforms implemented by a particular state. Durkheim argues that the theoretical consequence is that rather than an abstract economy grounded in '*a priori* suppositions' observation of *national* economy should be the focus of analysis.

Durkheim is critical of economics for the way in which its general propositions fail to take account of conditions of time and place, 'hence therefore of all social conditions' (1982: 205). He is also critical of the employment by economics of a notion of man in general ruled by self-interest – 'the sad portrait of an isolated egoist' (1978: 49). However, the social importance of economic factors was readily acknowledged by Durkheim, perhaps nowhere more so than in his observation that in 'contemporary societies ... economic relations form the basis of common life' (1959: 148). But while economic relations might form the basis of common life, ultimately it is social unity that is of most concern to Durkheim (1984). Social unity is dependent upon more than economic functions, as Durkheim's references to the importance of 'solidarity of interests' and 'bonds of interdependence', and related observations on the regulating influence of social forces and the necessity of moral authorities to achieve a curbing of appetites and to remedy the disorganization of economic life, confirm.

In the course of his criticism of economics for its analytic preoccupation with 'the construction of a more or less desirable ideal' and observational neglect of the complexity of real life, Durkheim (1978: 49) makes reference to the difficulties that derive from divisions between the various social sciences. In a manner that bears some comparison with the views I have already attributed to Georg Simmel and Pierre Bourdieu, Durkheim argues that contrary to the opinion expressed by economists, 'moral, legal, economic and political phenomena' do not 'unfold along parallel lines without intersecting' (1978: 51). Social phenomena such as these are closely related and in consequence it is not possible to study them separately. Durkheim adds:

> The result of this relatedness is that each of the social sciences loses some of its autonomy but gains in vitality and vigor. The facts which each had studied when the analytical framework had detached them from their natural milieu seemed to have no connection and to exist in a vacuum ... Now that they have been brought together according to their natural affinities, they appear as what they are: the various facets of a single, living reality, namely society.
>
> (1978: 51)

An approach that recognizes what Durkheim calls the 'relatedness' and Simmel describes as the 'multi-faceted' character of social life has the potential to be able to avoid what Bourdieu identifies as formulations 'totally inadequate to the objects of study'. In turn, such an approach is better placed to deal effectively with the complexity of social phenomena and to increase understanding of the 'economic and social determinants of the innumerable attacks on the freedom of individuals and their legitimate aspirations to happiness and self-fulfilment' (Bourdieu *et al.* 1999: 629). This has constituted the promise of sociology from its inception – the potential it contains to illuminate the contradictions intrinsic to social life and the social causes of individual experiences.

The impact of an emerging modern capitalist economy on social and cultural life is an important analytic theme for Durkheim. One of the sections of his *The Division of Labour in Society* (1984) provides an exploration of what are described as 'abnormal forms' of the division of labour. This section includes a discussion of anomie, inequality and disorganization as features, by implication problematic and remedial, of a developing modern industrial capitalism. The classification of such problems as abnormal or pathological is now recognized to be more controversial than Durkheim's initial discussion allows, for it is evident that experiences of normlessness and uncertainty, forms of inequality and concerns about disorder and disorganization have become frequent, if not endemic, features of modern capitalism.

Two years after the publication of his discussion of abnormal forms of the division of labour, Durkheim sought to outline more rigorously the rules for distinguishing between 'normal' and abnormal or 'pathological' social phenomena. In the course of his discussion of such rules, Durkheim observes 'to know whether the present economic state of the people's of Europe, with the lack of organisation that characterises it, is normal, or not, we must investigate what in the past gave rise to it' (1982: 95). The conditions that gave rise to the features identified by Durkheim persist, albeit in a more developed or aggravated form. The pace of economic change has accelerated dramatically and the consequences of the processes of transformation associated with the growth of a market economy have increased in scale and scope.

A number of the critical observations on aspects of late nineteenth- and early twentieth-century life provided by Durkheim continue to inform the experiences of a later generation of modern subjects encountering the complex consequences of continuing far-reaching processes of economic transformation. In his reflections on the forms of social disorganization and uncertainty arising from what subsequently has been called the 'great transformation' (Polanyi [1944] 1968 – see Chapter 2), Durkheim describes the relations between employers and employees, companies, and between companies and the public, as ruled by individual appetites, self-interest or egoism. In contrast to the classical economists' promotion of *laissez-faire* – the idea of a self-regulating market economy of 'overwhelming consequence to the whole organisation of society' (Polanyi 1968: 57) – Durkheim is critical of the notion that economic initiatives and interests should be free of regulation. In a discussion of the consequences he considers to be associated with the growth of the market economy and the unregulated expression of economic interests, he draws attention to the undermining of moral discipline and public morality. He argues that 'economic functions are not their own justification; they are only a means to an end; they constitute one of the organs of social life' (1957: 16). It is clear that for Durkheim the value of a particular form of economic activity is questionable if a disturbance of peaceful mutual relations, social disorganization and perpetual discontent with our lot is the inevitable price to be paid. Economic activity represents merely a means, the end of which in Durkheim's view is to bring about a 'harmonious community'.

In contrast to forms of economic analysis that endorse the idea and reality of a self-regulating market economy, Durkheim (1982) affirms the idea of a science of economics that recognizes the existence of society and concerns itself with the ways in which societal interests receive economic expression. From this standpoint individual economic activity is merely an abstraction – what is real, and of value, is 'the economic activity of society' (1982: 198).

Max Weber: questions of economy, culture and society

The relation between sociology and economics has been identified as the most complex and problematic of disciplinary differentiations (Giddens 1987: 40) and perhaps nowhere is this more acutely evident and better exemplified than in the writings and intellectual status of Max Weber. Weber is widely recognized to be a key figure in the establishment of the discipline of sociology for his contribution to sociological methodology and his substantive analysis of modern forms of life. Yet Weber conceived of himself first and foremost as an economist, as is evident from several of his texts, including the opening remarks in his 1918 Munich University address (Weber 1970: 129; see also Hennis 1988).

As to some extent is the case with the other thinkers discussed above, the intellectual configuration from which Weber's analytical practice emerged is one informed by moral philosophy, political science and political economy. Reflecting on this intellectual configuration, as well as the perspective and purpose of Weber's work, Hennis questions Weber's sociological credentials. He argues that Weber 'nearly always referred to sociology in a distancing fashion . . . Wherever he accepted the term for his own work he sought, by using specifying adjectives (*verstehend*, "interpretive") not only to isolate it, but actually to singularize it' (1987: 28). For good measure Hennis adds that while there is a sociology in Weber's work it is restricted to 'subjectively understandable phenomena' and the concepts and categories constructed are employed to make a contribution to 'social economics' (1987: 28–9).

If consideration is given to the question of Weber's central problem and thematic focus, it is evident that his work shares 'little with the specifically sociological traditions associated with the names of Comte, Spencer or Durkheim' (Hennis 1987: 27). The suggestion is that it is not possible to understand Weber properly if he is viewed simply as a sociologist. Hennis comments that it is not possible to understand Weber's work from the perspective of contemporary sociology, for in contrast to the intellectual division of labour current between the social sciences it is located within an 'unfractured tradition' in which economics is both a human science and a political science. As Weber remarks in his 1895 Freiburg inaugural lecture, economics as a '*human* science . . . investigates above all else the *quality of the human beings* who are brought up in those economic and social conditions of existence' (1989: 197). As a '*political* science' it is to be regarded as a 'servant . . . of the lasting power-political interests of the nation' (p. 198).

Hennis considers the formative influence on Weber's work of the unfractured tradition exemplified by the political economy of the German Historical School. He argues that what preoccupied Weber was 'questions concerning "values", "political" questions relating to the "cultural tasks of the present time" in so far as they are affected by the economy' (1987: 35). Weber's approach can be located within a long tradition of moral and political science concerned with the mutual relation of economic and social conditions of existence and the quality of man. Weber's work has been contrasted with what has been described as a 'science of "ascribed", "constructed" and "unrealistic" beings, the "mathematical ideal model" of "abstract theory"' (Hennis 1987: 38), signified by *homo oeconomicus*. Following the line of the German Historical School and the work of Karl Knies in particular, Weber's work contributes to the development of economics as a science of man, a moral and political science. It is in this historical context that Weber's work belongs and the development of his sociological writings is to be located.

Achieving an understanding of Weber's sociological writings is by no means an easy matter, for there are a number of contending readings claiming to have uncovered the thematic unity or central theme (Kalberg 1979; Hennis 1988; Tenbruck 1989). A number of texts have tended to be identified as constituting the core of Weber's sociological writings. Prominent among these is the widely read and influential study of *The Protestant Ethic and the Spirit of Capitalism*, a series of studies of 'world religions', and the diverse manuscripts posthumously assembled under the title *Economy and Society*. Weber's studies of the complex relationship between economy and society range widely across a number of concerns including capitalism and bureaucracy, relations between class, status and power, the growth of cities and increases in markets, and the significance of distinctions between different forms of rationality in social and economic life.

While Weber held that the economic sphere was a core feature of modern social life he argued that the development of modern societies could not be accounted for through a consideration of economic factors alone – on the contrary, other interrelated social and cultural processes had to be taken into account. This point of view is particularly evident in Weber's study of the development of modern western capitalism, a work which places emphasis upon the complex connection of economic, social and cultural phenomena. The development of forms of modern capitalist economic activity in the West is argued to have been closely connected with a particular cultural ethos, associated rationalizations of social conduct and the constitution of a 'new kind of individuality' (Sayer 1991: 119). In his discussion of the development of modern western capitalism, Weber drew attention to the importance of a number of factors that confirm a significant degree of common ground with Marx's analysis of the modern capitalist mode of production. According to Weber, rational capital accounting, identified as 'the most general presupposition for the existence of . . . present-day capitalism', is predicated on the following six conditions (Sayer 1991: 93–5):

- division of labour based on private property;
- formally free labour force;
- rational technology;
- calculable law;
- freedom of the market;
- commercialization of economic life.

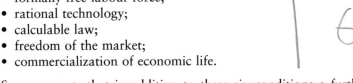

Sayer suggests that in addition to these six conditions a further three, to which Marx would surely have found it difficult to express any analytic objection, can be uncovered in Weber's work:

- modern bureaucratic state administration;
- rational ethos for the conduct of life;
- separation of business from household.

The key difference between Weber and Marx perhaps lies in the emphasis placed by Weber on the significance and impact of forms of rationalization on the development of modern forms of social life, and exemplified by his studies of religion, law, politics and economy. Although the notion of rationalization has frequently been at the centre of discussions of Weber's contribution to our understanding of modern social life, the meaning of the term and its significance in Weber's work as a whole has been a matter of considerable controversy (Hennis 1988).

Weber employs a notion of rationalization in his discussion of a number of related processes. These include the displacement of magical forms of thought following a process of 'disenchantment of the world', the bureaucratic or legal-rational organization of the state and the submission of more and more areas of human existence to systematic calculation and control. For Weber, capitalism constitutes one instance, albeit one of considerable significance, of a 'wholesale rationalization of western culture and institutions' (Sayer 1991: 113). Other instances noted by Weber include science, jurisprudence, music and art, but 'the most fateful force in . . . modern life, [is] capitalism' (1976: 17).

The conditions identified with the development of rational capital accounting include a number of non-economic ones, such as rational technology, calculable law, the development of the modern state and the constitution of an ethos or spirit conducive to the methodical and disciplined conduct of everyday life. These conditions assume a particular significance in Weber's work.

However, of all the analyses produced by Weber of the non-economic conditions associated with the development of capitalism it is *The Protestant Ethic and the Spirit of Capitalism* (1976), the articulation of a religious ethos, a particular economic mentality and a form of economic action, that has received most attention. What occupied Weber was the emergence of a distinctive form of economic activity that he considered a product of modern European civilization, namely 'sober bourgeois capitalism with its rational organization of free labour' (p. 24). It was the origins of the 'peculiar rationalism of Western culture' to which Weber directed his attention. To explain the particular features of western rationalism Weber remarked that it was necessary to take account of both the 'fundamental importance of the economic factor' and the processes through which 'the ability and disposition of men to adopt certain types of practical rational conduct' (p. 26) was formed. Reflecting on economy and culture at the beginning of the twentieth century Weber acknowledged that capitalism presented itself to individuals as 'an unalterable order of things' (p. 54) within which the individual had, of necessity, to live. Dominating the economic life of his day Weber remarked that capitalism 'educates and selects the economic subjects which it needs' (p. 55). The key question was how such a way of life had developed. The answer was sought by Weber through a study of the 'social ethic of capitalistic culture' (p. 54). This study led him to trace the formation of a disciplined, systematically rational conduct of life to the idea of a calling and a devotion to labour associated with the religious doctrines of ascetic Protestantism.

It was in and through the doctrines and associated practices of ascetic Protestantism that Weber (1978a) believed a rationalization of worldly conduct conducive to the development of modern capitalism was cultivated. In contrast to Catholicism, which places emphasis on the prospect of believers achieving redemption for their sins through confession, penance and prayer, and thereby clearly marks the path to salvation as in principle open to all, ascetic Protestantism leaves believers insecure about their status. At the heart of ascetic Protestantism the doctrine of predestination was located, which effectively stated that the fate of humanity had been predetermined by God:

> We know only that a part of humanity is saved, the rest damned. To assume that human merit or guilt play a part in determining this destiny would be to think of God's absolutely free decrees . . . as subject to change by human influence, an impossible contradiction.
>
> (Weber 1976: 103)

In so far as there was no way of knowing one's fate, believers were highly likely to suffer 'unprecedented inner loneliness (1976: 104) and to experience intense anxiety. It is in this context, Weber argues, that pastoral guidance commends intense worldly activity, for 'labour in the service of impersonal social usefulness' (p. 109) is assumed to promote the glory of God and to be willed by him. Attempting to lead a life of 'good works' also served as a means of reducing, if not removing, the fear of damnation.

In this way, through the emphasis placed on the moral value of worldly activity or work, the 'moral conduct of the average man was . . . deprived of its plan-less and unsystematic character and subjected to a consistent method for conduct as a whole' (Weber 1976: 117). The instruction to work hard in one's calling was at the centre of ascetic Protestantism. The value of one's labour might be measured in terms of 'the importance of the goods produced in it for the community', but also in terms of 'private profitableness' (p. 162). Weber notes that the accumulation of wealth is only regarded as ethically problematic within Protestantism when it is associated with idleness and 'sinful enjoyment of life', or is pursued in the hope of being able to live without a care. As in the parable of the talents, wealth creation or the accumulation of capital when recognized as a 'duty in a calling . . . is not only morally permissable, but actually enjoined' (p. 163). Worldly Protestant asceticism served to rationalize the attainment of private wealth through labour in a calling as a sign of God's blessing. The associated restrictions placed upon consumption, particularly of luxuries, and the limitations placed on enjoyment of possessions, combined with the religious valorization of 'restless, continuous, systematic work in a worldly calling' contributed to the expansion of that attitude Weber called the 'spirit of capitalism' (p. 172). The growth of acquisitive activity, coupled with limitations placed on the consumption of wealth, led inevitably to increasing productive investment of capital and further capital accumulation. In sum, one of the 'fundamental elements of the spirit of modern capitalism, and not only of that but of all modern culture: rational conduct on the basis of the idea of the calling, was born . . . from the spirit of Christian asceticism' (p. 180).

What had been a matter of choice for the Puritan – 'to work in a calling' – Weber suggests has become an inescapable feature of everyday life for subsequent generations of modern secular subjects, who have had no real option but to accommodate to the modern economic order and 'the technical and economic conditions of machine production which today determine the lives of all individuals who are born into this mechanism' (Weber 1976: 181). In the early twentieth century the notion of a dutiful performance of one's calling in accordance with the 'highest spiritual and cultural values' was increasingly out of step with the reality of a modern capitalist economic life. The pursuit of wealth had been 'stripped of its religious and ethical meaning . . . to become associated with purely mundane passions' (p. 182).

A century later the consequences of the developments identified are even starker. Ideas of duty and calling now appear to have little, if any, significant place in the fast-changing (disappearing) world of work – indeed they appear, for the most part, as an anachronism. In so far as our society is considered to be a consumer society then any residual sense of duty that might remain is likely to be found not in work or production but in the field of consumption. In view of the transformation of modern industrial capitalist society and the requirement for greater labour market flexibility, the strategy now is to 'dismantle the habits of permanent, round-the-clock, steady and regular work' (Bauman 1998a: 112). Now labourers need to 'forget, not to learn, whatever the work ethic in the halcyon days of modern industry was meant to teach them' (Bauman 1998a: 112). Such a society no longer has much of a need for mass industrial labour and increasingly individuals are shaped not so much by the requirements of work but 'first and foremost by the duty to play the role of the consumer' (Bauman 1998a: 80). The influence of material goods over people's lives has indeed grown exponentially and increasingly it is not restless, continuous work that is of value but ceaseless consumption, for 'the aesthetics of consumption . . . now rules where the work ethic once ruled' (Bauman 1998b: 32). In such a context the notion of a calling occupies a marginal position, for work as a calling, as a vocation, has become the preserve of a privileged few (Bauman 1998b).

The intellectual context in which the issue of the relationship between economy, culture and society is now being posed is in important respects significantly different from Weber's time. Economic life, cultural forms, processes and practices, and social interactions and relationships have all been affected by the continuing transformation of modernity. And whereas for Weber sociology was merely an emerging field of study, it has for some time now been accorded the status of an established specialized academic discipline. The process through which this status was realized was complex and had to include a settlement of boundary disputes between economists and sociologists. In short, the formal institutionalization of sociological research and teaching within the university was only realized with the achievement of an academic division of labour in which due recognition was given to the distinctiveness, if not the pre-eminence, of economics.

At the close of the nineteenth century, the question of the relationship between economics and sociology was at the forefront of debates between American social scientists. As they sought to establish sociology by designating its subject matter, methods and field of inquiry, American sociologists simultaneously had to acknowledge and accept the claims of the more established discipline of economics. And to that end it was necessary to surrender the Comtian ambition for sociology to be an all-encompassing science and to steer clear of topics that were considered to already belong within the domain of economics (Swedberg 1990; Bourdieu 1998).

Talcott Parsons and the differentiation of economic and
sociological analysis

The designation of a distinctive division of labour between sociology and
economics during the course of the 1930s involved a complex process of
intellectual negotiation to which the American sociologist Talcott Parsons
(1935a, 1935b) made a significant contribution. For Parsons the relationship between sociology and economics was considered to be complementary.
It was argued that sociology should not engage critically with mainstream
economics and it should not attempt to be a substitute for orthodox
economics. Parsons sided with neo-classical economists against institutional economics and proposed a clear division of labour between sociology
and economics. Orthodox marginalist economic theory was accepted by
Parsons, who argued that economics constituted the study of human
behaviour in terms of means allocation in the means–end relationship. In
contrast, sociology was to concern itself with values or ends, with 'ultimate
common ends and the attitudes associated with and underlying them, considered in their various modes of expression in . . . social life' (1934: 529).

Parsons was critical of institutional economics on two counts. First,
it was considered to operate with an inflated conception of the scope of the
discipline. Second, it was considered to be overly preoccupied with the
'concrete' to the neglect of the 'abstract', and in consequence to be 'disas-
trously wrong theoretically' (1935b: 661). In so far as the essence of science
was theory and the essence of theory was 'analytical abstraction' then
the claims of neo-classical economics were to be upheld and supported in
Parson's view. Institutions, the embodiment of values, were the legitimate
subject matter not of economics but of sociology.

Parsons made a significant contribution to the development of a distinct
division of labour between economics and sociology, his intervention serving to legitimate the neglect within neo-classical economics of social and
institutional dimensions, and effectively rendering the intellectual boundaries between the two disciplines impermeable. In consequence, relatively
little analytic attention has subsequently been devoted to economic sociology, institutional economics or the role of institutions in economic life.
Indeed, the tradition of economic sociology became intellectually marginal,
if not moribund, and in consequence, as one analyst has remarked, until
relatively recently 'the role of institutions in economic life remained virtually unexamined' (Velthuis 1999: 635).

Early in the twentieth century a comparable process of differentiation
between economics and sociology occurred in European social thought. By
the 1930s the two disciplines had drifted apart to such an extent that it
seemed to Schumpeter (1954b) that they knew little and cared even less
about what each other was doing. Although it might be argued that, briefly
during the early 1950s, ironically most prominently in the work of Parsons

and Smelser (1956), an attempt was made to bring economics and sociology closer together, the effort was ultimately to be regarded as a failure (Swedberg 1990: 15–16). However, in the closing decades of the twentieth century a new economic sociology began to emerge in both America and Europe. The 'great transformation' of the late nineteenth and early twentieth centuries had provided the stimulus for the initial development of a form of economic sociology. In a comparable manner, wide-ranging late twentieth-century economic transformations have provided the conditions within which a new synthesis of economics and sociology has begun to emerge under the banner of a 'new economic sociology' (Smelser and Swedberg 1994; Krier 1999; Beckert and Swedberg 2001).

The distinction and relationship between sociology and economics has become a matter of interest for two sets of analysts in particular. A concern with the interface between the disciplines of sociology and economics is *explicitly* addressed by those concerned about the limits and limitations of 'classical' economics and the lack of attention being given to economic sociology (Velthuis 1999; Zafirovski 1999). In contrast, the question of the relationship between sociology and economics remains more *implicit* for those critical of the cultural turn in social analysis and related relative neglect of economic aspects of social life in contemporary social thought. In the latter instance the call is for more recognition to be given to economic aspects of social life, for the relationship between economic processes and social and cultural practices to be accorded due consideration in contemporary social theory (Ray and Sayer 1999). My discussion represents a response to the latter call to acknowledge the prominence of economic processes and practices and to consider their impact on social and cultural life. The focus of my discussion is on the contribution classical and contemporary social analysts have made to an understanding of significant features of economic life as well as, in turn, the respects in which relations between economic, cultural and social processes have been transformed.

CHAPTER 2

NO ALTERNATIVE? CAPITALIST ECONOMIC LIFE AND THE CLOSING OF THE POLITICAL UNIVERSE

Introduction: the way things were

In the formative texts of key classical analysts like Marx, Simmel, Durkheim and Weber and in many of the narratives on social and economic life which subsequently have contributed to the development of modern social theory, an analysis of prevailing social conditions has necessitated a consideration of modern capitalism and its consequences and, in turn, an address of the possibility or prospect of realizing alternative forms of social and economic life. In the case of Marx, analysis of the character and development of the modern capitalist economy and its consequences for social and cultural life are at the centre of his work. But there is also a strong sense in Marx's writings of the dynamic and unstable character of capitalism, its vulnerability to crisis and the likelihood, if not the inevitability, of its transcendence. For example, in *The Communist Manifesto* Marx and Engels refer to the increasing 'revolt of modern productive forces against modern conditions of production' and the 'periodical return of commercial crises' (1968: 86), which threaten the entire society with disorder. But they also hold out the prospect of more positive forms of social transformation. In a related manner in *Grundrisse* Marx makes reference to the growing contradiction between the foundations of capitalist production and its development as

> the creation of real wealth comes to depend less on labour time and on the amount of labour employed than on the power of agencies set in motion during labour time, whose 'powerful effectiveness' is itself in turn out of all proportion to the direct labour time spent on their production, but depends rather on the general state of science and on the

progress of technology, or the application of this science to production.

(1973: 704–5)

This observation and related comments by Marx (1973: 708) anticipate aspects of more recent discussions of the long-running process of transformation to which work under capitalist conditions of production has continued to be subject (Castells 1996; Gorz 1999; Beck 2000). For Marx, the outcome of this process of transformation seemed to be relatively clear: just as the capitalist economy developed by degrees, so too would its negation, 'which is its ultimate result' (Marx 1973: 712). The continuing instability of contemporary capitalism, particularly in its global free-market phase, is not in dispute, but what the ultimate result will be must remain a matter of conjecture (Gray 1999; Hutton and Giddens 2001). Indeed, rather than the negation of capitalism, contemporary social and political discourse is preoccupied with coming to terms with the evidence of the durability of capitalism.[1]

Within the tradition of Marxist analysis it is socialism that has constituted the alternative to capitalism and an engagement with 'socialism as a social fact and socialism as a competing theory of society' is an important feature of the development of classical sociological thought (Turner 1999: 49). For example, in the respective writings of both Durkheim and Weber consideration is given to the question of socialism as a potential alternative form of life to capitalism. Durkheim (1959) approached the notion of socialism as a practical doctrine and as a programme for transforming society. In his work the notion of socialism is described as serving to mobilize opposition to capitalist economic conditions and to promote the idea of a more organized, regulated and unified form of economic life. Socialism constituted for Durkheim a potential means for socializing economic life, a way of installing morality within economic life, and as such represented the very antithesis of the free-market views of the classical economists of the time who insisted that economic interests were in no need of social regulation.

Durkheim might be regarded as adopting a 'sympathetic approach to socialism as a moral regulation of the economy which would restrain the anomic effects of utilitarian ideology and market conflicts' (Turner 1999: 49). In contrast, Weber was already concerned about the consequences of rationalization, and seems to suggest that a socialized economy would be even more vulnerable to the complex problems associated with a process of increasing bureaucratization. Whereas Marx presented the socialist alternative as promising to radically improve the lot of humanity, Weber depicted rational socialism as threatening to promote a 'monocratic bureaucratization of the whole of social life', a threat only forestalled by the continuing survival of free-market capitalism (Sayer 1991: 147–8). Whether Marx, Weber or Durkheim regarded the prospect of socialism with favour is not the point. What is important to note is that from the writings of the classics and running through social analysis for the greater part of the twentieth century, there has been a strong sense of a potential alternative to the capitalist mode of production. This controversial and problematic alternative achieved a form of realization in the aftermath of the October Revolution in Russia in 1917 and the subsequent establishment of what came to be known as the 'societies of actually existing socialism' (Bahro 1978; Arnason 1993).

The very idea of an alternative to capitalism now appears discredited, at best utopian. The forms of social and economic organization that had served as a representation of the possibility of socialism, if not exactly of 'what socialism ought to be and how it ought to function' (Jameson 1991: 208), have been steadily dismantled since 1989. The revolutionary events in Eastern Europe in 1989 and the defeat of the attempted coup in the former Soviet Union in 1991 lent weight to the view that socialism simply does not work. In the aftermath of the collapse of socialism in Eastern Europe it has been argued that there is now no alternative to capitalism, and that the only 'arguments that remain concern how far, and in what ways, capitalism should be governed and regulated' (Giddens 1998: 44). In a related manner it has been observed that

> No one today questions capitalism. Who indeed would risk doing so? The only powerful opponent of capitalism is profit-only capitalism itself. Bad news on the labour market counts as a victory report on Wall Street, the simple calculation being that profits rise when labour costs fall.
>
> (Beck 2000: 4)

In short, how to respond to and cope with a radically transformed global capitalist free-market economy has become the focus of analysis.

What forms of political and economic management might be able to avoid the detrimental consequences associated with both the interventionist and collectivist tendencies of a discredited socialism and the excesses of a market fundamentalism that are a defining feature of the dominant neo-liberal variant of contemporary capitalism? Given the extent and the intensity of the process of global economic transformation, Giddens argues that there is no prospect of saying 'no' to markets, and that the only realistic option is to try to make capitalism work for people economically, socially and culturally by 'modernizing social democracy' (2000: 29). The implication is clear – there is no radically different form of life open to us and all that can be achieved are merely adjustments to, rather than a more fundamental social transformation of, capitalist society.

The problem of living with(in) a capitalist market economy, and in particular of coping with its far-reaching consequences for social life, is one with which a substantial number of analysts, particularly within the Marxist tradition of inquiry, but also more broadly in the discourses of political economy and sociology, have been preoccupied (cf. Gailbraith 1963, 1993;

Harvey 1989; Bourdieu 1998, 1999; Gorz 1999; Gray 1999). A number of dilemmas and difficulties have been identified with 'market capitalism' and the economic and political programme of neo-liberalism. Specifically, that far from encouraging and perpetuating freedom the market merely serves to repress it (Jameson 1991: 273) and the 'reign of the market' brings about 'the destruction of a civilization' (Bourdieu 1998: 24, 25). Such criticisms recall aspects of a critical analysis of an earlier period of wide-ranging transformation of modern capitalist economic life, conducted by Karl Polanyi.

The Great Transformation: from the self-regulating market to social protection

Karl Polanyi's study, *The Great Transformation* ([1944] 1968) was published towards the end of the Second World War. It provides a critical analysis of the self-regulating market and the profit-maximizing economic logic associated with nineteenth- and early twentieth-century industrial capitalist civilization, and traces the development of interventionism and forms of 'social protectionism' to preserve the 'social fabric'. *The Great Transformation* can be read as a counter-discourse to Friedrich Hayek's *The Road to Serfdom* (1944). Hayek's text promotes the economic and political virtues of the free play of market forces and the freedom of individuals to pursue their own interests, and is critical of attempts by the state to intervene in or exercise regulation over economic activity. From Hayek's perspective, society needs to accommodate to the requirements of economic rationality. In direct contrast, Polanyi takes the view that 'normally, the economic order is merely a function of the social, in which it is contained' (1968: 71).

The analytic focus of Polanyi's study falls on the 'self-regulating' market system associated with nineteenth-century industrial capitalism. This system was compromised by, and ultimately disintegrated under, the impact of various forms of interventionism designed to provide a degree of social protection from market forces. The development of nineteenth-century industrial capitalism is argued by Polanyi to be exceptional in that the relationship between the economic system and social relations assumes a different form to that which historical and anthropological research has shown to exist in all other societies. Whereas in other types of society 'economy, as a rule, is submerged in . . . social relationships' (Polanyi 1968: 46), in the case of the industrial capitalist market economy '[i]nstead of economy being embedded in social relations, social relations are embedded in the economic system' (p. 57).

Outlining the distinctive features of modern industrial capitalism in the nineteenth century, Polanyi observes that 'gain' was elevated to a prominent position and, as a 'justification of action and behaviour in everyday life' (1968: 30), provided a basis for the self-regulating market system.

The idea that people act to safeguard their individual interest in respect of material goods and possessions is peculiar to a form of economic life controlled and regulated by markets. In such circumstances, where the economy is 'directed by market prices' or subject to market control, there are overwhelming consequences for the whole organization of society. Polanyi (1968: 57) adds that:

> it means no less than the running of society as an adjunct to the market . . . society must be shaped in such a manner as to allow the system to function according to its own laws . . . [for] a market economy can function only in a market society.

The shift from regulated to self-regulated markets took place at the end of the eighteenth century and precipitated a complete transformation in the structure of society, specifically an institutional separation of economic and political spheres. What took place was in effect a dismantling and replacement of longstanding market practices, that were subject to forms of regulation and restraint designed to prevent damage to the fabric of social life, by the institution of the free market that operated independently of questions of social cohesion and need. In the course of the nineteenth century, 'economic activity was isolated and imputed to a distinctive economic motive' (Polanyi 1968: 71). All the elements of industrial life – 'labour, land and money' – became subject to the control and direction of the market mechanism through a process of commodification. The process through which social and cultural life was subordinated to the 'laws' of the market turned virtually everything into a commodity and threatened 'the demolition of society' (Polanyi 1968: 73).

In his discussion of the ways in which the self-regulating market threatened to impact on the life of society, Polanyi describes the potential consequences for the human individual, the environment and business. As they are reduced to the commodity 'labour', a commodity that may be employed 'indiscriminately' or not all, human beings are deprived of their social being and their moral and psychological character. Human beings lose 'the protective covering of cultural institutions' and thereby become vulnerable to 'the effects of social exposure' (Polanyi 1968: 73). Recognition of the damaging consequences of the extension of the market mechanism to labour, land and money gradually led in the course of the nineteenth century to moves to introduce measures to restrict and regulate market forces. But while a movement emerged to 'resist the pernicious effects of a market-controlled economy' (Polanyi 1968: 76), momentum remained behind the market mechanism.

In the 1920s the prestige of economic liberalism was at its height with no price being considered too great to pay to achieve a sound budget and a stable currency: '[t]he privations of the unemployed made jobless by deflation; the destitution of public servants dismissed without a pittance;

even the relinquishment of national rights and the loss of constitutional liberties were judged a fair price to pay' (Polanyi 1968: 142). In this period (1924–9) Europe and America experienced an economic boom and there was confidence that the market system had been restored. However, by the 1930s the market economy was in crisis, Britain and America abandoned the gold standard and began to manage the value of their currencies, international debts were not honoured and the tenets of economic liberalism began to be disregarded. The events of the 1940s further served to undermine the budgetary and monetary orthodoxy of economic liberalism and led analysts, including Polanyi, to conclude that they had witnessed the end of the self-regulating market.

The circumstances of economic liberalism's demise also provided it with a counter-argument. This counter-argument (namely that it was interference with or an incomplete application of the self-regulating market system that precipitated difficulties) has subsequently resurfaced and contributed considerably to the emergence of neo-liberalism. Liberals argued that if various forms of intervention had not obstructed the working of the self-regulating market economy then there would not have been any difficulties. In short, in their view, problems were a product of 'interference with the freedom of employment, trade and currencies practised by the various schools of social, national, and monopolistic protectionism' (Polanyi 1968: 144).

In his discussion of the protectionist countermove against economic liberalism Polanyi draws attention to an 'economistic prejudice' which served to support the notion that it is lapses from economic liberalism that have been responsible for the 'ills of the time' (1968: 161). Economic liberals responded to the development of restrictions on the market system by contesting their necessity. Evidence of a need for measures to protect society was disputed. It was suggested that far from being exploited the working classes had gained substantially from liberal capitalism, which through the deployment of technological innovations was considered, on the whole, to have transformed people's lives for the better. Employing conventional criteria of economic welfare (wages and population figures), economic liberals argued 'how could there be social catastrophe where there was undoubtedly economic improvement?' (Polanyi 1968: 157). The critical response to economic liberalism offered by Polanyi is that social catastrophe is primarily a cultural rather than an economic phenomenon. The forms of degradation associated with the destructive consequences of the Industrial Revolution and the associated imposition of market forms of organization arose from the 'disintegration of the cultural environment' and key social institutions of the victims:

> The economic process may . . . supply the vehicle of destruction . . . but the immediate cause of undoing is not for that reason economic: it lies in the lethal injury to the institutions in which

social existence is embodied. The result is loss of self-respect and standards, whether the unit is a people or a class, whether the process springs from so-called 'culture conflict' or from a change in the position of a class within the confines of a society.
(Polanyi 1968: 157)

Drawing his analysis to a close, Polanyi remarks that the central problem with market society was that its social and economic life was predicated on 'self-interest'. Market society was based on the idea that individuals are motivated by self-interest, pursuit of profit and material gain. It was assumed that conduct would accord with the tenets of economic rationality and that 'markets were natural institutions' (1968: 249). Such an organization of social and economic life is at best exceptional. Rather than being a natural institution, the free market was in practice 'opened and kept open by an enormous increase in continuous, centrally organised and controlled interventionism' (1968: 140). In short, the market form of organization is revealed to have been imposed on society through the 'regulative system of mercantilism'; the *laissez-faire* economy is recognized to be the 'product of deliberate state action' (Polanyi 1968: 278–9, 141; see also Gorz 1999: 9 and Gray 1999: 5, 17).

The great transformation described in Polanyi's narrative is 'a development under which the economic system ceases to lay down the law to society and the primacy of society over that system is secured' (1968: 251). With the benefit of hindsight we can observe that the relationship between society and the economic system has not been, or at least has not remained, of the order anticipated towards the end of the Second World War. Society, once again, seems to be 'constricted by economics' (Polanyi 1968: 252) as it has been exposed to the unpredictable consequences of a deregulated global capitalist economy. Sixty years on we are living in another period in which the 'rhetoric of the market' (Jameson 1991: 263) has become a prominent, if not predominant, feature of social and political discourse. As the reality of a substantial degree of deregulation of market forces increasingly impacts on the structure and experience of everyday life (Gray 1999), we are perhaps better placed to respond to Polanyi's concerns.

A number of important economic transformations have taken place since Polanyi drew attention to the introduction of various social measures designed to protect society from being 'annihilated by the action of the self-regulating market' (1968: 249). The subsequent fate of human beings may not have been left in the hands of the market mechanism, but the last quarter of the twentieth century was marked by a resurgence of market forces. There has been a vociferous endorsement of the idea of a global free market by governments and transnational organizations, and it is increasingly assumed that 'democratic capitalism' is the inevitable destination of modernizing nations around the world. In short, market forces have once more been accorded a prominent place in both political discourse and the social and economic ordering of people's lives (Gray 1999).

The neo-liberal promotion of market forces and labour market flexibility towards the close of the twentieth century has been associated with the development of a global 'political economy of insecurity'. In reality this has come to mean that risks are redistributed 'away from the state and the economy and towards the individual' (Beck 2000: 3). As this has occurred, comparable signs of social dislocation to those identified by Polanyi in an earlier form of market society have become all too apparent and the victims no less evident (Elliott and Atkinson 1999).

It was the substitution of anonymous market 'laws' for 'laws which state-societies lay down for themselves' (Gorz 1999: 5) that opened the way for capital to become global and move unfettered beyond political regulation. The transformation of economic life associated with the shift from standardized mass production and mass consumption (Fordism) to a more disorganized, flexible, informational mode of production (post-Fordism) has meant that conventional forms of full-time employment and waged work have become increasingly vulnerable to replacement by temporary, casual, part-time jobs. With the introduction of new information and communication technologies, productivity can be increased without increases in work. Yet work has continued both to constitute 'the basis of social belonging and rights' and to represent 'the obligatory path to self-esteem and the esteem of others' (Gorz 1999: 5). In turn, there has been a re-emergence of the very forms of social dislocation associated with the advent of industrial capitalism at the end of eighteenth century. For example, 'forms of subproletarianization, of psychological misery, of "vagrancy" and "brigandage"' (Gorz 1999: 5), not to mention the destruction of subsistence labour and the forced migration of people in the Third World from the countryside to urban shanty towns. Moreover, with the development of post-Fordist capitalism even the impoverished commodity status of labour is threatened. Work in the form of abstract labour, 'invented and forcibly imposed by manufacturing capitalism from the end of the eighteenth century', work as 'measurable, quantifiable, and detachable from the person who "provides" it: work which can be bought and sold in the "labour market"' (Gorz 1999: 55) continues to disappear.

In a series of observations on the potential impact of the self-regulating market on the natural environment, Polanyi expressed concern that nature 'would be reduced to its elements, neighbourhoods and landscapes defiled, rivers polluted, military safety jeopardized, the power to produce food and raw materials destroyed' (1968: 73). Many of the fears expressed by Polanyi continue to haunt us. Forms of social protection have been eroded and 'the industrially forced degradation of the ecological and natural foundations of life' (Beck 1992: 80) has gathered momentum. The introduction and refinement of methods of social protection in the course of the nineteenth century and throughout much of the twentieth century may have compromised the 'self-regulating' operation of the market, as Polanyi anticipated. But market forces have continued to play a highly significant role in shaping social life. Evidence of the damaging impact of a relatively uncontrolled market economy on various aspects of the environment remains all too apparent. Consider the risks and hazards encountered in late modern capitalist societies and the examples of pollution (acid rain in Villa Parisi in Brazil), industrial accidents (Bhopal in India and Chernobyl in the Ukraine) and the contamination of food (DDT and lead in milk, and BSE in British beef) (Beck 1992).

A further concern expressed by Polanyi about the market economy – namely that 'the market administration of purchasing power would periodically liquidate business enterprise' (1968: 73) – has also proven to be well founded. Measures of social protection have been eroded and undermined by a resurgence of belief in the market economy that has received expression in the policies of neo-liberalism. As it has driven through a policy of 'destatization and debureaucratization of social protection' (Gorz 1999: 4) the economic and political programme of neo-liberalism has acquired considerable momentum and is now increasingly regarded as an 'inevitability' (Bourdieu 1998: 30).

At the heart of neo-liberalism is the notion that the regularities of the economic domain flowing from the free play of market forces – that is, 'the logic of markets' (Gorz 1999: 145) – should constitute the standard for, or the measure of, all practices. According to the neo-liberal narrative, exposing practices to market forces will ensure effective allocation of resources, efficient delivery of service and an economical production of commodities. Pursuit through the logic of the market of effectiveness, efficiency and economy in respect of resource allocation, service delivery and commodity production has not been without cost for individuals and communities. Ways of life have been disrupted, disorganized and rendered insecure by the transformation of economic life from organized, standardized and mass forms of production to more globally mobile, flexible, deregulated and, with the benefit of information technology, increasingly dematerialized forms of work and production. In the specific case of the public sector the increasing introduction of neo-liberal market 'reforms' has led to the dismantling of 'social welfare systems on the pretext that they are outdated "social entitlements" which are no longer fundable' (Gorz 1999: 21).

Other transformations: forms of capitalism from Fordism to neo-liberalism

The context in which Polanyi was writing was one informed by two significant developments. First, there was a widespread view that the market system was unreliable, a view that led to the emergence of Keynesian social democracy. With the adoption of Keynesian policies, markets were subject to regulation. When necessary, economic production and demand were stimulated by fiscal and monetary measures introduced by the state, which sought to redistribute a proportion of the wealth produced and create forms of employment through public expenditure to compensate for job losses in the private sector. The second important feature of the context in which Polanyi's analysis is located is the existence of a socialist economy in Soviet Russia, which for a time at least held out the possibility of socialist intervention in social and economic life as an alternative to the methods of liberal capitalism. Polanyi felt able to celebrate 'the passing of market-economy' (1968: 256) and confidently outlined the virtues of regulation and planning for achieving increases in justice, liberty and welfare. For good measure he criticized the way in which liberals had conflated the idea of freedom with 'advocacy of free enterprise', which in turn had been 'reduced to a fiction by the hard reality of giant trusts and princely monopolies' (1968: 257).

While a good deal has changed since Polanyi first outlined his criticisms of the 'market utopia', the capitalist mode of production has endured, passing through a series of complex processes of transformation. The post-war period from 1945–73 was one in which capitalist economies in the West experienced a long-running boom. This period of dramatic economic development is characterized by a particular economic and political formation that has been called Fordist-Keynesian – 'a certain set of labour control practices, technological mixes, consumption habits and configurations of political-economic power' (Harvey 1989: 124). It is a period marked by a dramatic increase in mass production and mass consumption and the refinement of a mode of state intervention in, and regulation of, economic life. A form of intervention that had been forged in response to an earlier crisis of capitalism in the 1930s, a crisis precipitated by economic depression and a lack of effective demand for goods and services. State intervention, following strategies based on the work of the economist John Maynard Keynes, sought to compensate for market fluctuations by managing economic demand and exercising control over economic development. Whereas the 'conventional wisdom' of economic liberalism had placed emphasis on the necessity of a balanced budget, Keynes offered a contrary view. He proposed that government might intervene to manipulate the level of aggregate demand, adding to it by 'spending in excess of taxation', subtracting from it by 'taxation in excess of spending', thereby influencing production (Galbraith 1963: 158–9). The role of the interventionist state in economic life, controlling demand for goods and services, was really only fully resolved after 1945. The subsequent deployment of state powers served to bring 'Fordism to maturity as a fully-fledged and distinctive regime of accumulation' (Harvey 1989: 129). But it was a regime that varied from country to country according to the precise form of articulation between 'Fordist accumulation and welfare-Keynesian modes of regulation' (Tickell and Peck 1995: 362).

For a considerable time during this period there was confidence that Keynesianism could effectively deliver stable economic growth in western societies, that through a combination of measures designed to have an impact on investment and savings, taxation and public expenditure, and the balance of trade between imports and exports, governments could successfully manage economic demand and, by determining the level of production of the economy, influence levels of (un)employment. Indeed, as J.K. Galbraith was able to note in the course of his discussion of *The Affluent Society*, even 'conservatives, save on the extreme right, have swallowed their distaste for the measures that the Keynesian programme requires and have implicitly adopted it' (1963: 160). For a time, (approaching 30 years) Keynesianism constituted the conventional wisdom, with western governments pursuing 'policies in which the state stimulated the growth of production and demand by fiscal and monetary measures' (Gorz 1999: 11). From the mid-1960s however, there were growing signs that the Fordist-Keynesian configuration was finding it difficult to deal with the contradictions of capitalism and there were increasing manifestations of what Gorz describes as an emerging 'crisis of governability' (1999: 11).

This crisis affected both the interventionist Keynesian state and the Fordist economic corporations. In so far as it intervened, regulated, sought to protect and arbitrate in respect of social and economic life, the state was vulnerable to being held responsible for social and economic outcomes. Signs of increasing social antagonism from the mid-1960s – riots in cities, sabotage and protest in factories and universities in America and Europe – called into question the notion that the 'Social State', through welfare and other social measures, could continue to reconcile people with the social consequences of capitalism. In turn, comparable problems subsequently began to arise in respect of the state's attempts to manage the performance of the Fordist economy, which became increasingly unresponsive to measures designed to promote economic expansion (Castoriadis 1997).

A distinguishing feature of the Fordist mass-production/mass-consumption system is rigidity, for the long-term and large-scale character of capital investment programmes and assumptions about 'stable growth in invariant consumer markets' (Harvey 1989: 142) tends to preclude operational flexibility. Associated problems of rigidity existed in Fordist labour markets, processes of labour allocation and labour contracts. They also existed in respect of 'state commitments . . . as entitlement programmes (social security, pension rights, etc.) grew under pressure to keep legitimacy at a time when rigidities in production restricted any expansion in the fiscal basis for state expenditures' (Harvey 1989: 142). In this setting the only source of flexibility was to be found in monetary policy and the decision to print money to keep the economy stable led to accelerating rates of inflation. Although the momentum of the post-war boom continued through the late 1960s and early 1970s the recession that began in 1973 brought the boom to a close. The limitations of managed capitalism were exposed; the corporatist compromise between state, capital and labour could not be sustained. What followed was a 'period of economic restructuring and social and political readjustment' (Harvey 1989: 145).

As economic expansion began to prove elusive, downturns in economies of scale and productivity followed and the expenditure of the Keynesian state increased as a percentage of gross domestic product and began to be regarded as a drain or burden on capital. Keynesian policies began to be seen as disadvantageous to the development of capitalism and increasingly, rather than corporatist centralized planning, flexibility and mobility came to be identified as vital for maintaining the competitive imperative of capitalism. In brief, capitalism needed to 'free itself from its dependence on the state and relax the social constraints it was under. The state had to be made to serve the "competitiveness" of companies by accepting the supremacy of "market laws"' (Gorz 1999: 12–13).

Early in the 1970s, with the advent of multinational companies, the flight of capital began to gather momentum. By the end of the decade, barriers to trade and controls on capital movements were being increasingly abolished and multinationals were turning into 'transnational global corporations' (Gorz 1999: 13). Such developments signal the end of the consensus over Keynesian-Fordist policies. The neo-liberal free-market process of transformation had led to 'the globalization of the economy and the divorce between the interests of capital and those of the nation-state. The *political space* (of states) and the *economic space* (of capitalist corporations) could no longer coincide' (Gorz 1999: 13).

Foremost among the changes in economic organization and practice set in motion during this period was a move to what has come to be regarded as a more flexible system of capital accumulation. In contrast to the greater rigidity and more visible centralized organizational structures associated with Fordism, the new form of accumulation is characterized by significant degrees of flexibility. Labour processes and markets, and production and consumption, are characterized by flexibility; organizational forms tend to be decentred and their 'watchword . . . [is] "deregulate"' (Gorz 1999: 11). In addition, flexible accumulation is characterized by the development of 'new sectors of production, new ways of providing financial services, new markets, and, above all, greatly intensified rates of commercial, technological, and organizational innovation' (Harvey 1989: 147). Elaborating on the shift of emphasis from Fordism to flexible accumulation, Harvey argues that capitalism has not become disorganized – on the contrary, it is becoming more 'tightly organised'. Innovations in the field of information have enhanced coordination and communication and have increased the capacity to identify and respond instantaneously to new social, cultural and economic developments, allowing fast responses to changes in taste, fashion and a variety of market conditions. The ready availability of accurate information, along with 'the complete reorganization of the global financial system and the emergence of greatly enhanced powers of financial co-ordination' (Harvey 1989: 160) have meant that imploding centralization has been accompanied by tighter forms of organization rather than disorganization.

After organized capitalism: from flexibility to reflexivity

A number of different periods, stages or phases of capitalism have been identified by social analysts. For example, Ernest Mandel (1975) draws a distinction between nineteenth-century market capitalism, twentieth-century monopoly capitalism and a late twentieth-century multinational or consumer capitalism. A parallel set of distinctions refers to nineteenth-century liberal capitalism, twentieth-century organized capitalism and finally a post-Fordist and postmodern ' "disorganization" of capitalism' (Lash and Urry 1994: 2). This latter set of distinctions suggests an increase in the scale, scope and reach of capital flows, from the level of the 'locality or region' to the national (and ultimately the international) scale. Such increases in the scale, scope and reach of capital flows ultimately lead Lash and Urry to argue that new economies of signs and spaces have emerged with the transformation of organized capitalism into a more disorganized form. The notion that disorganization has become a prominent feature of contemporary capitalism warrants further consideration.

In his discussion of the movement from Fordism to flexible accumulation, David Harvey contends that what is in the process of being worked out – 'in fundamentally new ways' – is the tension that has always existed within capitalism between 'monopoly and competition, between centralization and decentralization of economic power' (1989: 159). Signs of tensions being worked out should not, Harvey contends, be taken as evidence that a more disorganized form of capitalism is emerging – on the contrary, capitalism is becoming *more* tightly organized. Lash and Urry offer a two-fold response to Harvey's criticisms. First, they set out to clarify the respects in which contemporary capitalism is disorganized – notably in so far as 'the flows of subjects and objects are progressively less synchronized within national boundaries' (1994: 10). Then they present 'reflexive accumulation', as opposed to 'flexible accumulation', as the more appropriate term for describing the distinctiveness of contemporary capitalism. Notwithstanding the existence of 'massively powerful organizations affecting each individual country', Lash and Urry (1994: 10) contend that there are bound to be problems of synchronization, for organizations operate with(in) different times. With the advent of disorganized capitalism, societies are considered to be vulnerable to 'systematic de-synchronization' and in consequence everything is potentially exposed to disorganization. In sum, '[n]othing is fixed, given and certain, while everything rests upon much greater knowledge and information' (Lash and Urry 1994: 10–11).

Despite the development of increasingly complex forms of knowledge and information, Lash and Urry argue that the new economies of signs and spaces are 'increasingly uncontrolled'. Organized capitalism and the Keynesian-Fordist economic and political programme that constituted a necessary corollary are predicated on the notion that social and economic life is amenable to control through the application of modern rationality. This organized form of capitalism corresponds in important respects to the form of modernity Ulrich Beck equates with an industrial society where there is a 'demand to make human living situations controllable by instrumental rationality' (1994: 10). Beck describes industrial society as one form of modernity, an exemplification of a process of 'primary modernization' which has promoted a 'rationalization of tradition'. It is a form of life, or 'context of experience' that is dissolving or disappearing as the familiar standardized and interrelated roles associated with class, gender, family and occupation have become fragmented. For example, women are no longer automatically mothers, mothers are no longer necessarily the primary care providers for children they may have given birth to, and in many households mothers and fathers are now both wage earners. Moreover, in a not insignificant number of cases, the sole wage earner in the household will be female.

While industrial society as a 'model of the lifeworld' might be in the process of disappearing, Beck argues that industrial production and industrial dynamism continue. The difference is that we are now more conscious of living with the consequences – 'the industrial production society manufactures its opposite, the global society of industrial consequences' (1998: 27). To describe this new modern form of life, one in which there is a growing recognition of the threat posed by both the potential and the actual uncontrollability of industrial consequences, Beck has introduced the concept of 'risk society', which is characterized by a form of 'reflexive modernization'. In a risk society there is a recognition of the unintended and 'unforeseeable' after-effects of the modern industrial demand for, and pursuit of, control and these 'in turn, lead to what had been considered overcome, the realm of the uncertain, of ambivalence, in short, of alienation' (Beck 1994: 10). Such a society is increasingly self-critical, diagnosis confronts counter-diagnosis, experts line up to challenge experts and a new way of acting and thinking emerges that Beck terms 'reflexive modernization'. What is meant by this notion is a radicalization of modernity, a rationalization of rationalization, a modernization of modernization, or a process of 'self-confrontation with the effects of risk society that cannot be dealt with and assimilated in the system of industrial society' (Beck 1994: 6; see also 1998: 19, 2000: 261–2). It is on this broad notion of reflexive modernization that Lash and Urry draw to counter criticism of their idea that capitalism is disorganized.

Lash and Urry accept that 'risk society' constitutes an appropriate term for describing the current situation in which we encounter manufactured globally extensive problems and attempt to reflexively monitor the consequences and responses that follow. Drawing on the notion of reflexive modernization Lash and Urry argue that a concept of 'reflexive accumulation' more effectively represents the distinguishing features of contemporary capitalist socioeconomic processes than the competing notions of 'flexible specialization, flexible accumulation and post-Fordism' (1994: 60). These interrelated terms are considered to fail to adequately account for four significant and novel aspects of contemporary economic life concerning services, knowledge and information, consumption and the articulation of culture and economy. First, it is argued that analysis of contemporary social and economic life, guided by a notion of flexible accumulation, has tended to underestimate the significance of services. There has been a failure to register that within western societies 'most people . . . are now service providers . . . [and] everyone is now the service-receiver of a diversity of services' (Lash and Urry 1994: 204).

Second, there is a parallel underestimation of the crucial importance of knowledge and information to economic growth. Information processing and the organization of information is now at the heart of capitalist economic development and due recognition of this feature has the 'virtue of shifting attention away from flexibility and towards the reflexivity involved in the process' (Lash and Urry 1994: 221).

Third, Lash and Urry argue that the flexible accumulation argument tends to focus disproportionately on economic production to the neglect of consumption. In so far as this is the case, important issues concerning increasing consumer choice and the enhanced role of consumption in the formation and stylization of identity are neglected. In turn, questions concerning socially patterned differences in the consumption of goods and services, and other manifestations of 'aesthetic reflexivity', such as the impact of increased personal mobility (notably in relation to travel and tourism) are not addressed.

Finally, it is argued that there is a lack of appreciation of the extent to which culture, in the form of symbolic, aesthetically inflected processes, is now a significant dimension of both economic production and consumption. In short, economic life is increasingly becoming 'cultural and aestheticized' (Lash and Urry 1994: 109). Implied here is a process of radical socioeconomic transformation in which cultural and economic processes are, as Lash and Urry (1994: 64) remark, more than ever interlaced and inter-articulated; that is, that the economy is increasingly culturally inflected and that culture is more and more economically inflected. Thus the boundaries between the two become more and more blurred and the economy and culture no longer function in regard to one another as system and environment.

But is it the case that analyses operating with a notion of 'flexible accumulation' or 'post-Fordism' are necessarily unable to deal adequately with novel aspects of contemporary economic life? The analysis offered by David Harvey of the transition from Fordism to a more flexible form of capital accumulation appears to answer the charges outlined above. For there is recognition of a 'remarkable . . . surge in service employment', as well as the increasing significance of information for coordinating dispersed corporate interests (Harvey 1989: 156, 159–60). There is also acknowledgement of an acceleration in the pace of consumption and an associated relative shift away from 'the consumption of goods and into the consumption of services' (Harvey 1989: 285). Finally a closer articulation of culture and economy evidenced by the increasing significance accorded to 'differentiated tastes and aesthetic preferences' (1989: 77) in the process of capital accumulation is clearly identified. However, such novel aspects of contemporary economic life are not the focus of analysis. Ultimately for Harvey the objective is to document the ways in which Fordist forms of economic life have been eroded by the development of flexible forms of capital accumulation and the respects in which cultural life continues to lie 'within the embrace of . . . capitalist logic' (1989: 344).

However, what is striking about both forms of analysis is their relative neglect of any sustained critical consideration of the neo-liberal economic and political programme and its social and economic consequences. Harvey makes reference to the ways in which post-war Fordism was articulated with 'welfare statism, Keynesian economic management, and control over wage relations' (1989: 135), and identifies factors that have contributed to the dismantling of Fordism-Keynesianism. For example, transformations in global capitalism have increased the autonomy of the banking and financial system, empowering finance capital to the detriment of the economic sovereignty of the nation state. And innovations in communication and transportation have made possible 'the new international division of labour, shifting principles of location, and proliferating mechanisms of co-ordination both within trans-national corporations as well as between different sectoral commodity and product markets' (Harvey 1989: 165). There is a very brief acknowledgement of the contribution made by 'neo-conservatism' to this process of transformation in Western Europe and North America at the close of the 1970s, but for Harvey it is of the order of a 'consolidation' of changes that are considered to have been already underway.

In the analysis of transformations in economic life offered by Lash and Urry there is no direct address of neo-liberalism. However, reference is made to the issue of a restructuring of publicly provided services in what is described as 'post-industrial, postmodern and post-Fordist' disorganized capitalism (1994: 321). The main issue identified is the limitations associated with a programme of restructuring that seeks to impose post-Fordist, more flexible, private sector strategies on publicly provided services that are in substantial respects Fordist in nature. The objective of restructuring publicly provided services has often been regarded as a euphemism for reducing state expenditure or 'rolling back' the state, and it constitutes a prominent feature of the neo-liberal project to open up more and more areas of socioeconomic life to market forces. However, it is necessary to exercise a degree of caution on this issue, for underlying the apparent transition from a Fordist-Keynesian inflected capitalism to a new more flexible, reflexive or neo-liberal form of capital accumulation there are signs of possible forms of continuity to which Harvey (1989: 170) has drawn attention:

> The massive government deficits in the United States, mainly attributable to defence, have been fundamental to whatever economic growth there has been in world capitalism in the 1980s, suggesting that Keynesian practices are by no means dead. Neither does the commitment to 'free-market' competition and deregulation entirely fit with the wave of mergers, corporate consolidations, and the extraordinary growth of interlinkages between supposedly rival firms of different national origin.

However, notwithstanding the persistence of substantial US government expenditure deficits, particularly in the area of defence, there has been a turn away from Keynesian economic management and towards a global liberalization of trade and capital flows that has brought in its wake forms of disorganization and disorder. Harvey contends that there is evidence of capitalism becoming more tightly organized by virtue of a number of important developments in the fields of information and finance. These include the extended scale and increased speed of access to information – 'now a very highly valued commodity' – and the enhancement of financial coordination through the 'formation of financial conglomerates' (Harvey 1989: 159–60). However, it is evident that such developments, along with the deterritorialization, global dispersal of capitalist production and the 'dictatorship of finance capital' (Gorz 1999: 22) have simultaneously made instability and volatility more prominent features of social and economic life. The effects of disorder associated with these developments are manifest in most countries, for participation in global trade 'tends to project these features of disorganized capitalism into every country' (Gray 1999: 73; see also Lash and Urry 1994: 322–3).

The contradictions of global free-market capitalism

Transnational bodies such as the World Trade Organization (WTO), the International Monetary Fund (IMF), and the Organization for Economic Cooperation and Development (OECD) have sought to impose a particular version of free-market capitalism on the diverse forms of organization of economic life found throughout the world. However, the outcome of the development of a global free market has not been emulation of the American model of capitalism, but a disorderly emergence of 'indigenous types of capitalism that owe little to any western model' (Gray 1999: 4). There are now a variety of different market economies in East Asia, and Chinese, Japanese and Russian forms of capitalism can be seen to differ significantly from western 'democratic capitalism'.

The neo-liberal notion of a single global free market has been described as a 'Utopia that can never be realized' (Gray 1999: 2), for the promotion and attempted introduction of deregulated market economies leads not to convergence but to the development of new divergent forms of capitalism. As Gray observes, 'world economy does not make a single regime – "democratic capitalism" – universal. It propagates new types of regimes as it spawns new kinds of capitalism' (1999: 4). The introduction of measures to advance the development of the global free market serves to erode and undermine the sovereignty of nation states. The granting of powers to supranational or transnational agencies (IMF; WTO; OECD; World Bank) to enforce global laws and regulations to protect 'free competition' and facilitate the 'free circulation' of goods and capital limits the ability of nation states to regulate and control economic activity. The promotion of global free enterprise and deregulated markets has been associated with a range of other unintended consequences, in particular an increase in global crime and growing signs of 'global ecological disorder' (Beck 1992; Castells 1997, 1998).

The political upheavals, geopolitical transformations and forms of technological restructuring associated with the emergence of a global free-market economy have led to the development of a global criminal economy as well as to the globalization of ecological risks. As Castells reveals, criminal organizations have taken advantage of 'economic globalisation and new communication and transportation technologies' (1998: 168) to operate transnationally. Global networking of criminal organizations has led to expansion of the criminal economy, to crime becoming a global industry. While drug trafficking remains the paramount business within the global criminal economy there is now a diverse range of global criminal operations, including trafficking of weapons, nuclear material, women and children and body parts, as well as the smuggling of illegal immigrants and money laundering (Castells 1998: 174–8).

In a comparable manner, Beck has shown that the development of global free-market capitalism has led to an increase in environmental pollution and an associated 'universalization of hazards' (1992: 36). With the globalization of free-market capitalism, ecological risks have increased both in intensity and scope and now affect virtually everyone on the planet. As Beck observes, on the 'battlefield of market opportunities . . . everyone is pursuing a "scorched Earth" policy against everyone else' (1992: 38). In so far as global economic expropriation continues to be closely articulated with ecological expropriation and devaluation, if not devastation, then there is, as Beck remarks, a 'systematically intensifying contradiction . . . between the profit and property interests' intrinsic to the process and 'its frequently threatening consequences which endanger and expropriate possessions and profits (not to mention the possession and profit of life)' (1992: 39).

State intervention and the formation of free markets

The process of attempting to establish free markets, both in the nineteenth and the late twentieth century, required state intervention. Contrary to conventional neo-liberal rhetoric, 'free markets are a product of artifice, design and political coercion' and, unlike regulated markets that emerge spontaneously as a consequence of singular piecemeal responses to specific problems, they must be 'centrally planned' (Gray 1999: 17). The free market has to be engineered and the related ways in which neo-liberal economic policies were deployed by the state in America, Britain and New Zealand in the course of the 1980s provide appropriate examples of the explicitly political nature of the free market project. Effectively, states have contributed to their own impotence by endorsing the 'neo-liberal credo that all problems are best resolved by allowing free rein to the laws of the market' (Gorz 1999: 15). The subsequent development and impact of 'globalized capital' – that is, capital freed from political regulation – has undermined the role of the nation state and raised doubts about the effectiveness of democratic political institutions.

Revolutionary developments in information technologies and communications have contributed further to the erosion of 'economic nationalism'. Such developments have made it possible for companies to become transnational networks with the potential to move their registered offices promptly to advantageous locations anywhere in the world. An advantageous location is one that promises to provide the lowest rates of taxation on profits, the least burdensome labour laws, the most attractive subsidies and infrastructure and an effectively 'disciplined and cheap workforce' (Gorz 1999: 14). Economic insecurity is a corollary of the end of economic nationalism (Beck 2000). The balance of economic power has tipped decisively in favour of 'extra-territorial' transnational companies demanding labour flexibility and a deregulation of labour markets. Nation states continue to attempt to defend their economic territory only to find the effectiveness of the measures they are able to employ much reduced and their legitimacy increasingly called into question as they prove themselves 'unable to control . . . disorganized capital flows' (Lash and Urry 1994: 323).

Fear about the prospect of retaining a job, remaining in work, and/or successfully retraining and (re)gaining work is now a corollary of the cultivation of labour market flexibility for a growing number of people. Demoralization and despair seem to follow inexorably in the wake of the deregulation of work for a significant number of victimized individuals as the risks associated with capitalist economic activity are redistributed from the state and the economy onto the shoulders of individuals. Neo-liberal capitalism, emphasizing the economic, social and political virtues of the free market, has sought to further legitimate the removal of regulations and restrictions on trade by extolling the benefits of increases in consumer choice and consumer freedom that are deemed inevitably to follow. But the rhetoric equating increased consumer choice with freedom neglects to give any consideration to the critical issue of '*what* can be chosen and what *is* chosen' (Marcuse 1968: 23).

If there has been any enhancement of consumer freedom and choice as a consequence of the implementation of neo-liberal strategies to achieve economic growth, there have also been considerable unevenly distributed costs to bear. The neo-liberal disorganization of capitalism has gone 'hand in hand with the replacement of jobs by "flexible labour" and of job security by "rolling contracts", fixed-term appointments and incidental hire of labour' (Bauman 1998b: 40–1). Furthermore, the direct benefits of economic growth have tended to be distributed in favour of the already excessively wealthy members of the community and as a result 'the poor get poorer, the very rich . . . get richer still' (Bauman 1998b: 41). The pursuit of the neo-liberal utopia has created a widespread culture of insecurity and anxiety rather than a benign condition in which increased consumer freedom and choice can be exercised. Far from creating conditions in which everyone can express their 'sovereign' choices through the mechanism of the market, the neo-liberal programme has produced a free-for-all in which individuals compete with one another, fearing for their economic security as restructuring threatens to transform, if not eradicate, their jobs. In a comparable manner, states are pitched against one another to provide the most attractive conditions (in effect the lowest costs and most attractive incentives) for transnational companies seeking to accelerate their rates of capital accumulation (Bourdieu 1998).

The increasing deregulation of western economies that has taken place since the 1970s, along with the globalization of production and trade that has occurred, has undoubtedly meant that nation states have less control over what remains of their economies (Castoriadis 1997; Bauman 1998a; Gray 1999). Ironically, one area in which a degree of control has been retained to date – the public sector, and the social welfare system in particular – has itself steadily become a target for restructuring through a combination of increased centralization, imposition of market mechanisms and ultimately 'privatization'. In late twentieth-century Britain a number of locally governed services, including health, justice, law enforcement and education, were subjected to reorganization to make them more accountable to central government and, in turn, to allow market mechanisms to be imposed upon them (Gray 1999). Market reform of the welfare state was expressed in a variety of policy initiatives that also included the sale of nationalized industries and the contracting out of public service provision to private agencies. It is all part of a trend, as Gorz sees it, towards 'replacing social welfare systems by private insurance schemes and private pension funds . . . [and] substituting private management by finance for social management of social welfare by the political system' (1999: 20).

The programme of deregulation or liberalization that was initiated in Britain during the course of the 1980s by the Conservative administration of Margaret Thatcher attempted to create a framework of rules and regulations within which a free market could become self-regulating. Treating the US economy as a model, laws relating to employment were modified to increase the flexibility of labour markets. Restrictions were placed on entitlements to welfare benefits as a whole and unemployment benefits were redesigned 'specifically to compel recipients to accept work at market-driven rates' (Gray 1999: 29).

The consequences of measures such as these were as follows: unemployment and insecure forms of employment (part-time and contract work) increased as the prospect of a job for life or a career declined for a growing number of people; rates of pay for low-skill workers fell below the level required for sustaining a family; and diseases associated with poverty returned. These outcomes placed a considerable strain on key social institutions – indeed, Gray argues that the 'innermost contradiction of the free market is that it works to weaken the traditional social institutions on which it has depended in the past' (1999: 29).

One important implication of all this is that neo-liberal social and economic policies have contributed to the decline of the family. This is exemplified by: increasing divorce and cohabitation rates, as well as an increase in births outside marriage; the growth of an underclass of workless people; an increase in the level of recorded crime, the prison population and expenditure on law enforcement; and a rapid growth in inequality. In each respect the British experience seems to more closely parallel that of the United States and to differ in significant respects from other European countries that have not had such a prolonged exposure to neo-liberal policies. However, they too have been increasingly inclined to 'deify the power of the markets in the name of economic efficiency' (Bourdieu 1998: 100).

The closing of the political universe?

It has been suggested that the old political formulae of 'left' and 'right' provide little, if any, purchase on present conditions (Giddens 1994). A return to economic nationalism and a Keynesian interventionist state no longer constitutes a credible option to counter the consequences of a globally extensive and disordered capitalism (Gray 1999; Beck 2000). So what are the options? Is there a realistic prospect of an alternative form of social and economic life, or is it a case of accepting that 'there is now no alternative to capitalism, only its constantly mutating varieties' (Gray 1999: 195)? What are the prospects for countering the 'neo-liberal fatalism' that has brought history to a premature end (Fukuyama 1992), undermined politics and imposed upon us a 'set of unquestioned ends – maximum growth, competitiveness, productivity' (Bourdieu 1998: 50)? Social analysts concerned about the disorderly consequences of capitalist economic life are asking, and not for the first time, what if anything can be done (e.g. Galbraith 1996, 1998; Gorz 1999; Gray 1999; Beck 2000; Hutton and Giddens 2001; Philo and Miller 2001).

Writing in the early 1960s about social conditions in an 'advanced industrial civilization', Herbert Marcuse drew attention to what he described as the paralysis of criticism in a society lacking opposition. Describing social theory as being 'concerned with the historical alternatives which haunt the established society' (1968: 11), Marcuse proceeded to deliberate on the factors that he believed were bringing about a closure of the political universe. In many respects we now live in rather different times, in a different era. There have been significant processes of social, economic, cultural and political transformation since the 1960s. But perhaps most important of all, our society seems no longer to be 'haunted' by historical alternatives – rather, it seems increasingly resigned to living without *any* alternative. In so far as we are living with 'political closure', it is appropriate to reconsider aspects of Marcuse's analysis which appear to resonate with contemporary conditions.

Realization of the benefits of technical progress, or what amounts to much the same thing, experiencing, accepting and coming to appreciate, if not without a degree of ambivalence, what are (re)presented as benefits, coupled with the promise of yet more progress and further benefits to come, is identified by Marcuse as having brought about a reconciliation of opposing social forces and an erosion or refutation of social protest. The technical apparatus of production and distribution is held to determine both 'socially needed occupations, skills and attitudes' as well as 'individual needs and aspirations' and thereby institutes 'more effective, and more pleasant forms of social control and social cohesion' (Marcuse 1968: 13) – forms of control and cohesion that are more effective precisely because they are *not* experienced as control measures. What Marcuse has in mind is the way in which the generation or cultivation of particular needs, wants and desires, for which the prospect of satisfaction can be promised and then provided, serves the purpose of enhancing the economic and technical coordination of industrial capitalist civilization.

The category of needs is crucial for Marcuse and it leads him to make a controversial distinction between two sub-categories of 'true' and 'false' needs.[2] 'False', or what are sometimes termed 'repressive' needs are described as prevalent and as 'superimposed upon the individual by particular social interests' (Marcuse 1968: 21). There is recognition that beyond a biologically determined base level, needs have always been socially and historically preconditioned to accord with 'prevailing societal institutions'. The critical point Marcuse wishes to make is that the economic and political requirements of the existing system of production and distribution have led to the cultivation of needs and satisfactions that, notwithstanding the pleasure and happiness that individuals might experience and enjoy, remain in his judgement 'false' and 'repressive'. They remain so because the needs and satisfactions involved are regarded as 'imposed' – that is, they are not considered to be the expression of autonomous individuals, but a product of 'external powers' or 'dominant interests' over which individuals continue to have no control. Any happiness individuals may derive from the satisfaction of such manufactured needs has to be considered in relation to unseen, unanticipated and unintended consequences.

Marcuse has in mind the consequences both for individuals immediately immersed in the pursuit of consumer pleasures and the countless others who are directly and indirectly (and not infrequently detrimentally) affected by the complex circuits of capitalist economic production and consumption.[3] The argument is that where happiness derives from the satisfaction of needs that 'perpetuate toil, aggressiveness, misery, and injustice' and serves to prevent people from developing an awareness of the economic system of production and distribution that is responsible, the presence of false or repressive needs can be recognized. Marcuse remarks that '[m]ost of the prevailing needs to relax, to have fun, to behave and consume in accordance with the advertisements, to love and hate what others love and hate, belong to this category of false needs' (1968: 21, 22).

A couple of qualifications are in order here. The objection is not to people relaxing and having fun, but to the various ways in which needs for such experiences are externally constituted and effectively imposed upon individuals, and particular products (commodities), services and activities are (re)presented through advertising and marketing media as the means for achieving satisfaction of such needs and come to be regarded as so doing by persuaded consuming individuals. In particular, Marcuse is concerned that, as things stand, the price of happiness for some is toil, misery and injustice for others.

Consider as an example the McDonald's 'Happy Meal' experience designed for, marketed at and consumed by children around the world. Happy

Meals come with give-away promotional toys (frequently Disney characters appearing in contemporary movies). Many of these 'free' toys are produced in the Keyhinge factory in Vietnam. There, as Doug Kellner observes, the wage rates paid to the mostly young women 'average between six and eight cents an hour – well below subsistence levels' (1999: 200). In addition, management has continually refused to remedy unsafe working conditions, in particular poor ventilation that has led to several workers falling ill as a result of exposure to acetone. Through targeted advertising and marketing, children are made aware of and come to want a Happy Meal, not for its nutritional value but for the experience and pleasure promised by the give-away toy produced by young women whose '[w]ages do not even cover 20 per cent of the daily food and travel costs for a single worker let alone her family' (Kellner 1999: 200). The fleeting experience of happiness that may be gained from the 'Happy Meal' by the young consumer comes at a price that extends beyond the transaction in the fast-food restaurant. The price includes the poor nutritional value of the 'junk' food, the soon to be realized limited play value of the, by now, throw-away toy, and the toil, risk and injustice to which producers in remote locations are routinely subjected.

The process of consumption is represented to and experienced by consumers as an exercise of 'freedom of choice'. The reality in Marcuse's view is very different: consumption constitutes a form of control that is generally not experienced as controlling at all. In a consumer capitalist society, 'people recognize themselves in their commodities . . . The very mechanism which ties the individual to his society has changed, and social control is anchored in the new needs which it has produced' (1968: 24). In short, through the cultivation of needs and the provision of means for their satisfaction, consumption comes to constitute a significant means of social control.

What then are 'true' needs? By implication they are not imposed on individuals, they are not determined by 'external powers' and they do not serve 'dominant interests'. Marcuse argues that what they are cannot be decided by a tribunal that arrogates 'to itself the right to decide which needs should be developed and satisfied' (1968: 23). Rather it is a question that ultimately must be answered by 'autonomous' individuals, individuals free from indoctrination and manipulation, free from the needs and satisfactions associated with what is termed the 'repressive administration of society' (Marcuse 1968: 23). This society is one in which there appears little prospect of (true) needs requiring liberation being acknowledged, let alone expressed, for the imaginations of 'administered individuals' appear unable to extend any further than the mundane routines, rewards and seductive comforts of the consumer society. Through the processes of production and consumption of goods and services, 'prescribed attitudes and habits' are acquired along with 'certain intellectual and emotional reactions' that serve to bind people to the prevailing way of life. In such circumstances it becomes difficult to imagine an alternative form of social and economic life, let alone that people should want one, for the existing way of life seems 'much better than before – and as a good way of life, it militates against qualitative change' (Marcuse 1968: 27). In consequence, thought and behaviour become 'one dimensional'. The prospect of an alternative form of social and economic life has disappeared and the political universe is effectively closed. As Marcuse remarks, 'there is no reason to insist on self-determination if the administered life is the comfortable and even the "good" life' (1968: 53).

Describing western industrial capitalist societies in the late 1960s as combining 'the features of the Welfare State and the Warfare State' (1968: 32), Marcuse identifies two key elements as contributing to the closing of the political universe: technical progress and the external threat represented by international communism. The external threat of communism precipitated increased expenditure on defence by the 'Warfare State', stimulated production and employment and contributed to a raising of living standards. These in turn served to attenuate social class struggles and bring about an unprecedented degree of social cohesion. Since 1989 and the revolutions in Eastern Europe the external threat identified with 'communism' has all but disappeared. While defence expenditure has continued to be a significant component of the US Federal Government budget, the potential threat posed by 'rogue states' and the risks of international terrorism (notwithstanding 11 September 2001) cannot as yet be considered comparable to the challenge formerly posed by international communism.

In terms of the other element, there are throughout Marcuse's analysis several references to the economic, social and political impact of technical progress. These take the form of critical observations and analyses of 'technological processes' (mechanization, standardization and automation), the political character of 'technological rationality', the organization of the 'technological base' of industrial capitalist society and the increasingly technological character of social control. The prevailing technical structure and organization of production and consumption appears, Marcuse contends, 'to be the very embodiment of Reason for the benefit of all social groups and interests – to such an extent that all contradiction seems irrational and all counteraction impossible' (1968: 25). In short, there seems to be no alternative and the political universe appears closed.

Much has changed since the late 1960s. Industrial society is now regarded as a way of life that is 'disappearing' (Beck 1998: 20). The accelerating process of globalization that began in the closing decades of the twentieth century has undermined the relative stability of Fordist, organized capitalism and contributed to the development of a 'species of disordered, anarchic capitalism' (Gray 1999: 71). In the same period the threat of communism collapsed and instead of being considered as a 'worthwhile price for keeping the workers content and peaceful', welfare states in the west began to be regarded as an 'intolerable burden on capitalism' (Elliott and Atkinson

1999: 222). These and other comparable developments, including the growth of discontent with both the 'normalizing' aspects of Fordist standardization and the '"dictatorship over needs" . . . inherent in the bureaucratism of the welfare state' (Gorz 1999: 4), imply limitations to the contemporary relevance of prominent aspects of Marcuse's analysis of an administered society. However, his diagnosis of a closing of the political universe and many of his observations on the impact of innovations in technological rationality on work, consumption and culture continue to resonate with more contemporary analyses of social and economic life.

The impact of the progressive development of technological rationality on production is apparent initially through mechanization, which reduces the physical quality of labour, and subsequently through automation which displaces it. Marcuse describes automation as 'the great catalyst' that constitutes a 'change in the character of the basic productive forces' (1968: 43), one that transforms not only the character and availability of work, but also those who work, and also the place and meaning of work in their lives. The process of technological transformation of work identified by Marcuse has gathered considerable momentum since the late 1960s and the associated social, economic and political consequences have become a prominent focus of analytic concern (Castells 1996, 1997, 1998; Gorz 1999; Beck 2000).

Technological innovation in production and the disorganization and disruption it tends to bring along with it is generally (re)presented as necessary modernization which promises to deliver 'an ever-more-comfortable life for an ever-growing number of people' (Marcuse 1968: 35). In terms of the criteria set – increasing material wealth, rising gross national product etc. – it can be argued that the promise has retained its persuasiveness for a substantial proportion of people. That is, those for whom, in some shape or form, life continues to be experienced as having become more comfortable, those Galbraith (1993) has subsequently described as the 'contented majority'. However, there are others – the underprivileged, those to whom the promise is barely extended, let alone likely to be delivered. These are the people Marcuse (1968: 35, 56, 200) finds in the basement of society, the outcasts and outsiders, the poor, the unemployed and unemployable, those kept in line by more unpleasant means. The increasing contrast between the evermore comfortable and those 'whose life is the hell of the Affluent Society' (Marcuse 1968: 35) has subsequently been addressed in analyses of 'consumer society' (Bauman 1998b), 'network society' (Castells 1998), and the hidden economic production zones of the new 'branded' capitalism (Klein 2001).

The issue of social inclusion and exclusion in relation to consumption is explored in Bauman's (1992) analysis of the way in which the structure of domination in 'postmodern' capitalist society is reproduced through a combination of 'seduction' and 'repression'. Our society, Bauman (1998b:

24) remarks, is a consumer society and it engages the majority of people, those seduced by the promise of consumption, primarily as consumers. But again, there are others, those who are described as on the margins of society, those excluded from the consumer game. These are the 'non-consumers', those subject to forms of repression that serve to transform 'the market unattractiveness of non-consumer existence into the unattractiveness of alternatives to market dependency' (Bauman 1992: 98). In this way the widely held impression that there are indeed no realistic, attractive, practical alternative forms of social life gains additional confirmation.

Just as particular transformations in social and economic life have precipitated increasing political integration, so particular developments in culture, in a parallel manner, are held to be neutralizing 'oppositional and transcending elements' (Marcuse 1968: 58). As it has become increasingly exposed to a process of commodification, so culture has become subject to the order of exchange value and associated commercial pressures. Culture is now rarely a source of negation or 'protest against that which is' (Marcuse 1968: 63). This 'flattening out of the antagonism between culture and reality', identified as a corollary of commodification and associated developments in technological rationality by Marcuse (1968: 58, 63), serves to close off alternative imaginary possibilities by incorporating them into the prevailing order of things. Cultural forms and practices no longer stand apart from societal reality and call it into question. Rather than serving as a critical reference point for the generation of possible alternative forms of social life, cultural forms and practices are increasingly required to accommodate to market mechanisms. Commodified and incorporated within the market, cultural forms and practices effectively become 'commercials – they sell, comfort, or excite' (Marcuse 1968: 63).

Notwithstanding the 'aestheticization of everyday life', the proliferation of images and symbols, and the emphasis now placed on advertising, marketing and branding at the heart of the consumer society, there remains a dominant materialism (Featherstone 1991). Culture has indeed acquired a central position within late capitalist consumer society and a growing proportion of economic activity is now devoted to informational and symbolic work. But the commercialization of culture and the increased emphasis placed upon representation and symbolism in economic activity reflect the development of 'commodity aesthetics under late capitalism' (Haug 1986: 97).

Although Marcuse does not conceptualize the process of transformation to which cultural forms and practices are subject in quite these terms, what is identified in his work is 'the dissolution of an autonomous sphere of culture' (Jameson 1991: 48). It is a case of reality surpassing its culture through the wholesale incorporation of formerly oppositional and transcending cultural values into the established order of things 'on a massive scale' (Marcuse 1968: 58). The consequences of such a process of incorporation are that cultural ideals are compromised and transformed as they are assimilated and materialized. In short, the 'music of the soul' ultimately becomes the 'music of salesmanship' as priority is accorded to 'exchange value' over 'truth value' (Marcuse 1968: 59). As the increasing proliferation of capitalist market relations and the associated growth of a culture of consumption have led to a 'transformation of higher and popular culture', exemplified by 'the cultural centre . . . becoming a fitting part of the shopping centre' (Marcuse 1968: 69, 64), so critical distance has been erased. What is at stake here is the 'effacement . . . of the older (essentially high-modernist) frontier between high culture and so-called mass or commercial culture' (Jameson 1991: 2). This is a development that has been equated by Jameson with the emergence of a new cultural dominant, 'postmodernism', a corollary of the expansion of global capitalism.[4]

In his analysis of the transformations intrinsic to late capitalism Jameson focuses on the 'prodigious new expansion of multinational capital' and the associated 'expansion of culture throughout the social realm' (1991: 48–9). In particular, it is argued that to make sense of contemporary developments it is necessary to analyse both the powerful 'dynamic of the "culture of consumption"' and the impact of the 'culture of the market' on social life (Jameson 1991: 206–7). It is to a clarification of these two concerns – that is, the culture of consumption and the associated culture of the market at the heart of contemporary social and economic life – that discussion is directed in the following two chapters.

Notes

1 On the issue of the durability of capitalism and the potentially rejuvenating role of structural crises see the work of the 'regulation theorists', for example Boyer (1990); Lipietz (1987) and Tickell and Peck (1995). See also the collection of papers in *Thesis Eleven No. 66*, August 2001 on 'Rethinking capitalism'.

2 For a consideration of the appropriateness of a notion of 'need' for making sense of consumption in a consumer society see Bauman (2001b).

3 An important concern for Marcuse is the morality of consumption, the fact that consumption has social, ecological and personal consequences and that the happiness achieved by some is at the expense of misery, exploitation and injustice for others. For a wider-ranging consideration of the 'morality of consumption' see the special section of *Journal of Consumer Culture* (2001) 1(2): 225–60.

4 This issue is discussed in Chapter 1 of Jameson's book *Postmodernism or the Cultural Logic of Late Capitalism* (1991).

CHAPTER 3

CULTURES OF PRODUCTION AND CONSUMPTION

Introduction: capitalism and its consequences

What is produced and consumed in contemporary societies and how production and consumption are organized continue to be determined by a capitalist rationality whose historic significance Marx first noted in his study of nineteenth-century 'liberal' capitalism. Capitalism has changed in important respects since the nineteenth century. Liberal capitalism studied by Marx gave way to organized, mass production, mass consumption capitalism during the course of the twentieth century. This more organized 'Fordist' form of capitalism was itself subsequently displaced by a more flexible, reflexive and disorganized form in the closing decades of the last century (Harvey 1989; Lash and Urry 1994). Significant changes in the flows of 'money, means of production, consumer-commodities, and labour-power' (Lash and Urry 1994: 2) occurred as the circulation of capital grew from a local or regional level to a national scale, and then on to an international or global scale. However, notwithstanding the significance of such changes, Marx's work remains 'rich in insights' as we endeavour to understand the current situation (Harvey 1989: 339; see also Lash and Urry 1987, 1994).

In his nineteenth-century analysis of a developing modern capitalist mode of production and the impact it was having on social and cultural life, Karl Marx was influenced positively by the discourse of political economy. Reacting critically to the legacy of philosophical idealism and its tendency to approach the study of human existence in terms of abstract categories such as 'being', 'reason' and 'spirit', Marx placed analytic emphasis on the ways in which real living people went about their lives. Focusing on what he considered to be the real conditions of human existence, primarily the ways in which people (re)produced their means of existence, Marx sought to clarify the complex relationships that existed between social, cultural and economic forms of life, placing emphasis on the significance of economic production. In particular, Marx devoted detailed consideration to the distinctive characteristics and impact of capitalism, a modern mode of production, clarifying its distinctive economic features, developmental tendencies, and social and cultural consequences (Bottomore 1979; Sayer 1991).

Contemporary capitalism is different in some important respects from the mode of production Marx analysed (Castells 1992; Gray 1999; Hutton and Giddens 2001). Capitalism is a mode of production that cannot exist without constantly transforming 'the instruments of production, and thereby the relations of production, and with them the whole relations of society' (Marx and Engels 1968: 83). The continual pursuit of forms of social and technological innovation that promise to transform production and consumption – *how* things are produced and consumed, as well as *what* is produced and consumed – is a normal and necessary feature of capitalism. Within Marx's work it is the impact innovations in science and technology have on capitalist production that receives attention. The production of wealth is recognized to depend less on 'labour time and the amount of labour employed' and more on the way in which science and technology are applied in production and 'pressed into the service of capital' (Marx 1973: 704–5). Beyond a few brief speculative references to a possible increase in 'free time', Marx does not consider the consequences for consumption in this context.

The emergence of new modes of development is an integral feature of modern capitalism (Smart 2000) and the impact of transformations in the technological arrangements of capitalist production has contributed powerfully to the experience of modern life as a 'maelstrom' (Berman 1983). The experience of modernity has been described as one of 'perpetual disintegration and renewal, of struggle and contradiction, of ambiguity and anguish' (Berman 1983: 15). This is precisely what Marx was drawing attention to when he noted the 'uninterrupted disturbance of all social conditions' arising from the necessity under capitalism to continually 'revolutionize production' (Marx and Engels 1968: 83). Further references to the accelerating rate or pace of change, the transformation of prevailing relations and practices and the speed with which new relations and practices themselves, in turn, 'become antiquated', accord with the reality of contemporary social life subject to a disordered and disorganized capitalism. Likewise, identification of the need for a 'constantly expanding market' leading to the extension of capitalism around the globe anticipates the subsequent globalization of capitalism (Gray 1999; Hutton and Giddens 2001).

The consequences of this process, through which 'a cosmopolitan character [is given] to production and consumption in every country' (Marx and Engels 1968: 83), are an increasingly prominent feature of contemporary social life. In respect of production the 'national ground' of industry has indeed been eroded, national industries have been destroyed, and attracting new industries has become a vital matter. In turn, consumption long ago ceased to be confined to goods and services made available through local or national production and consumers have become well acquainted with, if not dependent on, 'the products of distant lands and climes' (Marx and Engels 1968: 84). An increasing 'inter-dependence of nations' has clearly displaced 'national seclusion and self-sufficiency' in both production and consumption, and this has become even more evident with the development of information technology and the deployment of powerful means of global communications. But while changes in technological arrangements and the increasing globalization of production and consumption have indeed transformed socioeconomic life, it has not been transformed beyond recognition – it remains fundamentally subject to a system of commodity production based on private ownership of property. Capital accumulation remains the primary objective, pursuit of profit continues to be the driving force. In short, socioeconomic life remains subject to capitalist relations of production.

Many of the aspects identified by Marx continue to be a prominent part of the system of production that it was anticipated all nations ultimately would be compelled to follow. However, a number of analysts have argued that there has been a notable shift of emphasis within contemporary capitalism from production to consumption, and that this calls for a more direct and sustained consideration of consumption to counterbalance Marx's preoccupation with production (Sayer 1991; Baudrillard 1998; Bauman 1998b).

Without production, no consumption; without consumption, no production

In his analysis of nineteenth-century capitalism Marx argued that 'production is also immediately consumption' (1973: 90) in the sense that in the course of production there is a consumption of energy and resources. Turning directly to what would more properly be regarded as consumption, Marx notes that 'consumption is also immediately production' (p. 90) in so far as the act of consuming produces effects – for example, the consumption of food reproduces the body. However, notwithstanding the apparent unity of production and consumption implied in these and other remarks, Marx adds that 'consumptive production' is different from and secondary to production proper, for the production that takes place in the course of consumption depends upon 'the destruction of the prior product' (p. 91).

While Marx accords priority to production in his analysis of capitalism there is recognition of the importance of consumption. Two respects in which consumption bears on production are discussed. First, it is argued that a 'product becomes a real product only by being consumed' (1973: 91) and second, that the need and/or motive for production is created by consumption. In short, 'no production without a need. But consumption reproduces the need' (p. 92). However, it is production that provides the object of consumption and, as a consequence of the specific features of the object, shapes the manner of consumption. Elaborating on the respects in which production creates the consumer, Marx observes that production 'produces consumption by creating the specific manner of consumption; and, further, by creating the stimulus of consumption, the ability to consume, as a need' (p. 93).

The analytic objective for Marx was to reveal the logic of capitalism, to show how it had to operate, and to that end the focus of his work fell on production. In consequence, while there is a recognition that production along with consumption, distribution and exchange form a 'totality, distinctions within a unity', ultimately the argument is that production predominates – 'The process always returns to production to begin anew. That exchange and consumption cannot predominate is self-evident' (1973: 99). However, as modern capitalism has developed, a number of the processes tentatively identified by Marx have become significantly more prominent features, calling into question the appropriateness of an analytic focus confined almost entirely to production. As science has been increasingly deployed in the service of capital the production of real wealth has become less and less dependent on labour time and the quantity of labour employed. In turn, work has become a less prominent feature of people's lives and less significant in determining their identity. The significance and impact of the application of science and technology to production has grown and appears to be increasing. This is particularly evident in the way in which 'the informational mode of development' has contributed to the restructuring of the capitalist mode of production and the emergence of an 'informational' capitalism (Castells 1996). Labour, as Marx anticipated, is no longer so directly involved in the production process – rather, the worker increasingly relates to the process of production more as 'watchman and regulator' (1973: 705–6).

As productivity increased with the development of productive forces so, Marx argued, there would be a requirement for the 'production of new consumption' (1973: 408). Elaborating on the process of expansion of consumption, Marx identifies three aspects:

> Firstly quantitative expansion of existing consumption; secondly: creation of new needs [markets] by propagating existing ones in a wide circle; thirdly: production of *new* needs and discovery and creation of new use values.
>
> (1973: 408)

The expansion of consumption along the general lines identified remains a central feature of contemporary capitalism. The necessity to continually create qualitatively different branches of production, along with newly-forged needs and desires that new products and services can be represented in marketing campaigns to satisfy, has led to a continuing process of

> exploration of all of nature in order to discover new, useful qualities in things, universal exchange of the products of all alien climates and lands; new (artificial) preparation of natural objects, by which they are given new use values. The exploration of the earth in all directions to discover new things of use as well as new useful qualities of the old . . . the development of the natural sciences . . . [and] the cultivation of all the qualities of the social human being.
>
> (Marx 1973: 409)

Such remarks undoubtedly open up the issue of consumption, but their ultimate purpose is to illuminate aspects of the general development of capitalist production. Production remains an important part of present-day society, but consumption has increased in significance and warrants more direct analytic consideration. Before turning to an analysis of consumption, further consideration needs to be given to the ways in which production and the world of work have been transformed.

On the transformation of work

It has been suggested that our society is now a 'consumer society' (Baudrillard 1998; Bauman 1998b). Whereas the industrial capitalist society that Marx studied was fundamentally one of production, a work-based society, a society that 'engaged its members *primarily* as producers', our society, in its 'late-modern, second-modern or post-modern stage . . . engages its members – again *primarily* – in their capacity as consumers' (Bauman 1998b: 24). Ours is a consumer society in so far as identity and status are acquired, and social inclusion or integration is achieved, through participation in consumer activity. The relative shift of emphasis from production to consumption, what Bauman terms the 'passage from producer to consumer society' (1998b: 24), is exemplified by the increasing prominence accorded to consumer activity. It is also reflected in the growing disaffection expressed by more and more people towards work and the respects in which individual identity now appears to be less and less bound up with job, work and career (Sennett 2001).

The passage from producer to consumer society was engineered – was made possible and necessary – by the way in which the world of work has been, and continues to be, transformed. Work in the sense of an activity that is considered sufficiently useful to warrant payment is a modern invention, 'invented then generalized only with the coming of industrialism' (Gorz 1989: 13). Within a modern industrial capitalist society, holding a job has been the basis on which individuals, generally adult males, 'belong to the public sphere, acquire a social existence and a social identity ... and are part of a network of relations and exchanges' (Gorz 1989: 13). But the current 'post-Fordist' process of capitalist development is radically transforming work, producing a spread of temporary, flexible and insecure forms of employment (Beck 2000) and increasingly creating low-paid, unskilled occupations, or 'McJobs' (Ritzer 1998). There is little sense of belonging, identity or satisfaction to be found in such forms of work. The new flexible form of capitalism has transformed the work experience and as a result 'people can't identify themselves with a particular labour or with a single employer' (Sennett 2001: 176, 183).

Feminization of work

As a flexible, informational capitalism has developed, work and labour markets have been transformed by the entry of women into the labour force on an unprecedented scale.[1] Changes in the organization and distribution of paid labour have been identified as part of the 'feminization of work' (McDowell 1997; Beck 2000). The feminization of work represents much more than an acknowledgement of the dramatic increase in women's employment. It signifies, in turn, that the new jobs and occupations in the service sector, the new more flexible and less hierarchical forms of organization and the new management structures and styles place emphasis on aptitudes and attributes stereotypically essentialized as 'feminine' (McDowell 1997). An aptitude for serving and caring is an asset in service sector employment. Likewise an empathetic and cooperative managerial practice is more appropriate following the shift from 'vertical bureaucracies to the horizontal corporation' (Castells 1996: 164). More broadly it has been suggested that the rapid increase in women's employment is a consequence of

> the informationalization, networking, and globalization of the economy ... [and] the gendered segmentation of the labour market taking advantage of specific social conditions of women to enhance productivity, management control, and ultimately profits.
>
> (Castells 1997: 162)

More precisely, the growing involvement of women in the labour force is identified by Castells with three main factors. First, although there are only small differences in occupational profiles, a significant wage differential exists between men and women in all countries. In short, for employers women represent an attractive labour pool because there is the prospect of 'paying less for similar work' (Castells 1997: 169).[2] Second, the new informational economy requires a labour force capable of adapting to new demands and tasks and possessing relational skills suitable for service-related person to person work. As Castells remarks, 'the new economy requires increasingly the skills that were confined to the private domain of relational work to be brought to the forefront of management and processing of information and people' (1997: 169). In sum, given their relational skills and conventionally lower rates of pay, women workers are very attractive to employers.

However, it is a third factor that Castells argues has contributed most to the rapid growth of women's employment – namely a structural congruence between the needs of women workers for flexible employment and the requirements of the new economy for a 'flexibilization of work'. It is not surprising that women account for the bulk of part-time and temporary employment, for there is a fit between their need for 'working flexibility . . . and the needs of the new economy' (Castells 1997: 173).

Adult males in full-time employment with 'a wife in the background to take care of "everything else"' (Beck 2000: 58) have ceased to be the norm in the world of work. What has been called 'monogamous work' has been steadily replaced by new patterns of employment and distributions of work (shorter hours and lower pay; part-time work; flexible, casual, temporary forms of employment). A corollary of this 'feminization' of the world of work, as Beck (2000: 64, 93) notes, has been an increase in precarious forms of employment.

Reflecting on the way in which production and work have been transformed in the wake of the break up of the Fordist-Keynesian configuration that regulated the process of capital accumulation during 1945–73 (Harvey 1989), Naomi Klein notes that multinational corporations no longer boast of being 'engines of job growth'. Rather, they are now inclined to present themselves as 'engines of economic growth' and to regard labour as a 'burden' (2001: 261, 262). According to Klein, the means corporations increasingly employ to produce economic growth include 'layoffs, mergers, consolidation, and outsourcing – in other words . . . job debasement and loss' (p. 261). Innovations in technology have undoubtedly contributed to the current situation in which 'productivity grows together with the tapering of employment' (Bauman 1998b: 24). But it is the neo-liberal imposition of flexibility in relation to labour processes and labour markets, to both production and patterns of consumption, which has precipitated job debasement and loss. Neo-liberal capitalist management of technological innovations has meant that

> increasing gains in productivity generate falling wages, deteriorating living and working conditions, a rapidly growing underclass of working poor, destitute, jobless and homeless people on one side, and rising profits, affluence and conspicuous luxuries on the other.
>
> (Gorz 1999: 145)

As the world of work has been transformed and we leave the 'work-based society' behind, so the insecure worker has become an increasingly prominent figure. As companies have sought to increase their scope for 'flexibility', frequently a euphemism for minimizing responsibility for employees in order to 'keep overheads down and ride the twists and turns in the market', so jobs have been replaced by 'casualized', temporary or part-time forms of work (Klein 2001: 231, 254). The insecure worker, a product of this process, is unable to identify with work and tends to regard as 'his/her "true" activity the one he/she devotes himself to in the gaps between . . . paid "work"' (Gorz 1999: 53). Increasingly it is with non-work life, in the spaces and endless cycles and circuits of consumption, that individuals are inclined, and indeed encouraged, to identify themselves and find meaning in their lives. Increasingly, identity, social recognition and integration are achieved not through productive activity in the form of employment, career or job, but through the activity of consumption. However, the possibility of finding fulfilment and meaning in consumption is far from guaranteed, and is likely to be at best partial and transitory. For a necessary feature of the process of reproducing consumer subjects is the maintenance of the pursuit of fulfilment and meaning as a project without finality. Furthermore, while the gates to the shopping mall are open to all, some – 'the flawed consumers' – do not have the means to truly enter into the consumer game, and in a consumer society 'inadequacy . . . as a consumer . . . leads to social degradation and "internal exile"' (Bauman 1998b: 38).

Beyond the work ethic

As the nature of work and production has been transformed and consumption has become a markedly more prominent feature of contemporary social life, it has been argued that an 'aesthetics of consumption . . . now rules where the work ethic once ruled' (Bauman 1998b: 32). When, in the early years of the twentieth century, Max Weber (1976) published his contribution to an understanding of the origins of modern capitalism, the 'work ethic' constituted an important and influential feature of social and economic life. The work ethic promoted the idea that waged work constituted a duty and contributed to the (re)production of a disciplined labour force, to the internalization of habits and patterns of conduct conducive to the efficient performance of tasks within industrial capitalist workplaces (Thompson 1967). The work ethic placed emphasis on the virtue of work, on the importance of working to provide for oneself and/or one's family, and in turn condemned those who sought to evade their responsibility to work. It is worth recalling that for most workers within an industrial capitalist context work was poorly paid and not likely to be a source of intrinsic satisfaction. For a substantial number, waged work was undertaken in the face of considerable risks to their health and safety. It is in this context that the significance of the work ethic can be appreciated, for it accorded meaning and moral value to waged work. The work ethic contributed to the process whereby work came to occupy a pre-eminent significance in the lives of adult male members of modern society. Work represented the primary source of their identity – determining who they were from what they did – and contributed powerfully to their sense of self-esteem. In short, the work ethic got people to work, or perhaps more accurately it contributed to a cultural setting in which to work was regarded as the normal state of affairs, and being out of work, or not working, was likely to induce feelings of guilt and arouse anxiety.

The lives of pre-industrial workers were shaped by the rhythms and forces of nature, as well as by the customs and practices enshrined in tradition. The transformation of such workers into the docile and disciplined factory operatives of industrial capitalism, whose working lives were determined by 'the foreman, the clock and the machine', required nothing less than a crusade (Bauman 1998b: 6). At the forefront of the constitution of the new more disciplined way of life and the new form of subjectivity lay the work ethic. In his examination of the conditions that nurtured 'a manner of life so well adapted to the peculiarities of capitalism', Max Weber refers to a 'social ethic of capitalistic culture' and to a spirit of capitalism as a 'definite standard of life claiming ethical sanction' (1976: 55, 54, 58). What Weber sought to do was to explain how a particular form of conduct conducive to the development of a specific form of economic activity, notably the relentless drive to accumulate capital intrinsic to modern rational capitalism, had emerged within western Europe after the Reformation. Weber explains how 'worldly Protestant asceticism', with its promotion of methodical, disciplined work, or labour as a 'calling', and condemnation of idleness, 'irrational use of wealth' and unrestricted consumption, had contributed to the formation of cultural conditions conducive to the development of modern capitalism (1976: 63, 171).

As Weber acknowledges in his concluding remarks, 'the Puritan wanted to work in a calling; we are forced to do so' (1976: 181). The world into which individuals are now born is one in which the capitalist economy constitutes a seemingly 'unalterable order of things', a way of life to which there appears no alternative but to accommodate (Weber 1976: 54–5). Reflecting on the relationship between religious precepts and modern capitalist activity, Weber comments that from a 'religiously influenced life-style' had emerged individuals ready, willing and able to 'live up to the demands of early modern capitalism' (1978a: 1124). But by the turn of the twentieth century, Weber was able to note that modern capitalism no longer needed the support of a religious ethic; that 'on the whole, modern capitalism . . . is emancipated from the importance of such ethical factors' (1978a: 1125).

By this time, material goods had begun to assume 'an inexorable power' over people's lives 'as at no period in history' (1976: 181).

The capitalism of today that dominates social and economic life has manufactured a world in which material goods and services appear to exercise even more power over people's lives. In contemporary capitalism it seems that 'consumer freedom' has moved into the central place formerly occupied by work in the coordination of 'individual motivation, social integration and systemic reproduction' (Bauman 1992: 49). Hence the suggestion that rather than focus on the work ethic and production, analytic attention now needs to be directed to the development of a 'consumer society' (Baudrillard 1998) and an associated 'aesthetic of consumption' (Bauman 1998b).

Conditions of consumption

An increasing range and diversity of material goods and services is now available for consumption, and the shopping mall and the activity of shopping have become prominent features of contemporary social life, the cultural centre of which is consumption (Baudrillard 1998). For a capitalist economic system that increasingly needs consumers more than it needs producers, the 'spending-happy consumer is a necessity' and for the 'individual consumer, spending is a duty' (Bauman 1992: 50).

To explain the strategic importance accorded to consumption in the latter part of the twentieth century, Baudrillard recalls the lack of effective demand that produced economic depression and a crisis of capitalism in the 1930s. He suggests that at that time modern industrial capitalist societies 'knew how to make people work . . . [but] did not know how to make them consume' (1975: 144). The realization that it was no longer production but circulation that was the central problem for capitalism led to the identification of consumption as the strategic element and the mobilization of people as consumers as a necessity – 'their "needs" became as essential as their labour power' (Baudrillard 1975: 144). And just as labour power is produced through a process of cultural conditioning – that is, accommodated to the routine requirements of the modern industrial capitalist workplace through the work ethic and related disciplinary technologies that produce appropriate forms of human subjectivity – so consumer 'needs' have to be continually conditioned (Galbraith 1963, 1969; Marcuse 1968; Baudrillard 1998; Klein 2001).

Consumer needs or wants have become a strategic element because the basic predicament confronting contemporary capitalism is 'no longer the contradiction between "profit maximization" and the "rationalization of production" . . . but that between a potentially unlimited productivity . . . and the need to dispose of the product' (Baudrillard 1998: 71). Decisions about the purchase of goods are strategically too important to be left to uncondi-tioned consumer choice. So demand is managed through 'a huge network of communications, a great array of merchandising and selling organ-izations, nearly the entire advertising industry [and] numerous ancillary research training and other related services' (Galbraith 1969: 205; see also Packard 1957; Klein 2001).

Contemporary society remains 'objectively and decisively a society of production, *an order of production*', but it is now closely articulated with an '*order of consumption*' (Baudrillard 1998: 33). While production remains decisive, 'heroes of production' are considered by Baudrillard to have been displaced by those of consumption, as 'movie stars, sporting or gambling heroes . . . [and] a handful of gilded princes[ses] or globe-trotting barons' (1998: 46) have become our cultural icons. Notwithstanding the emphasis placed on market forces and enterprise culture in the closing decades of the twentieth century and the prestige acquired by a new genera-tion of entrepreneurs, contemporary society continues to be fixated with the lives of consumer culture 'heroes'. Media representations of the life-styles and forms of conspicuous consumption of celebrity figures continue to serve the function of providing 'economic stimulus for . . . consumption' (Baudrillard 1998: 46).

The culture of early capitalism promoted ascetic conduct and demanded that you 'work hard in your calling'. Pleasure constituted a potential prob-lem, a distraction from the requirement to work hard. In contrast, con-temporary capitalism quite deliberately promotes the idea of pleasure and encourages its pursuit through consumption, for it needs an endless supply of consumers continually pursuing satisfactions promised in the marketing and advertising of an expanding range of products and services. As I have indic-ated, an appropriate supply of happy-to-spend consumers, eager to exercise their consumer freedoms and express their consumer choices does not emerge spontaneously but through a complex process of cultural constitution. Reflecting on the changing culture and economy of the Fordist-Keynesian industrial capitalist configuration that was made necessary with 'the applica-tion of increasingly intricate and sophisticated technology to the production of things', Galbraith (1969: 13) drew particular attention to the importance of the process of consumer demand management.

The conventional wisdom of economic analysis has been that the con-sumer is sovereign and that there is a 'unidirectional flow of instruction from consumer to market to producer' (Galbraith 1969: 216). In contrast Galbraith reveals consumer conduct to be subject to a process of social and economic management. Through the psycho-sociological apparatus of advertising and marketing, consumer demand is stimulated and shaped and behaviour is accommodated to 'the needs of the producers and the goals . . . of the system' (Galbraith 1969: 217). Endorsing this view, Baudrillard (1998: 72) remarks that the freedom and sovereignty of the consumer are mystification pure and simple. This carefully sustained mystique (preserved first and foremost by economists) of individual satisfaction and choice, which is the culmination of a whole civilization of 'freedom', is the very ideology of the industrial system, justifying its arbitrary power and all the collective nuisances it generates.

However, while Baudrillard endorses criticism of the notion of consumer 'freedom' or 'sovereignty' he is, in turn, critical of Galbraith's assumption that a distinction can be drawn between 'authentic' and 'artificial' needs and that, in turn, the 'needs of the individual can be stabilized' (1998: 73). From the standpoint of the consumer the distinction between 'authentic' and 'artificial' satisfactions is groundless. Furthermore, Baudrillard continues, the notion that capitalist economic development has required 'forced acculturation to the processes of consumption' does not explain 'why consumers "take" the bait' (1998: 74).

Rather than consider needs or wants as conditioned in relation to particular objects and depict the individual consumer as a passive victim of the system, Baudrillard argues that consumption is now central to the constitution of social status, identity and difference. Consumption is an 'unlimited social activity' and 'needs are reorganized around an *objective* social demand for signs and differences' (Baudrillard 1998: 74). Needs do not emerge as discrete singular phenomena, rather they constitute a system and it is in this sense that they are the product of the system of production:

> needs, taken one by one, are *nothing* . . . there is only a system of needs, or rather . . . needs are only *the most advanced form of the rational systematization of the productive forces at the individual level*, where 'consumption' takes over logically and necessarily from production.
>
> (1998: 75)

This formulation allows Baudrillard to avoid a crude conditioning thesis and acknowledge that consumers may resist specific advertising and marketing campaigns encouraging them to consume a particular product. Resistance to particular products and substitution of others to meet needs is a routine feature of consumer activity, but the 'consumption power' ultimately exercised remains a 'propensity . . . within the more general framework of the productive forces' (Baudrillard 1998: 75).

In so far as needs assume the form of a system, Baudrillard argues it is necessary to realize that needs are 'radically different from enjoyment and satisfaction' (1998: 75). From this perspective, needs are system elements and do not signify a relationship of individual to object. Consumption is 'not a function of enjoyment, but a *function of production*' and in so far as this is recognized to be the case Baudrillard adds that it should come as no surprise to find that the puritan ethic '*haunts* consumption and needs' (1998: 78, 76). It is in this sense that the notion of consumption as a duty, 'perhaps the most important of duties' (Bauman 1992: 50), becomes understandable, as, in turn, does the compulsive quality and seemingly limitless character of consumption.

Consumption as a meeting of biological need and subsistence has been displaced by what Baudrillard terms 'consumption proper' – that is, a sociological system of signs. Consumption is a 'system which secures the ordering of signs and the integration of the group . . . both a morality (a system of ideological values) and a communication system, a structure of exchange' (Baudrillard 1998: 78). In consumption, individuals unavoidably enter into a 'generalized system of exchange and production of coded values' (p. 78) and it is this that constitutes the distinctiveness of our society, the basis on which social life now increasingly revolves.

Seduction and obligation

While there is a significant level of agreement about the prominent place consumption now occupies in contemporary society, there are important differences in both the conceptualization and explanation of the processes involved (Featherstone 1991). What is clear from Galbraith's account is that consumption is dependent on production in a number of respects that have subsequently increased in significance. The 'urge to consume is fathered by the value system which emphasizes the ability of the society to produce' and the close articulation of production and consumption is realized through 'the institutions of modern advertising and salesmanship' (Galbraith 1963: 133). The contention is that consumer wants or desires are dependent on the system of production, and that they are continually created through the very processes that present themselves as the means for achieving satisfaction.

After noting the paramount position of production and the importance of ensuring that there is an adequate level of consumer demand for goods and services, Galbraith draws attention to the ways in which corporations attempt to influence decisions about consumer purchasing. It is chiefly through market research, advertising and branding, as well as by 'devising a product, or features of a product, around which a sales strategy can be built' (Galbraith 1969: 208) that corporations have attempted to influence consumer decisions. Anticipating developments that have become a particularly prominent feature of late twentieth-century commercial corporate practice, Galbraith (1963) notes the increasing significance of manufacturing demand for a product and adds that the outlay involved is no less important than that incurred in the manufacture of the product itself. Increasingly, the aim is to recruit 'a loyal or automatic corps of customers', to build 'customer loyalty or *brand recognition*' (Galbraith 1969: 210, emphasis added). This aim, as Klein's (2001) analysis of 'branding' culture has subsequently demonstrated, has only increased in scale and intensity as capitalist economic life has become more competitive, market-driven, and insecure (Beck 2000).

Galbraith's analysis not only challenges the conventional wisdom of economic analysis and political commentary – that the consumer is the 'ultimate source of power in the economic system' (1969: 221) – it also calls into question the status of the individual at the pivot of modern western culture. The notion of consumer freedom – that the individual consumer exercises sovereignty over producers through the market – simultaneously serves to legitimate particular practices (the subordination of workers to corporations; the unintended consequences of increased production) and misrepresent the underlying reality of economic life. In reality, it is the continued manipulation and management of consumer demand that is being protected, 'not the individual's right to buy' (Galbraith 1969: 222).

With the establishment of consumption as the principal medium for the expression and experience of freedom within late twentieth-century modern capitalist societies there has been a relative shift of emphasis from more evident, intrusive and at times explicitly repressive forms of social regulation to more subtle and 'efficient methods of seduction' (Bauman 1992: 51). These are methods of which people seem to be largely unaware, methods which have led to consumption being experienced as an exercise of choice, as a freedom, rather than as a managed activity. As Galbraith observes, 'people need to believe that they are unmanaged if they are to be managed effectively' (1969: 223). What is implied here is the way in which the constellation of ideas, practices and experiences associated with 'consumer freedom' (re)produces behaviour that is both 'functionally indispensable' and harmless for the capitalist system (Bauman 1992: 51).

The significance for social integration of a relative shift of emphasis from 'a regime of work governed by constraint' to a regime of consumption governed by incentives (Gorz 1989: 44) is reflected in the increasing importance consumer activity assumes in the constitution of modern forms of subjectivity. Gorz argues that if consumer goods and services once served to compensate individuals for the sacrifices incurred in work, there has now been a cultural transformation. No longer do we 'want commercial goods and services to compensate for functional work, we want functional work so that we can afford commercial goods and services' (Gorz 1989: 46). This represents a sign of the 'efficiency of incentive regulation by consumerism' (p. 46). Seduced by the promised personal satisfactions of consumption, individuals are content, if not eager, to retreat into the private sphere. Increasingly, priority is accorded to 'the pursuit of "personal" advantages' to the detriment of the public domain and associated 'networks of solidarity and mutual assistance, social . . . cohesion and our sense of belonging' (Gorz 1989: 47). The broader question of the consequences for the public domain (and in particular public services) of consumers being encouraged to pursue their own satisfaction through their own agendas is addressed in Chapter 5.

A common denominator in the analyses of production and consumption considered in this chapter is that the needs, wants and desires of consumers are in significant ways deliberately cultivated or contrived. For example, in one case it is argued that increasing wants or needs are the consequence of 'aggressive management of the consumer' (Galbraith 1969: 348). In a comparable manner, making the 'needs of consumers grow at least as quickly as the production of commodities and commodified services' has been identified as an imperative for capitalist economic rationality (Gorz 1989: 114). This line is effectively endorsed by the observation that consumers cannot be allowed to be idle. Consumers need to be continually 'exposed to new temptations' (Bauman 1998b: 26). They must be kept in a suspended state. Never quite satisfied with what they have, always on the lookout for more, and anticipating the purchases that they believe will make them happier, while forgetting the many times that previous purchases have failed to live up to promised expectations. However, for consumption to be so appealing, so seductive, there need to be 'customers who are ready and keen to be seduced' (Bauman 1998b: 26). The process of seduction in play in the consumer game involves a complex array of subtle and not so subtle techniques of persuasion exerting influence over conduct. The process leaves consumers sublimely believing that they are exercising freedom of choice and in consequence they remain unaware that they are exposed and vulnerable to more of the same. The power of seduction is effectively exemplified by a remark attributed to the chairman of the American advertising agency J. Walter Thomson, that the consumer process involves 'creating in the minds of people needs of which "they haven't got the faintest idea"' (quoted in Gorz 1989: 120). Advertising and marketing effectively allow corporations to exercise a significant influence over consumer decisions about the purchase of goods and services. Rather than consumer subjects exercising sovereignty in the market-place, corporations are confident that 'if they make it we will buy it' (Galbraith 1969: 210). And most of the time we do, because that is our purpose as consumer subjects, that is how a sense of identity and belonging are continually achieved and expressed for those participating in the consumer society.

While emphasizing the importance of consumption in contemporary culture and reaffirming the idea that consumer needs and satisfactions are economically and culturally constituted, Baudrillard's analysis tends to give more weight to the respects in which consumption constitutes a core component of the reproduction of the capitalist system of production. Where it was once necessary to socialize 'the masses as labour power', now it is equally necessary to 'socialize them (that is, control them) as consumption power' (Baudrillard 1998: 82). In his discussion of the way in which consumption has come to occupy such a strategic significance within the system of production, Baudrillard argues that for the individual consumer 'enjoyment', achieved in and through consumption, becomes an 'obligation', a 'duty'. The suggestion is that this is the 'equivalent in the new ethics of the traditional imperative to labour' (1998: 80). The implication is that consumption corresponds in some way to a calling, a vocation, and that just like early modern workers who were forced to work in a calling (Weber 1976: 181), late modern subjects are required to consume and to find pleasure from doing so.

Baudrillard remarks that 'consumerist man . . . regards enjoyment as an obligation' and that there is no prospect for the modern consumer of 'evading this enforced happiness and enjoyment' (1998: 80). Undoubtedly the rationale for a great deal of consumption in a modern society, beyond, that is, the meeting of material needs deemed fundamental, is the achievement of individual enjoyment, happiness or satisfaction. The consumer is encouraged to be narcissistic, to be self-preoccupied and to systematically exploit 'all the potentialities of enjoyment' (Baudrillard 1998: 80). However, while it is appropriate, as Baudrillard does, to challenge the notion that the 'finality of consumption' is in practice enjoyment or pleasure, it is questionable whether consumers actually *regard* the achievement of enjoyment as an obligation, or the attainment of happiness as a duty. Rather than refer to a relationship of duty or obligation it might be more appropriate to place emphasis on the ways in which a *raising of expectations* of enjoyment and pleasure on the part of consumers constitutes a fundamental and necessary feature of the system of production. Anticipation of enjoyment and expectation of pleasure on the part of consumers have to be continually cultivated, the more so because satisfaction is at best a fleeting experience, if not one that perpetually recedes the more we consume.

It is not possible to be content with what one already has within a late modern capitalist society for which built-in obsolescence is both an economic necessity and a cultural virtue. The emphasis placed on technological innovation in modern culture leads to a high premium being placed on the 'new' or the latest, and there is a commonly held assumption that 'any "new" product is inherently superior to an old one' (Galbraith 1969: 208, Note 4). An incitement to consume is further stimulated by what Baudrillard describes as a 'revival of a *universal curiosity*' (1998: 80) in respect of an increasing range of goods and services. Curiosity is continually cultivated to ensure that consumers will 'try everything' and not 'miss out'. The methods and media employed to ensure consumers continue to do their 'duty' now extend well beyond management of demand through the medium of television on which, as Galbraith argued, the 'industrial system is profoundly dependent' (1969: 213). With the development of a post-Fordist, more flexible form of capitalism, a system that in many respects has moved beyond industrialism, there has been an increasing commercial co-optation of cultural life. What has been described as 'creeping ad expansion' is evident in the 'branding of entire neighbourhoods and cities' around the globe as well as in the increasing 'colonization . . . of mental space' evident in an increasing expectation and acceptance that cultural life comes packaged with commercial sponsorship (Klein 2001: 37, 38, 65–6).

On credit

In a further development of his argument that consumption is learnt through a 'new and specific mode of *socialization* related to the emergence of new productive forces and the monopoly restructuring of a high productivity economic system', Baudrillard (1998: 81) identifies the crucial role increasingly played by credit. Capitalism is a system of production 'characterized by continuous efforts to shorten turnover times, thereby speeding up social processes while reducing the time horizons of meaningful decision-making' (Harvey 1989: 229). Potential barriers to the achievement of a reduction in turnover time include 'consumption lags', and a number of technical and organizational innovations have been introduced to overcome such obstacles. These include 'planned obsolescence in consumption (the mobilization of fashion and advertising to accelerate change) [and] the credit system' (Harvey 1989: 229).

However, it is not the contribution that the credit system makes to the acceleration of the turnover time of capital that is of immediate analytic concern to Baudrillard. Rather, it is the contribution of credit to the emergence of a process of systematic and organized consumption to which attention is directed. Credit is important in so far as it constitutes a 'disciplinary process of the extortion of savings and the regulation of demand' (1998: 81). Taking advantage of credit consumers effectively receive training in saving and economic calculation which corresponds in some respects to the rational and disciplinary 'ethos' crucial to the earlier formation of modern capitalism (p. 81). In so far as consumption is a duty or an obligation and 'Spending [and] Enjoyment ("Buy now, pay later") have taken over from the "puritan" themes of Saving [and] Work' (p. 82), credit has become an increasingly prominent feature of consumer capitalism.

The one consumer 'freedom' contemporary capitalism cannot afford to promote is the freedom *not* to consume. Stopping shopping is a cost that cannot be endured. Capitalist consumer culture employs all the means at its disposal to conjure up appealing images and persuasive signs, to 'summon up dreams, desires and fantasies' of the potential for fulfilment through a process of 'narcissistically pleasing oneself' in and through the consumption of symbolic goods and services (Featherstone 1991: 27). But fulfilment has to be limited in duration, partial and continually disrupted by the realization that there are endless other ways of pleasing oneself, other potential satisfactions that cannot wait. Credit certainly allows consumer subjects to 'take the waiting out of wanting', but in so far as it does that it may have other, rather different and additional effects to those identified by Baudrillard. Marketing hype promotes credit as facilitating immediate gratification in advance of saving up to buy. The crucial role of credit according to Baudrillard is to provide 'a systematic socio-economic training in enforced saving and economic calculation' for those individuals who might otherwise have not been 'exploitable as consumption power' (1998: 81). Credit from this standpoint is a disciplinary process that provides a mental training in 'economic foresight, investment and "basic" capitalist behaviour' (p. 81).

While the credit process may have effects of this order on some consumers, there is evidence of a range of other effects. These include chronic levels of indebtedness and a reduced rate of savings, effects that have led to expressions of public concern and calls for restrictions to be placed on the marketing and issuing of credit cards (Ritzer 1995, 1998). As Ritzer remarks, 'when we have credit available to us, we are far more likely to spend to excess and to plunge into debt' (1995: 59). Credit, and credit cards in particular, lead to increased levels of spending. While responsibility lies in part with the unrestrained consumption of those consumers who get into unmanageable levels of debt, the aggressive marketing of credit card companies and easy availability of credit undoubtedly contribute significantly to rising levels of indebtedness. The increasing promotion of consumer culture in contemporary capitalism is a key factor, for 'modern capitalism has come to depend on a high level of consumer indebtedness' (Ritzer 1995: 19).

There is a system contradiction between the need for a continual increase in consumers willing and able to purchase goods and services and the fact that new information and communication technologies make it possible to 'increase productivity *without* work' (Beck 2000: 42; see also Gorz 1999), thereby reducing the security of employment and income. As Gorz observes, 'the purchasing power of a growing proportion of the population is falling' (1999: 89). How are the 'irreplaceable' consumer and the necessity of consumption to be reconciled with transformations affecting the world of work – for example, the increasing insecurity of employment and the growth of part-time, short contract, poorly paid McJobs? It is to this question that credit constitutes the answer.

The consumer society that Baudrillard described has continued to develop. There is a continuing need for individuals as 'workers' (wage labour). However, the world of work is changing fast and employment is becoming increasingly insecure. Analysts now refer to the prospect of a declining requirement for wage labour as science-based information technologies are increasingly deployed in production, and to the prospect of a 'capitalism without work' (Beck 2000) or the end of a 'wage-based society' (Gorz 1999). But if the demand for individuals as workers is uncertain it remains the case that where they are 'practically irreplaceable today is as consumers' (Baudrillard 1998: 83).

Reflecting on the transformation of social and economic life from the competitive stage of capitalism, Baudrillard observes that the hybrid of individualistic and altruistic values that characterized the 'great transformation' (Polanyi 1968) is impossible today. Along with an altruistic morality, Baudrillard felt able, writing in 1970, to add that 'the "free market" has virtually disappeared' (1998: 84). The principal societal tension identified at the time by Baudrillard was between the exercise of 'bureaucratic, state monopoly control' and the various manifestations and excesses of individualism. In Baudrillard's words there is a 'deep contradiction between political and civil society in the "consumer society": the system is forced to produce more and more consumer individualism, which it is at the same time forced to repress ever more harshly' (1998: 84). There are today continuing tensions between individualism and collective provision and constraint, but the balance of forces has shifted considerably. The subsequent regeneration of 'free market' philosophy and the promotion of market forces in neo-liberal political rhetoric and economic policy have led to a number of changes. These include a reduction in some aspects of the role of the state, an increasing accommodation of social policy to the values of the free-market economy, a revalorization of individualism, an erosion of collective provision and an undermining of the public sector (Bourdieu 1998).

More and more 'consumer individualism' is being produced, as Baudrillard anticipated, but increasingly it is only at the margins, in dealing with the various categories of 'inadequate' or 'flawed consumers' – the unemployed, the poor, the underclass, the criminal – that harshly repressive measures are being employed (Bauman 1998b). For the majority, 'consumer individualism' represents a relationship of dependency, a relationship that emerges from acceptance of seductive proposals to consume goods and, increasingly, services. Although it is a relationship of dependency it is experienced and regarded as freedom; it is a 'do-it-yourself-dependency; people gladly, willingly, joyfully enter the dependency relation' (Bauman 2001a: 26). The contradiction that Baudrillard identifies between individual consumption and collective responsibility continues to be a prominent and troubling feature of contemporary social life. The perpetual promotion and satisfaction of individual consumption continues to sit uneasily alongside calls for collective responsibility and collective provision. Whether as a contrast between 'private affluence' and 'public squalor' (Galbraith 1963) or 'self-interest' and 'public interest' (Bell 1976), the contradiction endures – indeed, with the advent of neo-liberalism it has been exacerbated (Bourdieu 1998; Gray 1999).

The end of the Fordist-Keynesian configuration led to the emergence of a globally extensive, disorganized and flexible capitalism, guided by a neo-liberal programme of deregulation and promotion of market forces. In turn, the end of ' "Fordist" growth' led to the introduction of 'lean production' methods (reductions in manning levels, more worker self-management and a pursuit of maximum flexibility in the production process) which have transformed the productivity of labour through processes of technological and organizational innovation (Gorz 1999). The emergence of a disordered global free-market capitalism, unleashing what has been described as a 'global gale of creative destruction' (Gray 1999: 76), has had a significant impact on consumption. It has placed an even greater premium on the importance of ensuring that there is a buoyant demand for products and services, that customers remain loyal and that brands are not simply continuing to be recognized, but are extending their reach.

Global capitalism and the branding of consumption

Market research prior to production, and advertising, marketing and branding after production, are transforming culture (virtually a process of commodity consumption) into an increasingly branded form of life (Klein 2001). The process by which consumer demand for further products is created through the 'psycho-sociological apparatus' of advertising and marketing is effectively concealed behind a political rhetoric of 'consumer choice', which is itself represented as the organizing principle of an accommodating market-place. The reality is quite different from the 'accepted sequence' that has become an established feature of economic discourse and political commentary.

With the increasing commercialization of culture around the world, it has at times become almost impossible to differentiate between the commercial and the cultural. As the commercial has intruded on the cultural, so culture has been transformed into 'little more than a collection of brand-extensions' (Klein 2001: 30). With the global shift from manufacturing a product as the core activity to marketing and branding as the focus of the successful corporation, the primary objective has become to present products 'not as "commodities" but as concepts: the brand as experience, as lifestyle' (Klein 2001: 21). To achieve this end, production has increasingly been contracted out to locations that can guarantee low-cost labour, few if any restrictions on production and the incentive of low- or no-tax concessions, and corporate activity has increasingly been redirected and concentrated upon marketing and branding. In a world that is so pervasively and persuasively marked by brands in the form of cultural ideas, attitudes, values and experiences, what is the meaning of consumer choice? Where corporate sponsorship has expanded its reach to encompass activities as diverse as concerts, papal visits, zoos and after-school sports activities (Klein 2001), and where more and more areas of life are subject to corporate branding, it is becoming difficult to regard consumer choice as anything other than a process of brand(ed) selection, part of a wider-ranging process of commercial co-optation that leads us 'in "uniform" . . . into the global mall' (Klein 2001: 129; see also 140).

Branded multinationals like Nike, Gap, McDonald's, Starbucks, Microsoft, Ikea, Coca-Cola, Swatch, Toys 'R' Us and the Body Shop have increasingly displaced small, independent retail outlets around the world and now account for a rising share of consumer transactions. Such companies operate in a global market-place, marketing a carefully contrived style of life rather than a particular commodity, and striving to create the impression that their mission is to contribute to the enhancement of consumer choice. However, behind the appearance of increased consumer choice lie 'new restrictions on cultural production and public space' (Klein 2001: 130). In short, branded consumption is radically transforming, if not undermining, the idea of consumer choice – both the meaning and the manner of its expression. Reflecting on the different factors now affecting consumption, Klein (2001: 130) argues:

> This assault on choice is taking place on several different fronts at once. It is happening structurally, with mergers, buyouts and corporate synergies. It is happening locally, with a handful of superbrands using their huge cash reserves to force out small and independent businesses. And it is happening on the legal front, with entertainment and consumer-goods companies using libel and trademark suits to hound anyone who puts an unwanted spin on a pop-cultural product. And so we live in a double world: carnival on the surface, consolidation underneath, where it counts.

Through the growth of advertising and marketing budgets and the proliferation of franchises and chains, undermining small and independent businesses by engaging in price wars, 'setting up chain-store "clusters"' (Klein 2001: 132) and developing flagship superstores, consumer choice is being continually contrived, channelled and regulated.

Changes in the retail landscape have had a significant impact on consumption. There has been a growth of large cut-price retail stores, exemplified by the big box, category killer 'Wal-Mart model'. Another retail strategy has been to set up several outlets in areas already well provided with comparable retailers – the clustering, cannibalizing, 'Starbucks model'. And then there is the branded superstore, where the emphasis is not simply on selling something but on 'imprinting an experience on you', effectively branding you – the 'Nike/Disney model'. These different retail strategies have transformed the process of consumption. However, while these innovations in retail practice have had important consequences for consumer choice, the significance of their impact extends well beyond changes to the way we shop. As Klein observes, '[t]hey are key pieces of the branding puzzle that is transforming everything from the way we congregate to the way we work' (2001: 140), to the ways in which we think about ourselves and our identities.

Consumption and identity

An important feature of the cultural turn in social analysis has been a tendency to regard consumption as an activity in and through which identity is constructed. Identity is argued to be unstable, fragmented and constantly in the process of becoming, constantly being (re)constituted. As one cultural analyst has remarked, identities are formed through

> resources of history, language, and culture in the process of be-coming rather than being: not 'who we are' or 'where we came from' so much as what we might become, how we have been represented and how that bears on how we might represent ourselves. Identities are therefore constituted within, not outside representation.
>
> (Hall 1996: 4)

From this perspective, identities are constructed in and through discourse, in and through narratives 'produced in specific historical and institutional sites' (Hall 1996: 4). Increasingly it is in and through the process of consumption that a sense of identity is achieved. Identity has ceased to be something permanent, a product of a steady and consistent process 'proceeding through a succession of clearly defined stages' (Bauman 1998b: 27). Identities are now rarely built to last, and increasingly lack the foundation of a permanent job, secure work or a career. In circumstances where work is increasingly insecure, where jobs come and go, what are the prospects for identity? Bauman argues that in so far as identity has a provisional or temporary quality it is advisable to 'embrace it lightly' and that it might be more appropriate to 'speak of self-identity in the plural' (1998b: 28), for during the course of their lives individuals are likely to adopt and discard a number of identities.

The transformation in identity corresponds in many respects with the passage from a modern producer society to a postmodern consumer society (Kellner 1992; Bauman 1998b; Beck 2001). There is a striking correspondence between the qualities intrinsic to consumer society – the increasingly temporary and transitory character of commodities and services produced for consumption – and the flexible, for-the-time-being, character of identity. As Bauman (1998b: 29) notes:

Identities, just like consumer goods, are to be appropriated and possessed, but only in order to be consumed, and so to disappear again. As in the case of marketed consumer goods, consumption of an identity should not – must not – extinguish the desire for other, new and improved identities, nor preclude the ability to absorb them. This being the requirement there is not much point in looking any further for the tools than the market place.

Increasingly, the resources employed in what Hall (1996) terms the process of becoming – shaping what we might become and how we might represent ourselves – derive from the capitalist market-place of the consumer society. While choice is clearly exercised in relation to the purchase of consumer goods and services, the uses to which they are put and the place or meaning they may be accorded in people's lives, choice is continually exposed to the seductive influences and suggestive powers of advertising, marketing and branding. The choices made by consumers are 'free' only in the sense that they could have chosen otherwise. The available range from which a choice is made, the potential uses and the cultural meanings that might be accorded are powerfully influenced by the 'entire process of the production, distribution, retailing and consumption of goods' (Philo and Miller 2001: 66).

The consumer process and advertising, marketing, fashion and popular culture in particular, contribute significantly to the instability of identity through the promotion of new products, images and values suggestive of new identities. The process of post-Fordist commodity production and 'market segmentation of multiple ad campaigns and appeals reproduces and intensifies fragmentation and destabilizes identity which new products and identifications are attempting to restabilize' (Kellner 1992: 172). Furthermore, while it is possible to note the increasing element of choice in consumption implied above, it is important to emphasize the *limitations* on choice represented by the range of available goods and services. It is also important to recognize the *limits* within which consumer choice needs must be exercised – 'limited/partial information about products, limited access to types of shops and limitations of resources' (Philo and Miller 2001: 67).

The movement from Fordist mass production to post-Fordist, flexible, small batch production and niche marketing can be regarded as having increased consumer choice, in so far as the range from which choices are made has been extended (Lash and Urry 1994). However, it is also evident that with the emergence of a deregulated global market-place, large corporations have sought to work out how to sell 'identical products across multiple borders' (Klein 2001: 115). The solution global corporations have come up with is neither to be seen to be forcing their culture upon others, nor to customize their marketing campaigns to fit the different markets.

Instead, global corporations have tended to opt for diversity marketing, to respond to the problems of cultural identity and cultural differences by appearing to 'sell diversity itself, to all markets at once' (Klein 2001: 117). But while global corporations endorse the need for greater diversity and present themselves as bending over backwards to avoid offending local cultures, there is a growing recognition that their activities are contributing to the creation of an increasingly homogenized global consumer culture. There are, as Ritzer (1998: 88; see also 77) notes, 'powerful homogenizing trends in the world today', exemplified by the similarity of the operations of global corporations such as McDonald's, Nike, Gap, Ikea, Toys 'R' Us, Coca-Cola, Starbucks etc., wherever they are located around the world. Notwithstanding cultural differences, consumers around the world are increasingly exposed to a branded culture, to what Klein describes as 'in effect mono-multiculturalism' (2001: 117).

Noting the increasing prominence of a 'One World placelessness', Klein remarks on the way in which, notwithstanding cultural differences, 'middle class youth all over the world seem to live their lives as if in a parallel universe' (2001: 117, 119). They are dressed in Gap sweatshirts, Levi's or Diesel jeans, wearing Nike/Adidas/Timberland footwear, and listening to a Sony CD player. But a factor crucial to the process of successfully selling the 'same products, in the same way, all around the world' is that the potential consumers must 'identify with their new demographic' (Klein 2001: 119–20). In consequence, diversity marketing takes the form of global advertising campaigns promoting, in this particular instance, the notion of a 'global teen market':

> A kaleidoscope of multi-ethnic faces blending into one another: Rasta braids, pink hair, henna hand painting, piercing and tattoos, a few national flags, flashes of foreign street signs, Cantonese and Arabic lettering and a sprinkling of English words, all over the layered sampling of electronic music. Nationality, language, ethnicity, religion and politics are all reduced to their most colourful, exotic accessories, converging to assure us . . . there is never an 'us' and 'them', but simply one giant 'we'.
> (Klein 2001: 120)

In short, there is a common hybridized consumer identity that overrides distinctive local cultural identities.

Increasingly it is through the medium of television and in particular the global reach of media organizations like CNN (which is available in 212 countries) and, in relation to the global teen market, MTV (which broadcasts in 83 countries) that the possibility of the global consumer is made a reality. It is young consumers who represent the first truly global consumers. It is the popularity of media such as MTV with its 'vision of a tribe of culture swapping, global teen nomads' (Klein 2001: 121) that has done much to form a homogeneous market in which global corporations can sell their wares. The enormous reach and popularity of MTV International, watched every day by 85 per cent of teenage consumers around the world according to the 'New World Teen Study', leads Klein to conclude that it has 'become the most compelling catalogue for the modern branded life' (2001: 121), the source of a hybridized global identity that is based on consumption.

The consumer is not 'sovereign', but more like a 'postmodern' serf – not bound to the land, but bound to consume. With the growth of branded consumption it is not products that are being marketed and sold but increasingly lifestyles, experiences and identities. Whereas advertising hawks the product, branding promotes a way of living, a way of doing something, a way of being. The branding of culture and the marketing of identities has not escaped criticism, but as Klein notes, 'identity politics weren't fighting the system, or even subverting it. When it came to the vast new industry of corporate branding, they were feeding it' (2001: 113). Cultural movements stressing the politics of identity effectively weakened organized labour and indirectly influenced 'individualized, decentralized uses of technology . . . [thereby] facilitating capitalist restructuring' (Castells 1998: 340). Ultimately the demand articulated within identity politics for a greater recognition of diversity has been welcomed and accommodated within the culture industries – indeed, it has become the 'mantra for global capitalism' (Klein 2001: 115).

Consumption in the service of production

In a discussion of theories of consumer culture Featherstone argues that 'the production of consumption approach has difficulty in addressing the actual practices and experiences of consumption' (1991: 15). What Featherstone seems to mean by this is that there are 'differentiated audience responses and uses of goods', that there are 'socially structured ways in which goods are used to demarcate social relationships' (1991: 15, 16). Undoubtedly there is evidence of differentiated responses to and uses of goods and these need to be subjected to analysis. In short, there are indeed different modes of consumption. There are differences between 'durable' and 'non-durable' goods and the meaning of consumption is complex and includes a range of attributes with which a good may be associated through advertising, marketing and the acquisition of symbolic value. For example, Featherstone mentions the search for prestige that may be the motivation for the purchase of a high exchange-value good. However, such observations are not at all incompatible with an analysis that places emphasis upon the production of consumption. Indeed, many of the features identified – for example, differentiated responses to and uses of goods – are a part of the process of the production of consumption. For instance, the cultivation of diverse tastes, consumption preferences and lifestyle practices is precisely the focus of the activities of the 'cultural intermediaries' (Bourdieu 1984) working in media, design, fashion, marketing and advertising businesses. Such services are an increasingly significant component of the production process and the cultivation of a demand for consumer goods expressive of a diversity of cultural lifestyles.

It is important to recognize the emergence of a new post-Fordist, more flexible form of capitalism which is not oriented to mass production and the nurturing through the culture industries of a homogeneous mass consumer culture. However, it is also necessary to acknowledge that Fordist forms of production have not completely disappeared and that it might be argued that there is an 'interpenetration of opposed tendencies in capitalism as a whole' (Harvey 1989: 338). In other words:

> two rather different regimes of accumulation and their associated modes of regulation (including the materializations of cultural habits, motivations, and styles of representation) might hang together, each as a distinctive and relatively coherent kind of social formation.
>
> (Harvey 1989: 338)

But in both instances there remains an imperative to expand consumption, to ensure that there are purchasers for ever-increasing levels of production. In both cases production is organized on the basis of capitalist economic rationality and it is vital that 'the needs of consumers grow at least as quickly as the production of commodities and commodified services' (Gorz 1989: 114). In short, it is necessary that consumption is in the service of production, that consumer demand is continually cultivated through 'methodically orchestrated . . . commercial advertising', marketing and branding (Gorz 1989: 115).

Normal everyday life in a consumer society is 'the life of consumers, preoccupied with making their choices among the panoply of publicly displayed opportunities for pleasurable sensations' (Bauman 1998b: 37). But this is a life that is both made possible and made necessary by the increasing productive capacity of contemporary capitalism and the associated requirement to ensure that products can be disposed of. The economic system has changed in significant respects, particularly with the deployment of information technology, but notwithstanding the emergence of 'informationalism', a new mode of development, 'capitalism is still operating as the dominant economic form' (Castells 1996: 198). Consumption is without doubt a vital economic and cultural aspect of the restructuring and reorganization of capitalist economic life, but it constitutes an 'organized extension of the productive forces' (Baudrillard 1998: 76). Analytic recognition of the overriding significance of production not only reveals the limitations of 'consumption-oriented models of capitalism' but in turn provides a foundation from which to take issue with both the rhetoric and the reality of 'the market'.

Notes

1 Between 1973 and 1993 the participation rate of women aged 15 years or more in the labour force in OECD countries rose from 48.3 per cent to 61.6 per cent. In the USA between 1973 and 1994 the increase was from 51.1 per cent to 70.5 per cent (Castells 1997).
2 In the 1960s in the USA, women's earnings were 60–65 per cent of men's and although they had risen by 1991 to 72 per cent of men's earnings, Castells notes that it was on the back of a decline in men's real wages. Comparable differentials exist in the UK, where in the mid-1980s women's pay was 69.5 per cent of men's. In Germany it was 72 per cent in 1980 and 73.6 per cent in 1991, and in France it was 79 per cent in 1980 and 80.8 per cent in 1991 (Castells 1997: 169).

CHAPTER 4

WITHOUT REGARD FOR PERSONS: THE MARKET ECONOMY

Introduction: the culture of the market

The origins of the term 'market' can be traced back to the Latin *mercatus*. The notion of the market has been associated with a number of meanings. These include 'buying and selling in general'; a particular physical space (the market-place); and in the case of the discourse of modern economics, an 'abstract price-making mechanism that is central to allocation of resources in an economy' (Swedberg 1994: 255). A market can be said to exist where there is competition and the opportunity for exchanges between a number of potential agents. It is also worth emphasizing that markets, facilitating exchanges between agents, involve social processes and are *social institutions*.

In an analysis of the complexity of the phenomenon of the market, Swedberg notes both the diverse types characteristic of modern capitalist societies – financial, consumer, labour and industrial – and how the market form has become 'directly associated with dynamic economic growth' (1994: 256). But while the market is a central economic institution it has not been a prominent focus of analysis within the history of economic thought. Moreover, where there has been consideration of the notion of the market it has tended to be primarily as a price-making and resource allocating mechanism rather than as a social institution. A few exceptions can be found in the discourse of the 'New Institutional Economics', most prominently in the works of North (1990) and Hodgson (1994). In both cases an attempt is made to consider the market as a social institution by examining the power relations, rules, routines and norms, and the unintended consequences that are intrinsic features of economic life (Swedberg 1994; Slater and Tonkiss 2001).

Sociologists, as Swedberg observes, have paid even 'less attention to the market than economists' (1994: 264). An outline of a sociological approach to the market can be found in the classical writings of Max Weber. Employing an 'interpretive' sociological approach, Weber remarked that the market represented 'a coexistence and sequence of rational consociations, each of which is specifically ephemeral insofar as it ceases to exist with the act of exchanging the goods' (1978b: 635). A number of important lines of inquiry concerning exchange, regulation, calculation and ethics in relation to the market situation and modern rationality are opened up in Weber's sociological writings. What is of most concern to Weber is the dominance within modern society of one particular type of rationality – 'formal' or 'instrumental' – that is, directed towards the development of the most technically effective means to achieve a given end. Modern rationality for Weber is synonymous with the pursuit of efficiency, calculation or quantification, prediction and control. And in conception, if not in practice, the market exchange process is regarded as the very exemplification of the logic of modern 'instrumental' rationality (Weber 1978b). For Weber (1964) not every type of action that is rational in its selection of means is considered to be 'rational economic action'. But 'market situation' in the modern western capitalist economy – that is, where 'money calculations are highly developed' – is at the forefront of analysis when conditions of formal rationality and their consequences are being considered (Weber 1964: 180, 211).

As Weber acknowledged, in the course of the nineteenth century, market forms of organization had spread around the globe as nation states sought to create the conditions in which an economy controlled and regulated by markets alone could develop. Towards the close of the nineteenth century concern was beginning to be expressed about the impact of the market system on social life. In the 1930s the notion of the self-regulating, self-righting market economy was undermined by the 'Great Depression'. The policy response to the lack of effective demand for goods and services that threatened economic collapse, subsequently identified as Keynesianism, was to deploy a set of 'managerial strategies and state powers that would stabilize capitalism' (Harvey 1989: 129). These interventionist strategies and powers achieved their optimum configuration in the period during 1945–73, during which time various compromises between the state, corporate capital and organized labour made possible a prolonged period of economic growth.

During this period the state assumed a variety of responsibilities and deployed fiscal and monetary policies to stabilize business cycles and demand conditions. Public sector investment ensured relatively full employment and expenditure on welfare and social security systems provided a 'strong underpinning to the social wage' (Harvey 1989: 135). Although the precise form and degree of state intervention varied from one advanced capitalist country to another, all the national governments concerned sought to engineer 'stable economic growth and rising material living standards through a mix of welfare statism, Keynesian economic management, and control over wage relations' (Harvey 1989: 135).

For their part, large business corporations were committed to enhancing rates of productivity, increasing economic growth and raising standards of living through steady increases in levels of investment, the primary objective being to create a stable foundation for profit-making. The requirement to achieve these objectives was 'steady but powerful processes of technological change, mass fixed capital investment, growth of managerial expertise in both production and marketing, and the mobilization of economies of scale through standardization of product' (Harvey 1989: 134). Organized labour, for its part, was required to discipline its membership and cooperate with management to achieve productivity gains in return for wage rises.

Under the auspices of the Fordist-Keynesian configuration of 'organized' capitalism, which prevailed until the mid-1970s, big business tended to seek justification for its activities in terms of social values, placing emphasis on its contribution to the 'common weal' – providing jobs, raising standards of living and meeting the needs of consumers. On the subject of the fundamental realities of capitalist economic life – 'profits, interest, monopoly, inequality' – big business was more reticent, if not defensive (Elliott and Atkinson 1999: 57). However, by the end of the century, following the deployment of neo-liberal economic policies and the development of a new form of capitalism ('Post-Fordist', 'disorganized', 'flexible' and 'global'), market values, once again, had become dominant. As with the earlier period analysed by Polanyi, deregulation and marketization have not taken place spontaneously. It is not a case of a natural order being restored – to the contrary, 'free markets are creatures of state power, and persist only so long as the state is able to prevent human needs for security and the control of economic risk from finding political expression' (Gray 1999: 17).

Increasingly it is in terms of the values and ethos of commerce, enterprise and entrepreneurialism – in short, the market – that organizations, including those in the public sector, have to justify themselves and their activities. We are now, as Frederic Jameson has remarked, completely 'inside the culture of the market' and so thoroughly immersed in its alter ego, the 'culture of consumption . . . we are unable to imagine anything else' (1991: 206–7). More and more people are required to accommodate to 'market testing', and in the case of public sector employees and the users of public services, to accept an extension of market mechanisms beyond the private sector to the public domain. What are the features of the 'market ethos' that returned to a position of such dominance in the closing decades of the twentieth century? Three interlocking elements have been identified (Elliott and Atkinson 1999: 58):

- The market has come to be regarded as an 'objective external reality against which all human activity can be judged' and as such it increasingly constitutes the primary source of authentication and validation. In contrast, non-market criteria are deemed to be 'artificial' and likely to 'distort' this reality.

- Conduct that accords with market criteria is considered to be more beneficial or advantageous ('efficient') than conduct that is 'in defiance or ignorance of it'.
- Given the above, the practices, structures, values and assumptions of organizations that operate in accordance with the disciplines of the market – i.e. 'large-scale business organizations' – are regarded as those that other organizations should seek to emulate.

It is to a critical consideration of the idea of the market and the forms of life associated with the culture of the market in contemporary society that the following discussion is directed.

Since the 1970s, neo-liberal economic ideas have become increasingly prominent in the formulation of social and economic policy. With the discrediting of Keynesian social democracy, economic debate has been constituted increasingly in terms of neo-liberal ideas and assumptions and there has been a widespread promotion of the idea of the 'free' market by economists, policy makers and governments. As one critic of the rhetoric that has accompanied the regeneration of the notion of the market has commented, 'surrender to the various forms of market ideology . . . has been imperceptible but alarmingly universal. Everyone is now willing to mumble . . . that no society can function efficiently without the market and that planning is obviously impossible' (Jameson 1991: 263). The notion of the independence or autonomy of markets has come to be regarded not only as a potential reality but also as an unquestionable virtue to which the organization of economic life should be directed. The market is regarded as a decentralized yet organized process of exchange, subject to a general system of law, in which calculating agents compete, take decisions, enter into transactions and reach agreement on contracts and prices. The market process is considered 'neutral' and 'beneficial' in so far as it represents an impersonal mechanism for achieving an orderly outcome from a multitude of individual decisions.

What emerges from the market process as a whole does not directly correspond to the intentions of the individual agencies involved – rather, the outcome is an unintended consequence of the complex articulation of a multiplicity of individual decisions, unanticipated conditions and unforeseeable circumstances. From the perspective of the individual agent/agency, the market is experienced as an external totalization '(which no one wanted, anticipated or planned) . . . of the actions of serialized individuals' (Gorz 1989: 34). Elaborating on the issue of spontaneous regulation through the market process, Gorz argues that the market represents a 'systemic mechanism'. Spontaneous market regulation 'imposes its laws from without on individuals who are then ruled by them and are forced to adapt and to modify their conduct and projects according to an external, statistical and totally involuntary balance of forces' (Gorz 1989: 34).

There is a recognition of this quality of regulation through a mechanism that is neutral in relation to individuals, one that does not correspond to the intentions of individuals, in Max Weber's discussion of the contribution of bureaucratic organization to the capitalist market economy. Reflecting on the technical conditions necessary for the ' "objective" discharge of business', Weber remarks that ' "Without regard for persons" is . . . the watchword of the "market" and, in general, of all pursuits of naked economic interests' (1970: 215). The institution of the market, necessarily neutral or impersonal in its operation, is unable to show any regard for persons. As the institution of the market has become a more prominent feature of modern social life, so have its impersonal effects. The diffusion of impersonal market exchange relations into more and more areas of social life has contributed significantly to the increase in indifference shown and ethical disregard displayed towards others in contemporary society (Bellah *et al.* 1996; Smart 1999).

Max Weber on market relations

In Weber's work there are a number of fragmented narratives on different aspects of the market, including the impersonal character of market relations, the significance of calculation and the forms of regulation to which the market situation may be exposed.

For Weber, the market relationship is the most impersonal form of life people can enter. This is not due to the competitive nature of market activity or the potential for conflict between interested parties, but because such interaction is oriented solely towards the commodity. In the market individuals do not focus on the personal characteristics of other participants but on the commodity alone. As Weber (1987b: 636) comments:

> there are no obligations of brotherliness or reverence, and none of those spontaneous human relations that are sustained by personal unions. They would all just obstruct the free development of the bare market relationship, and its specific interests serve, in their turn, to weaken the sentiments on which these obstructions rest. Market behaviour is influenced by rational, purposeful pursuit of interests.

But while the operation of the market is oblivious to personal relationships and associated forms of ethical responsibility, there is a requirement for 'market ethics' in the sense that the reliability of transactions is predicated on a framework of rational legality and the inviolability of agreements.[1]

A corollary of the tendency for business in a capitalist market economy to be conducted objectively, or 'without regard for persons', is that economic activity is subject to a formal rationality of calculation. Calculation in terms of money is central to the exchange process in the market situation and is identified by Weber as the 'most rational means of orienting economic activity' (1978b: 86). Money accounting makes possible differentiation between alternative means by facilitating a calculation or an evaluation of their potential effectiveness in the achievement of a productive outcome to economic action. However, as well as providing the 'most "perfect" means of economic calculation' (Weber 1978b: 86) of anticipated and actual outcomes of courses of economic action, money has other significant socially and economically consequential qualities. By virtue of its 'infinite flexibility and divisibility' (Simmel 1990: 297) money makes possible the range of complex forms of interdependency between people that is a prominent feature of modern economic life. In turn, money, as Simmel remarks, is 'conducive to the removal of the personal element from human nature through its indifferent and objective nature' (p. 297).[2] The process of economic exchange that takes place in the market and by means of money produces an order of values that is not reducible to the subjective or personal feelings of individuals. It is an order that individual agents encounter as an 'objective realm' determined by a market mechanism that eliminates all elements that escape calculation (Weber 1970). In so far as social values are increasingly reduced to the 'mediating value of money', then cynicism and a blasé attitude are the inevitable result (Simmel 1990: 255). And in so far as the market and the money economy now intrude into most aspects of public and private life, then that ethical quality of responsibility for others, the sensitivity of one subjectivity to another that constitutes a foundation for moral-political order, is increasingly compromised (Smart 1999).

Weber identifies four respects in which a regulation of the market may be exercised: through tradition, convention, by law, and as a consequence of 'voluntary action arising from the structure of interests' (1978b: 83). Restriction on market activity may reflect the acceptance by participants of traditional limitations on exchange. Limitations may also arise as a consequence of an acceptance that it is inappropriate to submit specific services or objects to the process of market exchange. Legal restrictions on market exchange processes may take the form of price regulation or the exercise of limits on 'the possession, acquisition or exchange rights of control and disposal over certain goods to certain specific groups of persons' (Weber 1978b: 83). Finally, regulation of the market arises where some participants are able to control possession of, or opportunities to acquire, goods or services, and thereby 'influence the market situation in such a way as actually to abolish the market freedom of others' (Weber 1978b: 83).

The significance of market regulation through custom and convention has declined with the 'disintegration of tradition' (Weber 1978b: 337). The neo-liberal programme to free market forces has further reduced the significance of conventional disapproval of the subordination of particular goods and services to market forces. But 'conventional' concerns have not entirely disappeared – rather, they have resurfaced in arguments about the moral limits of markets, to which further consideration needs to be given. In contrast, the regulatory framework of law has grown in significance, reflecting the predominance of the capitalist market economy and its requirement for 'a legal system the functioning of which is *calculable* in accordance with rational rules' (Weber 1978b: 337). Lastly, but perhaps most significantly of all, there is a form of market regulation that derives from the exercise of monopoly power, a form of regulation that remains a prominent, if too often unacknowledged, feature of the reality of the modern market economy (Monbiot 2000; Hertz 2001; Klein 2001).

Key features of the market

Analysts have attributed a number of specific features to the market process. These include:

- exchange
- calculation
- organization
- competition
- freedom or autonomy of the parties involved
- pursuit of self-interest
- impersonality or neutrality

The market is considered to constitute a complex exchange system in and through which resources are allocated in response to changing relationships between supply and demand, guided by the calculus of price and profit and the law of contract. Essential to the notion of the market is the existence of calculative agency, organization and a process of coordination and compromise conducted in a spirit of competition (Callon 1998). No less important is an assumption of the freedom of agency to voluntarily participate in economic transactions, guided by self-interest, in a market situation that is deemed to be neutral in regard to the particular characteristics of individuals or agencies involved and the outcomes that might emerge.

Markets operating without hindrance are considered highly ordered systems of exchange. Order is believed to emerge spontaneously – that is, without design or social engineering. The market is represented as a mechanism for reconciling the expression and pursuit of self-interest on the part of both buyers and sellers. Acknowledging our increasing interdependence, in particular the needs that we have for the assistance or help of others, Adam Smith argued that we could not simply rely on benevolence:

It is not from the benevolence of the butcher, the brewer or the baker that we expect our dinner, but from their regard to their own interest. We address ourselves, not to their humanity but to their self love, and never talk to them of our own necessities, but of their advantages.

(1776: 13, quoted in Mackintosh *et al*. 1996: 25)

The implication is that unintended beneficial consequences follow spontaneously from individual self-interested courses of action occurring in and through the market. Hence the metaphor of the 'hidden hand' of the market that ostensibly allows unintended mutual benefit to emerge from the complex interactions of individuals in pursuit of their self-interest.

The notion of the market invoked above is based upon a number of assumptions, notably of competition between a multiplicity of agencies – sellers and buyers, firms and consumers – all small in size relative to the market and therefore unable to exercise influence over the market process. The implication is that as consumers are generally unable to do anything other than treat market price as a given, so small producers are required to sell their produce at a price that they are unable to influence because their output is relatively small in relation to the total market. For a competitive market to exist – that is, one free from the influence of producers exercising monopoly power – it is not only the size of firms that matters. In addition, it is vital that potential participants in the market have unhindered access to necessary information about the market, the range of products and the prices at which they are available. But such market assumptions are rarely, if ever, realized in practice.

It is vitally important to differentiate between the rhetoric and the reality of the market, or more appropriately, it is necessary to recognize that the market is in an important sense both rhetoric *and* reality. As Frederic Jameson has observed, the market is 'at one and the same time an ideology and a set of practical institutional problems' (1991: 260). There are a set of associations and understandings that are closely articulated with the market, if not generated by it. In particular, 'freedom' is represented as a fundamental feature of the market system; it is a key component of the rhetoric of the market. However, as Jameson (1991: 266) remarks:

the slogan of the market . . . is . . . virtually always a misnomer. For one thing, no free market exists today in the realm of oligopolies and multinationals . . . market as a concept rarely has anything to do with choice or freedom, since those are all determined for us in advance, whether we are talking about new model cars, toys or television programs: we select among those, no doubt, but we can scarcely be said to have a say in actually choosing any of them.

A self-regulating 'free' market economy is an economy directed solely by market prices, but save for the exceptional case of the competition of many sellers and many buyers, the necessary conditions are rarely (if ever) fulfilled. Where the producers of goods are 'numerous and small' and the goods concerned are 'easily substitutable' then the 'competitive ideal' is perhaps approximated (Galbraith and Salinger 1981). But with the emergence of oligopolies and monopolies the economic system has come increasingly under the influence of large corporations. Moreover, while participants in the market, particularly consumers, may have access to 'information', its status, quality and purpose will vary. There is some information available on the prices and qualities of products and on regulations and tests to which goods are subjected if they are to reach required safety standards. Also there is some information available on the potential hazards and risks associated with the consumption of particular goods and services. But compared to the volume of advertising and the scale of the promotion of products and services to which consumers are increasingly routinely exposed, independent sources of information on markets and products remain relatively scarce and generally far less readily accessible. Indeed, much of what passes for information readily accessible to consumers comes through the medium of advertising, the primary purpose of which is not to create more knowledgeable and discerning consumers but to increase the demand for and the sale of products and services. In short, advertising is directed towards the management of demand, although how it goes about the business of achieving this end has changed 'from delivering product news bulletins to building an image around a particular brand-name version of a product' (Klein 2001: 6; see also Galbraith 1963: 133–4, 1969: 276–7). However, while it is clear that there is no longer a competitive market in the classical sense, the notion survives and continues to inform economic analysis and policy, and political rhetoric and commentary (Galbraith and Salinger 1981).

The objective of creating 'free' markets accumulated considerable support among economists, policy makers, non-governmental organizations (NGOs) and governments around the world in the closing decades of the twentieth century (Gray 1999). Increasingly the proclaimed objective has become the promotion of economic freedom and enterprise through the deregulation of markets. The ultimate aim of deregulation and marketization is the creation of a globally extensive free market. The existence of wide-ranging support for freeing up the market system demonstrates the appeal of a philosophy that has sought to represent market behaviour as 'natural' – in effect as in accord with human nature. In market philosophy the ordering of social and economic life by means of the 'hidden hand' of the market is presented as in harmony with, and as an enhancement of, human freedom itself.

Free-market philosophy

Leading protagonists of free-market philosophy such as Friedrich Hayek (1944, 1949, 1960) and Milton Friedman ([1962] 1982) have argued that the market, free from state intervention or regulation, constitutes the complex result of the decisions and courses of action of diverse individuals. Simultaneously, the market constitutes a mechanism that collates and reacts to a complex assortment of data – information, initiatives and action – to which 'pointers', in turn, individual producers and consumers, may respond as they take decisions and adjust or change their courses of action (Hayek 1949: 87). It is this apparent capacity of the market to deal with and respond to a great quantity of complex data that leads Hayek and Friedman to argue that it is an intrinsically more efficient mechanism than state planning, regulation or intervention. The latter are considered to merely disrupt market forces and to 'distort the market's tendency to perform optimally' (Gorz 1989: 128). The complexity of modern social and economic life is such that economic calculation on a societal scale is deemed to be inadvisable on both economic and political grounds. Quite simply the economic argument advanced by Hayek and Friedman is that there is no way of accurately anticipating the multiplicity of initiatives that may be carried out by individual agents possessing partial knowledge of a limited part of the relevant field of action. It is argued that in such circumstances attempts to intervene in and regulate economic activity are destined to prove deficient and less effective than market-led solutions. In so far as economic calculation on a societal-wide scale is deemed to be subject to inescapable inaccuracy, the implication is that the only feasible alternative is to let market forces determine things.

A related view of the difficulties encountered by states attempting to intervene in economic life is provided by Durkheim in a discussion of the consequences associated with the 'anomic' division of labour. Although there is recognition that development of the 'organ of government' is a necessary corollary of increases in the division of labour, there is a simultaneous identification of inescapable limitations to the governmental sphere of action. On this matter Durkheim (1984: 297) remarks:

> It is not the government that can at every moment regulate the conditions of the different economic markets, fix the prices of goods and services, regulate production to the needs of consumption etc. All these practical problems throw up a mass of details, depend upon thousands of special circumstances that they alone are aware of who know them intimately. *A fortiori* the government cannot effect an adjustment between these functions and make them work harmoniously together if they themselves are not in harmony.

The particular objection to state intervention outlined in the above remarks is primarily epistemological. The central issue is that there are inescapable limitations to the knowledge available to individuals and, in turn, to any centralized governmental planning authority. Hayek (1949) argues that these limitations derive from two sources. First, the division of knowledge in modern society impairs communication of knowledge and presents a problem of coordination. However, another form of division in respect of knowledge is implied in Hayek's account, notably between universalizing and local forms of understanding. Some forms of knowledge – 'practical knowledge embodied in skills and know-how . . . knowledge of particulars, local to time and place' (O'Neill 1998: 130) – cannot be expressed in terms of abstract propositions or communicable universals. In so far as this is the case then there will be forms of knowledge in society of which particular individuals and organizations will be unaware. The second source of limitation on the knowledge available to individuals and organizations arises from the difficulty of determining existing needs or wants and of anticipating future needs or wants. In contrast, the market is presented as a self-regulating mechanism that provides, through the medium of price, 'informational feedback between economic actors necessary for the mutual adjustment of their activities' (O'Neill 1998: 129).

Friedman: capitalism and freedom

The market is not only regarded as economically more efficient by Hayek and Friedman, it is simultaneously considered to enhance the scope for human freedom. Economic activity in contemporary capitalism typically takes the form of competition between private enterprises operating in terms of a notion of a free market, although with the increasing marketization of the public sector competition is not confined to the private sector alone. In discussion of the respective merits of the market and government in the organization of economic life, Friedman comments that 'History suggests that capitalism is a necessary condition for political freedom' (1982: 10). Competitive capitalism is considered to be conducive to both economic and political freedom. The central thesis is that economic freedom is not only a desirable end in itself, but that, in turn, it is an 'indispensable means' to the realization of political freedom. Competitive capitalism as a specific form of organization of economic life separates economic from political power and thereby, Friedman argues, the one is able to offset the other and, in consequence, political freedom is promoted. The biggest threat to freedom is perceived to lie with the tendency for governmental intervention in social and economic life to increase in scale and intensity as modernity increases in complexity. The argument is that while government promises to *preserve* freedom, and may in practice serve as an instrument to that end in certain limited respects, it simultaneously represents a concentration of political power that constitutes a serious *threat* to freedom. Friedman's concern is that, notwithstanding the best intentions, interventions emanating from centralized government end up doing more harm than good.

To avoid the threat posed to freedom by a concentration of political power, limitation on the scope of government is advocated. This is to be achieved in two ways. First through the utilization of 'voluntary co-operation and private enterprise in both economic and other activities' (Friedman 1982: 2). Second through a dispersal or decentralization of governmental power. The acceptable parameters for the exercise of governmental influence are argued to be 'to protect our freedom both from the enemies outside our gates and from our fellow-citizens: to preserve law and order, to enforce private contracts, to foster competitive markets' (p. 2). The promotion of voluntary cooperation and private enterprise in economic and non-economic activities brings the private sector into play as a check on the powers of government. Countering the tendency towards an increasing centralization and concentration of governmental power through a strategy of dispersal likewise represents a potential limitation on government.

In addition to the two 'protective' reasons for limiting governmental influence briefly outlined above, Friedman (1982) identifies a third more 'constructive' rationale, namely the inability of government to respond to, nurture or enhance the 'variety and diversity of individual action' (p. 4). There is an acceptance that governmental intervention may have produced benefits in the form of improvements in housing, nutrition, schooling and sanitation, to the advantage of many individuals and communities. However, such improvements are criticized for simultaneously substituting 'uniform mediocrity for the variety essential for that experimentation which can bring tomorrow's laggards above today's means' (p. 4). In essence, Friedman considers that collective forms of provision interfere with individual freedom and impair economic performance.

At the heart of the neo-liberal view outlined is the notion that free markets necessarily enhance human well-being in both economic and political terms. The idea that market economies are more effective in promoting human welfare than other forms of organization of economic life runs through economic theory from the work of classical economists such as Adam Smith to contemporary neo-liberal economic thought. In so far as the market is assumed to be procedurally neutral in its operation then it is deemed to be the most appropriate mechanism for allowing individuals to pursue their own interests and conceptions of the good life in a pluralistic modern social context. The neo-liberal argument is that the market effectively coordinates and organizes the activities of large numbers of individuals pursuing their own economic interests. The market is represented as a mechanism of coordination that is voluntary and of mutual benefit to all the parties involved in the exchange process, 'provided the transaction is bi-laterally voluntary and informed' (Friedman 1982: 13). The contrast drawn is generally with what is represented as the only alternative, namely economic coordination through centralized state direction employing, where necessary, coercive techniques.

The key problem of social organization in Friedman's view is how to achieve effective coordination of the economic activities of large numbers of people. But the solution ultimately proposed is derived from an oversimplified contrast between the alternatives outlined, namely the market or the state – that is, coordination through 'voluntary cooperation', or coordination through 'coercion'. In his argument, Friedman generalizes from a model of a simple exchange economy. In a simple exchange economy each independent household is able to use resources in its control to 'produce goods and services that it exchanges for goods and services produced by other households, on terms mutually acceptable to the two parties to the bargain' (Friedman 1982: 13). Households are described as having the scope to decide whether to satisfy wants directly or indirectly – that is, by deciding whether (and in what proportion) to produce goods and services for self-consumption or for exchange in the market-place. The existence of the option to satisfy wants directly through the production of goods in the household means that the exchange process will not be entered unless there is a perceived potential benefit to be gained. Friedman remarks that 'no exchange will take place unless both parties . . . benefit from it. Co-operation is thereby achieved without coercion' (1982: 13).

The suggestion is that much like the simple exchange economy, cooperation remains individual and voluntary in a 'complex enterprise and money exchange economy', providing, that is, that the following conditions are met:

> (a) . . . enterprises are private, so that the ultimate contracting parties are individuals and (b) . . . individuals are effectively free to enter or not to enter into any particular exchange, so that every exchange is strictly voluntary.
>
> (Friedman 1982: 14)

There is a brief acknowledgement of the difficulty of specifying the precise 'institutional arrangements' required for satisfying these conditions. There are references to the necessity of law and order both to 'prevent physical coercion of one individual by another' (Friedman 1982: 14) and to ensure contractual compliance. There is also a brief recognition of the potential problems arising from monopoly and effects on third parties. But there is no recognition of the reality of contemporary capitalism as a competitive, private enterprise exchange economy that operates in a significantly different manner from a simple exchange economy composed of independent households. Commercial enterprises are much more than benign or neutral 'intermediaries between individuals in their capacities as suppliers of service and as purchasers of goods' (Friedman 1982: 13–14). The ultimate point of commercial enterprise within a capitalist economic system is capital accumulation, profiting from the circuits of production, distribution, exchange and consumption. Individuals are involved as producers and consumers of goods and services only in so far as they contribute effectively to that end.

Friedman (1982) assumes freedom of exchange can be achieved and maintained as the 'central feature of the market organisation of economic activity' (p. 14). It is asserted that the market form of organization prevents interference in people's lives 'in respect of most . . . activities' (p. 14). The existence of other sellers in the market protects consumers from coercion by the seller – the assumption being that they can literally 'shop around'. Likewise, producers and sellers are protected from consumer coercion by the existence of other consumers to whom goods and services can be marketed and sold. In turn, employees are described as protected from coercion by employers by the market form of organization in so far as there will be other employers in the market offering job opportunities.[3]

From this standpoint it is asserted that the free market simply 'gives people what they want' (Friedman 1982: 15). The assumption being that everyone ends up being satisfied with their lot, that everyone obtains 'what they want'. In so far as the organization of economic activity is market based, then the role of government is minimized, effectively reduced to ensuring a level playing field by outlining rules and acting to enforce them. The market 'permits wide diversity' and promotes economic freedom. In contrast, centralized governmental forms of organization are portrayed as requiring or enforcing conformity and as promoting political coercion. Where economic activity is organized through the market the potentially 'coercive power' that might be exercised by political authority is considered to be effectively neutralized. As Friedman remarks, 'economic strength [becomes] . . . a check to political power rather than a reinforcement' (1982: 15). However, no convincing analytic justification is offered for the equation of the market with voluntary cooperation and the state with coercion. Furthermore, there is no consideration of the issue of how discriminating the exercise of economic strength might be in practice. The idea that economic strength might be employed in such a manner as to erode and undermine democratic political freedoms is not entertained at all. In consequence there is no consideration of the possibility that rather than being a precondition for political freedom, the development of capitalist economic life might have other more undesirable political effects. For example, Soros notes how 'the untrammelled intensification of *laissez-faire* capitalism and the spread of market values into all areas of life is endangering our open and democratic society' (1997: 45). Rather than preventing interference in people's lives, the market form of organization now represents one of the most significant and intrusive influences, a potentially coercive force to which people are increasingly and involuntarily exposed.

Another significant and no less problematic assumption present in the narrative on the articulation of economic and political freedom is that, unlike political power, '[e]conomic power can be widely dispersed' (Friedman 1982: 15). The reality of economic competition between companies on the one hand and countries on the other suggests otherwise, as does the fast-growing imbalance exemplified by the rising economic and political influence of multinational companies and the declining economic and political sovereignty of nation states. Friedman's assertions on the dispersal of economic power are not convincing, particularly in a context where the development of an informational capitalism has led to the emergence of a 'Fourth World' of over-exploitation, poverty and social exclusion (Castells 1998). The policy of unrestricted market logic advocated by Friedman has led to rising inequality and poverty, as well as to 'black holes' of social exclusion (Castells 1998: 162). It has enabled corporations to become powerful political forces. In some cases the budgets of multinational corporations now exceed the gross domestic product of nation states, indeed 'of the top hundred economies, fifty-one are multinationals and only forty-nine are countries' (Klein 2001: 340). The movement towards a globally extensive free-market economy has led to a range of economic and political developments that radically challenge Friedman's view that 'free market capitalist society fosters freedom' (1982: 19).

Hayek: market order and autonomy

To fully understand the spontaneous order associated with the market, Hayek argues that it is necessary to 'free ourselves of the misleading associations suggested by its usual description as an "economy"' (1976: 107). In Hayek's view the notion of economy suggests a deliberate organized allocation of means by an agency in order to realize a particular end or ends differentiated in terms of relative importance from other competing ends through recourse to specific value criteria. While such a usage of the term makes sense in relation to an individual household, farm or enterprise, it is argued that it is misleading when utilized in reference to the complex and diverse economic activities of a society. For Hayek, reference to the economy of a country, or 'national economy', necessarily implies a form of socialist organization, a singular ordering of ends according to a unitary plan. In so far as market order cannot be equated with a unitary system of ends, Hayek suggests that it might be necessary to employ a new term – 'catallaxy' – to describe the spontaneous order 'brought about by the mutual adjustment of many individual economies in a market' (1976: 109).

The market is not governed by a single scale of objectives. It serves, Hayek (1976) argues, 'the multiplicity of separate and incommensurable ends of all its separate members' (p. 108). It is this quality that is considered to make possible the 'Great Society', nurturing individual freedom and all its associated values. This society achieves its coherence not through design but through the market and its processes of exchange, through supplying goods and services for others and seeking, in turn, goods and services from others. In such a society, Hayek argues, we satisfy needs of which we have no knowledge and contribute to the achievement of ends of which we might not approve if we had knowledge of them:

> That we assist in the realization of other people's aims without sharing them or even knowing them, and solely in order to achieve our own aims, is the source of strength of the Great Society.
>
> (p. 110)

Reflecting on the unintended mutually beneficial effects identified with the process of exchange, Hayek (1976) notes that one response has been to draw attention to the selfish motivations of people. The pursuit of self-interest is undoubtedly an important driving force in the provision of goods and services for others in the market, but there is more going on in Hayek's view. In particular it is necessary to note the benefits of the division of labour intrinsic to market exchange processes, the respects in which differences of knowledge and purpose are beneficially reconciled in the emergence of an 'overall order . . . superior to any deliberate organization' (p. 110).

Such a society, Hayek notes, has no 'common concrete purposes', rather the 'Great Society' is 'means-connected not ends-connected' (1976: 110). The idea that a modern society requires a 'solidarity' that derives from a common set of values and shared purposes is firmly rejected by Hayek. While there is an acknowledgement that this may be regarded as a moral defect it is implied that such a diagnosis signifies the persistence of a moral tradition that owes more to 'end-connected tribal society' than to the reality of life in a complex modern setting. For Hayek, common purpose and common goals are matters of which to be wary, save for exceptional moments of sudden emergency (e.g. war). What from this standpoint holds the Great Society together, what gives it its coherence, its interdependence, are economic relations:

> The suggestion that . . . the only ties which hold the whole of a Great Society together are purely 'economic' (more precisely 'catallactic') arouses great emotional resistance. Yet the fact can hardly be denied; nor the fact that, in a society of the dimensions and complexity of a modern country of the world, it can hardly be otherwise. Most people are still reluctant to accept the fact that it should be the disdained 'cash-nexus' which holds

the Great Society together, that the great ideal of the unity of mankind should in the last resort depend on the relations between the parts being governed by the striving for the better satisfaction of their material needs.

(Hayek 1976: 112)

It is the ordering made possible through the market process that is considered to be the source of a 'peaceful reconciliation of divergent purposes' deemed beneficial to all.

Anticipating aspects of the discourse on the globalization of capitalism, Hayek proceeds to argue that 'interdependence', which has led to the emergence of 'One World', could only have been an effect of the market order. In sum, what links 'the life of any European or American with what happens in Australia, Japan or Zaire are repercussions transmitted by the network of market relations' (Hayek 1976: 112–13). By implication the nurturing of increased interdependence in the form of globally extensive market exchange processes promises to deliver a free 'global' society at peace with itself.

Critical reflections on the association of the market with freedom

The association of the market with economic and political freedom warrants critical consideration. It has been suggested that 'the market provides economic freedom' (Friedman 1982: 15) and that a 'free society' is held together by a market ordering of economic relations (Hayek 1976). But what precisely is meant by 'freedom' in each instance is not satisfactorily clarified. By implication it seems to be a condition in which there are no constraints on the conduct of individuals, where there is no intentional interference. In short, the conception of freedom employed is negative, the primary virtue of the market organization of economic activity being that it 'prevents one person from interfering with another in respect of most of his activities' (Friedman 1982: 14). As with Hayek's account of the virtues associated with freedom of exchange, the primary emphasis is placed upon the absence of interference or 'coercion by the arbitrary will of another or others' (1960: 11). The freedom of the individual is not to be equated with material preconditions or access to resources. For Hayek such an equation signifies a 'confusion of freedom with power' (1944: 19) typical of socialism.

In a critical analysis of market philosophy, John O'Neill (1998) sets out to clarify the cluster of values and assumptions that have informed discussion of the relationship between the market and freedom. At the heart of the liberal and neo-liberal promotion of the market is the assumption that a dynamic commercial society 'fosters social independence' and 'frees individuals' (p. 77). Reflecting on the arguments that have been advanced in favour of the freedom-enhancing qualities of the market, O'Neill draws a distinction between neutrality-based and perfectionist forms. The neutrality-based argument for markets conceives of freedom and autonomy as prerequisites for individuals pursuing their own versions of the good life. In contrast, in the perfectionist case, 'the dispositions of character that form the virtues constitutive of the autonomous person – the powers to reason for oneself, to be self-reflective, to act as the author of one's own life – form a central component of the good life' (p. 64). The implication is that social and political institutions should be so organized as to cultivate such virtues while undermining 'the opposing vices of heteronomy – passivity, self-abnegation, deference to authority' (p. 64).

Both Hayek and Friedman make an explicit appeal to a negative concept of freedom in which emphasis is placed on the individual in pursuit of a chosen objective not being subject to the interference of another or others. A more positive conception of freedom that identifies the importance of possessing a capacity or attributes necessary to pursue a chosen objective appears to be rejected. It is in this context that O'Neill poses a basic question: 'What is the good of "negative" freedom?' Two liberal responses to this question need to be distinguished. In the first, freedom is not a basic value. Rather it constitutes a 'condition of the procedural neutrality of political and economic institutions' in which constraint or interference is absent and individuals can pursue their own versions of the good life, providing they do not prevent others from so doing (O'Neill 1998: 65). The central issue here is *choice*, the possibility of following one's own choices. The second response treats the value of unrestricted freedom of choice as beneficial to the process of building the moral character of the individual. The implication here is that the market economy contributes to the constitution of the moral character of individuals in so far as it makes exercise of autonomy and possession of the ability to make choices a necessity.

O'Neill (1998) argues that Hayek and other exponents of free-market philosophy are inclined to conflate having choices or being in a position to follow one's chosen path with being in possession of the necessary capacities or attributes constitutive of autonomy or self-determination. In short, there is a failure to distinguish between the question of 'whether or not one is coerced by others' and having 'the dispositions and powers to be one's own person' (p. 67). This has meant that a positive aspect of the value of freedom in Hayek's work in particular has tended to be neglected. Hayek places emphasis on the importance of the neutrality of the mechanism of the market, in particular on leaving individuals with the scope to follow their choices free from interference. In consequence the issue of autonomy or self-determination is left implicit and is thereby effectively reduced to a 'procedural matter of having choices' (O'Neill 1998: 68). But the availability of choice does not signify that individuals have the capacity to act as autonomous agents. Preoccupation with negative conditions conducive to the exercise of free choice means that the crucial issue of the conditions in and through which autonomous agency is (to be) constituted is not addressed.

However, there are traces in Hayek's work of a 'perfectionist' regard for 'autonomous character' and recognition of the market as a necessary condition for the development of independent individuals with 'the capacities and powers to formulate their own values and thoughts' (O'Neill 1998: 69). The implication is that the qualities that constitute autonomy are not simply given, they are associated with specific conditions. Notably with modern market economies that not only require, but nurture, self-directed individuals with a distinctive self-identity able, to a substantial degree, to shape the ways in which their lives develop. But there are problems with such a defence of the market. O'Neill identifies three areas of difficulty associated with:

- the value of autonomy;
- the conditions necessary for the development of autonomy;
- the existence of different conceptions of autonomy.

First, for autonomy to have value there have to be a range of adequate valuable options from which choice(s) can be made. This means that the non-market institutional spheres (educational, cultural, familial and associational) in which people pursue valued projects and relationships need to be protected from market forces. These non-market spheres are 'undermined if they are colonised by markets, either directly by being transformed into commodities that are subject to sale in the market, or indirectly by being subject to the norms and meanings of the market' (O'Neill 1998: 70). In short, there need to be limits to the extension of markets.

Second, autonomy requires individuals to possess particular attributes – for example, the capacity to reason, to determine the adequacy and appropriateness of criteria of evaluation and to make qualitative judgements between different courses of conduct. In so far as this is the case, there is a need for 'non-market domains of informal and formal education, and material, cultural, familial and working conditions that develop the capacity for self-determination which a free market will fail to deliver' (O'Neill 1998: 70). While the capitalist market economy is regarded as a necessary condition for autonomy it does not constitute a sufficient condition, as Friedman (1982) acknowledges. However, while acknowledging that capitalist economic forms of organization may exist alongside forms of political life that are not free, both Hayek and Friedman neglect to consider the significance of non-market relations for the development of the capacities required to exercise self-determination.

Finally there is the question of the conception of autonomy itself. O'Neill suggests that both neo-liberal defenders of the market and their critics are guilty of employing 'one-dimensional contrasts between autonomous and non-autonomous persons' (1998: 71). The autonomous person is characterized as one who has, in significant respects, shaped or determined self-identity and who is able to independently arrive at decisions, judgements and choices. The contrast drawn is with the individual whose identity derives from 'external circumstances' and who is 'excessively dependent' on the authority, judgement and choices of others (O'Neill 1998: 71). The criticism developed by O'Neill is that the simple contrast drawn between autonomy and its absence neglects other possible ways in which autonomy might be eroded. The possibility of autonomous character rests not only upon the absence of external imposition but also upon what O'Neill describes as the presence of 'settled dispositions'. The problem identified is that preoccupation with autonomy might take 'the excessively individualistic form which understands its scope to include the very standards by which the self and its works is to be judged: the resulting excessive self-conceit is as much opposed to autonomy as excessive dependence' (O'Neill 1998: 71). Rather than assume that markets enhance autonomy, O'Neill cautions that it is necessary to examine the effects of the market system. In particular, consideration needs to be given to the growth of narcissistic forms of individualism that make a virtue of 'the self who plays with identity' and the individual who claims to be 'the authentic author of his own values' (O'Neill 1998: 71). Evidence of the increasing instability, fragility and fragmentation of identity, of the transitory or provisional character of the contemporary sense of identity, suggest that rather than being conducive the market system may be contributing significantly to the undermining of autonomous character (Sennett 1998).

In a broadly comparable manner it has been argued that behind the proliferation of 'increasingly unstable, fluid, shifting, and changing identities' lies the inexorable process of capitalist commodification:

> The market segmentation of multiple ad campaigns and appeals reproduces and intensifies fragmentation and destabilizes identity which new products and identifications are attempting to restabilize. Thus, it seems that it is capital itself which is the demiurge of allegedly postmodern fragmentation, dispersal of identity, change and mobility.
>
> (Kellner 1992: 172)

The development of modern market societies has freed individuals from the constraints of traditional fixed social positions and seems to have given them an 'independent' identity. In so far as this is the case it is argued that free-market institutions have contributed to the constitution of conditions in which forms of self-determination can be exercised. However, the dynamic character of modern capitalist market-ordered societies produces constant movement and a perpetual pursuit of innovation. The associated 'uninterrupted disturbance of all social conditions' (Marx and Engels 1968: 83) leads to uncertainty and agitation, not least in respect of identity and the sense individuals have of who they are, where they belong, where they are going and what it is that matters to them. In such a context, as O'Neill notes, settled dispositions and commitments constitutive of the character of the autonomous person are increasingly undermined. In place of identity, anchored in the dispositions of character whose development requires time and commitment, the market society promotes the formation of 'social identity' which is both preoccupied with and a product of 'the appearances that commodities create' (O'Neill 1998: 80). Rather than enhancing autonomy the market system's perpetual promotion of movement and innovation, a necessary corollary of the competitive pursuit of capital accumulation, is associated with an equation of identity with appearance. In sum, far from enhancing autonomy, under the influence of the modern market system identity becomes 'more a question of appearances and the capacity one has to buy them' (O'Neill 1998: 81).

Autonomy and authority

Market philosophy contends that the capitalist market system promotes freedom, in so far as it makes it possible for sovereign consumers to exercise choice in both their consumption of goods and style of life. A suspicion of authority as constituting a constraint on the 'freedom of the authentic agent' (O'Neill 1998: 85) is a corollary. The ideas that the individual should not be constrained by any authority other than that of their own 'reason, conscience or will' and that the consumer subject is indeed sovereign are frequently invoked in defence of the market. Such views have also served to legitimate an extension of market principles into spheres that formerly have been exempted. For example, O'Neill notes the pressure to extend market logic to 'cultural and educational fields', to which list the fields of health and welfare can be added.

Where an excessively individualistic form of autonomy gains currency, where self-authorship is considered to extend to the very criteria by which conduct and associated consequences are to be evaluated, a tendency towards excessive self-assertiveness is likely to develop, and an unwarranted contrast tends to be drawn between 'autonomy' and 'authority'. In his development of a 'less heady picture of the autonomous person' O'Neill argues that there are times and circumstances in which it is both necessary and appropriate to 'trust claims that call on authority' (1998: 87). In consequence an important attribute of autonomous character is to know when and where this is reasonable and when and where it is not. In turn it is crucial to be able to distinguish

> between authority that is founded on competence and that an-
> swers to standards independent of the person, and authority
> that is founded on mere power, status or wealth. The latter are
> never sources of competence nor grounds for deference . . . one
> of the problems of modern market societies . . . is that legitimate
> authority is compromised by association with wealth and the
> social power it confers.
>
> (O'Neill 1998: 87)

The distinction drawn above between 'epistemological authority' based on impersonal standards or grounds and 'social authority' that derives from social or institutional position is pivotal to O'Neill's argument that there are contexts in which assent to authority is rationally justifiable and consistent with the exercise of autonomy. For example, O'Neill suggests that autonomy may be exercised in considering whether to assent to the 'epistemological' authority of those with medical, educational and technical competencies. The implication being that before seeking and following the advice of professionals – doctors, teachers, technicians etc. – or before making use of resources they have provided, there is a potential to question whether or not to trust their claims to authority. In this respect informed assent to authority may be regarded as an exercise of autonomy that avoids the potentially disabling effects of professional dominance (Smart 1992).

What is at issue here is trust in abstract systems and, in particular, forms of expert knowledge. People are increasingly reliant on expert systems. The attitudes of trust shown by people towards such systems and forms of knowledge have been described as 'usually routinely incorporated into the continuity of day-to-day activities and . . . to a large extent enforced by the intrinsic circumstances of everyday life' (Giddens 1990: 90). In so far as trust in practice constitutes a 'tacit acceptance of circumstances in which other alternatives are largely foreclosed' (Giddens 1990: 90), the question arises as to where scope for autonomy to be exercised is located. The answer offered by Giddens is that experiences at 'access points' give rise to tensions between what is described as 'lay scepticism' and 'professional expertise' and, by implication, that it is at these points that an exercise of autonomy may lead to a withdrawal, maintenance or development of trust.

The contrasting of autonomy and authority, and in particular the identification of potentially coercive consequences of authority for individual autonomy, have constituted the basis on which the case for extending market forces has been developed. A more radical exploration of the relationship of autonomy and authority allows consideration to be given to the possibility that there are spheres of social life that need to be protected from market forces. At stake here is the question of potential limits to markets and the issue of market boundaries.

Marx, market exchange and the experience of autonomy

The assumed interrelationship of capitalism and freedom, of markets with autonomy, is vulnerable to another line of criticism. In developing his analysis of markets and autonomy O'Neill cites Marx as an analyst for whom the system of market exchange represented a powerful source of the liberation of individuals from traditional social roles. While this is an uncontroversial observation, attributing to Marx the view that 'markets develop autonomy' is more contentious. In 'The Chapter on Money' in the draft work published as *Grundrisse* Marx spells out the importance of the transformation of production, consumption and associated activities with the development of capitalist market exchange processes. In particular Marx notes the respects in which these are articulated with 'the dissolution of all fixed personal (historic) relations of dependence' (1973: 156). The dominance of market exchange only develops fully, and continues to develop 'ever more completely' in what Marx describes as 'the society of free competition' (p. 156). In this society individuals become increasingly interdependent as a result of the constant necessity for exchange. Marx notes how economists have tended to regard this outcome as a beneficial consequence of the pursuit by individuals of their private interest, which serves 'the general interest, without willing or knowing it' (p. 156). In response, Marx argues that private interest cannot be treated as given, as reflecting an essentially autonomous nature – rather it is 'socially determined'. It is only achieved 'within the conditions laid down by society and with the means provided by society' (p. 156). From this standpoint it is the process of market exchange that increasingly constitutes the basis of the interdependence between indifferent individuals, their social bond.

The social bond, Marx argues, is 'expressed in exchange value' and materialized in the form of money – 'the individual carries his social power, as well as his bond with society in his pocket' (1973: 157). The generality of market exchange means that there is an increasing tendency for all activities to lose their individuality. In turn, the dominance of exchange value means that individuals increasingly encounter the social character of productive activity 'as *their subordination to relations which subsist independently of them* and which arise out of collisions between mutually indifferent individuals' (p. 157, emphasis added). In such circumstances it is the general process of exchange of activities and products that assumes autonomy, not individual producers and consumers.

In a series of further comments on the market system, Marx observes that increasing interdependence in production and consumption coincides with the growing independence and indifference of producers and consumers to one another. But how is such 'independence' to be interpreted? Does it signify support for the view that markets develop autonomy? In discussing the way in which the capitalist market system has developed,

Marx provides a number of observations on the emergence of institutions that provide information which allow individuals to adjust their activities in the light of their knowledge of the activity of others. As individuals inform themselves about markets, their knowledge shapes their conduct and 'reacts back in practice on the total supply and demand' (1973: 161). However, it would be a mistake to regard such observations as supporting the view that such independent individual producers and consumers are the beneficiaries of market enhanced autonomy.

In Marx's work a distinction is drawn between the more personal social relations that were a feature of an 'undeveloped system of exchange' and the social relations that are characteristic of a more developed, modern capitalist system of exchange. However, Marx cautions against an oversimplified contrast between a social formation in which there is a predominance of relations of 'personal dependence' and one in which there is a prevalence of 'independent' individuals able to exercise autonomy. Marx argues that while the developed system of exchange dissolves 'ties of personal dependence' and within it individuals seem to be independent, 'this is an independence which is at bottom merely *an illusion*' (1973: 163, emphasis added). Individuals are 'free' to interact and exchange with one another, but Marx adds that

> they appear thus only for someone who abstracts from the *conditions*, the *conditions of existence* within which these individuals enter into contact (and these conditions, in turn, are independent of the individual and, although created by society, appear as if they were *natural conditions*, not controllable by individuals).
>
> (1973: 164)

In place of the constraints of personal ties and relations the individual is defined and restricted by an order of external, objective and independent relations. Rather than regard these relations as exemplifying an abolition of dependence Marx suggests that they represent the 'dissolution of these relations into a general form . . . the elaboration and emergence of the general *foundation* of the relations of personal dependence' (1973: 164). In short, where formerly individuals were ruled through relations of personal dependence, now they are subject to, and indeed subjects of, abstractions. From Marx's standpoint the illusion of autonomy is a necessary corollary of the market system's development of objective dependency relations.

Rather than nurturing the development of autonomy the market constitutes an abstraction that serves as a mechanism of regulation. The ordering that is achieved through the market is not a product of the intentions of individual buyers and sellers – rather, it constitutes a form of coherence that is 'a product of chance', one that exercises a 'spontaneous regulation' over the conduct of individuals (Gorz 1989: 34).

Autonomy, authority and the question of boundaries

There is another dimension to the argument on the issue of autonomy and authority in relation to the market: that of market boundaries. What is broadly at stake here is the question of whether limits need to be placed on the extension of market forces. In short, are there goods and services for which provision through the market is inappropriate?

For the most part the production of goods and services in the public sphere, production for or by government, has tended to be located outside of the market (Galbraith and Salinger 1981). However, with the cultivation of a culture of enterprise and the adoption of neo-liberal economic policies the market has been accorded greater significance, and renewed emphasis has been placed on the value of market competition and the role of the consumer (Heelas and Morris 1992). The equation of the development of free markets with an enhancement of economic efficiency has led to an extension of the market mechanism into a number of formerly non-market spheres. In particular, in addition to an intensification of market forces there has been an extension of their scope into a number of formerly non-market or 'professional territories' like education and health (Heelas and Morris 1992; O'Neill 1998).

As the market mechanism has been imposed upon formerly non-market spheres of public life so the provision of services, whether of education, health, welfare or whatever, has become subject to the logic of the market. As education or health is reconstituted as an industry in the market-place,

> what matters is attending to 'production' to increase efficiency and quality. The intention is that people will have to exercise initiative; compete for 'consumers'; cost their activities and think of themselves as 'producers', if they are to prosper, let alone retain their jobs. In this fashion, the discipline and rigour of the market helps to construct a mode of selfhood defined in terms of the virtues of enterprise.
>
> (Heelas and Morris 1992: 5)

Complementing the educational and health 'producers', the teachers, the nurses and the doctors, are the 'consumers', the students and the patients. With the extension of the market mechanism the traditional roles of professionals in a number of formerly non-market spheres such as education and health are effectively being redefined. Through the imposition of a process of 'marketization' in the public sector the autonomy of professionals is being steadily eroded. The objective, ostensibly, is to improve service provision and enhance the sovereignty of consumers. In practice the turn to market mechanisms and market forces probably owes more to a sense that the problem of achieving adequate taxation revenue to fund public service provision is unlikely to be resolved and that in its current form 'the welfare state has become unsustainable' (Giddens 2000: 102–3).

For example, in higher education there are increasing signs of the presence of 'norms and institutional forms characteristic of commercial society' (O'Neill 1998: 93). The institution of the university is becoming a 'means of educational consumption' (Ritzer 1998: 151) and is more and more dependent on corporate funding and commercial sponsorship (Smart 2002). In turn, the student now brings a consumer mentality to higher learning, indeed has become a 'consumer' of courses. With the extension of market forces and the associated growth of a consumer culture what it means to be a student, what counts as worth knowing and what value is to be placed on knowledge, are all being transformed:

> Property rights on the products of intellectual research are increasingly being defined in terms of the norms of markets. Forms of quality assessment and control borrowed from management techniques in the commercial world are being applied to teaching and research. Universities increasingly are under pressure to 'market' themselves to their prospective 'customers'.
>
> (O'Neill 1998: 93)

The issue of autonomy can be turned against those who would argue for an increasing extension of market freedom by asking why the interest of the consumer should prevail over that of the producer. This is precisely what O'Neill intends when he argues that the 'independence of educational and cultural spheres from markets is a question itself of autonomy, of those within particular practices and institutions to pursue particular projects and activities independently of consumer choices' (1998: 94). Two reasons are offered by O'Neill in support of the idea that there should be limits to the extension of markets.

First, limits are deemed necessary to ensure reproduction of the very conditions necessary for the nurturing of autonomy, for the development of those 'capacities and dispositions of character . . . constitutive of autonomy' (O'Neill 1998: 94). What is at stake here is the nurturing of qualities conducive to exercising choice – for example, the ability to critically consider information, to weigh it up, be discriminating and order preferences, and arrive at independent decisions or judgements. In turn, O'Neill suggests that the very 'existence of valuable options over which choices can be made' requires that some spheres, notably 'educational, cultural and associational' (1998: 94), be protected from the potentially all-consuming influence of market forces. What is at issue here is the question of whether or not there are values that involve more than consumer preference or taste. The notion of *valuable* option' implies the presence of a criterion or criteria through which a judgement of value is reached and accorded to a course of action, a practice, an experience, object or artefact, that cannot be reduced simply to an expression of consumer preference. Affirmation of authoritative standards is not incompatible with autonomy – on the contrary, the very possibility of autonomous existence requires a degree of reason-based trust in the appropriateness and effectiveness of the specific abilities, skills and capacities of a range of providers in a variety of diverse fields.

A response to the issues outlined above requires not only a consideration of the benefits to be gained from limits or restrictions being placed on the extension of market forces, but also that attention be given to the broader operation of the market system, its consequences and human impact. Market philosophy provides insight into rationales for the market and an ideal typical sense of how the market mechanism might operate, *ceteris paribus*. However, other things are not equal – the reality is that free impersonal competitive markets are, at best, exceptional. Large corporations exercising excessive leverage over markets and the economies of nation states is increasingly commonplace, if not the rule (Galbraith and Salinger 1981). In short, 'markets which function problematically seem to be the "general case" in the real world' (Mackintosh *et al.* 1996: 29).

In the conclusion to his narrative on the apparent freedom enhancing effects of capitalism, Milton Friedman briefly acknowledges 'the difference between the actual operation of the market and its ideal operation' (1982: 197). However, this admission merely constitutes a pretext for further criticism of forms of government intervention, where the differences between actual and intended effects are argued to be substantially greater than in the case of the market. In a comparable fashion Hayek makes a contrast between fecundity attributed to the market and futility ascribed to government intervention. The discussion that follows is directed, in contrast, to the reality of the market and its consequences.

The market system and the quality of social and economic life

In contrast to the idea of markets enhancing human well-being, critical analysts have drawn attention to the problematic consequences of market forces (Castells 1996, 1998; Soros 1997, 1998; Bourdieu 1998; O'Neill 1998; Gray 1999; Philo and Miller 2001). The prominence of a 'culture of the market', the valorization and deployment of the market as the pre-eminent mechanism for organizing economic activity and social priorities, is increasingly evident in contemporary society and now intrudes into and affects most aspects of the majority of people's lives. However, a number of specific problems have been identified in respect of contemporary forms of life subject to the 'culture of the market' and an associated 'culture of consumption' (Jameson 1991: 206).

Pursuit of self-interest in a competitive process of market exchange is argued by both Hayek and Friedman to have the unintended consequence of creating a spontaneous order of mutual benefit to all market participants. The notion of 'free' and 'efficient' markets that are beneficial to all is however far removed from the reality of market processes. Rather than being associated with order, markets frequently exhibit disorder and produce disorganization in social and economic life. For example, inflation and unemployment have been identified as two forms of market disorder which cause 'anxiety for both economists and citizens' (Mackintosh *et al.* 1996: 27). Other aspects of the market process have also attracted criticism for the consequences with which they have been associated.

The emphasis placed upon competition and self-interest in pursuit of material rewards and personal satisfactions within the culture of the market has been argued to have contributed significantly to the development of a society in which inequality is on the increase, financial reward is the principal source of motivation, and '[c]onsuming becomes more important than caring' (Heelas and Morris 1992: 11). Paralleling concerns expressed about the increasingly unequal distribution of wealth in a market-oriented society (Castells 1998; Beck 2000), analysts have drawn attention to the ways in which the culture of the market has affected the quality of social and personal life (Sennett 1999). In turn, this has opened up the question of the moral dimension of markets, in particular the issue of moral limits to market activity (Plant 1992; Keat 1993).

The emphasis placed upon individual self-interest and the virtues of competitiveness and commitment towards the realization of material values and goals reflects the extent to which everyday social life has become subject to market processes. Within the culture of the market,

> life becomes a perpetual endeavour; where stress, guilt and fear of failure are likely to loom large; where the workaholic ethic threatens familial and personal relationships . . . where companionship in the workplace is constantly threatened by rivalry and suspicion.
> (Heelas and Morris 1992: 13)

The regeneration of a 'production' ethic, an ethic of enterprise and wealth creation that has become an increasingly prominent part of contemporary social life, is however only one part of the story. Conspicuous consumption is also a corollary of the culture of the market and pivotal to the development of an increasingly consumer-led capitalism. As consumption has become a more significant aspect of contemporary social life, individuals have become socially engaged primarily in their role as consumers. The key requirement is that the capacity of individuals for consumption is never exhausted and is continually replenished or enhanced. It is not so much that consumers must not be allowed to rest, as that while resting they continue to consume products and services, as well as the seductive signs that help replenish their capacity for further rounds of consumption. Consumers, as Bauman remarks, 'need to be constantly exposed to new temptations in order to be kept in a state of a constantly seething, never wilting excitation and, indeed, in a state of suspicion and disaffection' (1998b: 26).

In a comparable manner, Ritzer draws attention to the way in which consumers are increasingly encouraged to enter the market-place, 'to spend more than they should, and often more than they can afford, on consumption in order to keep the economy operating at a high and ever-increasing level' (1998: 120). The condition of being satisfied or contented with one's lot is anathema to a society that requires its members to be actively participating consumers. The consumer market needs customers, it needs individuals for whom the attraction of consuming an endless supply of goods and services is never diminished, nor finished. It requires individuals for whom consumption is experienced, not as a temptation to which they cannot help succumb, but as a matter of choice that has been freely exercised. Undoubtedly for the consumer there is an internalized pressure to consume. However,

> that impossibility of living one's life in any other way, reveals itself to them in the form of a free exercise of will. The market might have already picked them up and groomed them as consumers, and so deprived them of their freedom to ignore its temptations, but on every successive visit to a market place consumers have every reason to feel in command. They can, after all, refuse their allegiance to any one of the infinite choices on display – except the choice of choosing between them that is. The roads to self-identity, to a place in society, to life lived in a form recognisable as that of meaningful living, all require daily visits to the market place.
>
> (Bauman 1998b: 26)

The objective of increasing consumer freedom of choice has been a key feature of the extension of the market system to formerly non-market spheres involving the delivery of professional services. Such an extension is a characteristic feature of late modern capitalism which has continually sought to remove the 'limits impeding the deployment of economic rationality' (Gorz 1989: 127) and to give free rein to the 'logic of the pure market' (Bourdieu 1998: 96). In response to the implementation of a neo-liberal programme of deregulation directed towards the cultivation of conditions in which markets can operate relatively unhindered, critical analysts have sought to open up discussion of the moral parameters within which markets operate.

Morality and the market

There are three respects in which the question of morality arises in terms of markets (Plant 1992). The first is in relation to the moral foundations of the market. The contractual relations intrinsic to the operation of the market are themselves grounded in non-contractual shared moral understandings (Durkheim 1957). For markets to be able to operate there has to be a degree of trust between participants, there has to be confidence that promises made will be kept, that people can be taken at their word. As Durkheim recognized, it is the non-contractual moral element that is crucial to contractual relations. It is on the basis of the assumption and practical confirmation of shared moral values and attitudes towards the inviolability of contracts that the pursuit of self-interest in and through market activity is ordered. The pursuit of self-interest alone represents a potential threat to the 'moral assumptions on which . . . market exchange rests' (Plant 1992: 87). Indeed, as a culture of self-interest has developed in tandem with capitalism the moral values essential to capitalist market economy have become vulnerable and subject to compromise.

The pursuit of self-interest by market participants may also lead to monopolies or to attempts to gain subsidies or privileges from government. Plant argues that such expressions of self-interest threaten the integrity of the market and underline the need for some sense of 'civic virtue' – that is, the maintenance or regeneration of values that are not self-regarding, 'without which the market itself cannot function effectively' (1992: 90). The alternative is greater regulation of market behaviour to protect the integrity of the market. The possibility of regenerating such an ethos is made problematic by the fact that a sense of civic responsibility has been steadily undermined by the culture of self-interest nurtured by market relations. The problem identified by Plant (1992: 90) is that

> the growth of market relationships may gradually displace those forms of civic virtue and responsibility, which, if they were internalised, could constrain individual behaviour in the interest of the market in an informal way; and may, in the longer term, erode the social basis of consent necessary for formal legal regulation when informal mechanisms have failed.

The second respect in which morality has become an issue is in relation to the matter of limits to market forces. As a number of analysts have noted, considerable concern has been expressed about the moral propriety of allowing human organs, blood, or reproductive services to be offered for sale (Plant 1992; Keat 1993). From a capitalist perspective all the elements are present for a market in body parts. There is a demand for human organs, the donor system does not always provide a sufficient supply and 'if markets are usually construed as exchanges in property rights, then if a person owns anything, he or she owns the parts of his or her own body' (Plant 1992: 91). The potential commodification of human organs is the issue that has brought the question of the moral limits of markets most clearly to people's attention. Notwithstanding support for the idea of a market in organs and tissues from those promoting the free market, Plant contends that most people would probably object on moral grounds to body parts being subject to market forces and relations. Elaborating on the grounds for regarding a market in body parts as inappropriate, Plant comments that it might reflect 'an underlying attachment to the idea of respect for persons: that people should not treat themselves as commodities, or as a means to the ends of others' (1992: 92). However, the existence of prostitution, pornography and other manifestations of body commodification, along with the growth of a market for health care, in which ability to pay rather than need is ultimately important, suggest otherwise. It is difficult to find any consistency in regard to moral boundaries on this score, as Plant is forced to acknowledge.

The issue of limits to the extension of market forces has also surfaced in relation to goods and services provided in the public sector. For example, it has been argued, on the grounds of distributive justice, that education, health care and welfare goods should be available on a non-market basis. By implication, the availability of such essential goods should reflect need rather than ability to pay and to that extent such goods should be protected from expansive market relations (Walzer 1983). A parallel argument has focused on the way in which a public sector 'ethos' of service and care is threatened by an extension of market forces, through either a privatization of public service provision or by the introduction of market principles within the public sector (Plant 1992).

The third respect in which the issue of limits to an extension of market principles has been addressed is in regard to the consequences of market exchange processes. Free market philosophy, as I have indicated, suggests in its defence that markets are simply neutral mechanisms through which individual acts of free exchange take place. The outcome of a market exchange process constitutes a summation of freely expressed individual choices. It is an unintended outcome, an unintentional result of a multiplicity of individual decisions and actions. In so far as this is the case, from this perspective, whatever the outcome, the market process cannot be regarded as vulnerable to moral criticism. In other words, it is deemed inappropriate to invoke criteria of justice in relation to market outcomes. And even if the case for a moral criticism of markets is allowed to proceed, it is likely to run into the objection that we simply lack 'agreed criteria of distributive justice' (Plant 1992: 95).

However, the rationale for free markets begs a number of questions. The notion that the outcome of the market process can simply be treated as the aggregation of decisions and actions on the part of individuals exercising their freedom to engage in exchange is not convincing, particularly when consideration is given to the unequal terms on which participants enter the market. The market process is an exchange of property rights and if this is to have legitimacy then, in turn, property titles must be regarded as legitimate. The market exchange process takes place in a social context where there is a substantial inequality of ownership of goods and a lack of agreed criteria of distributive justice that might provide a basis on which property redistribution could be considered. There is a tendency to believe, as Hayek and Friedman do, that markets are beneficial even where wide inequalities in property exist, the assumption being that the existing distribution of property is more likely to promote economic dynamism and allow the needs of the less wealthy to be met through an alleged 'trickle-down effect'. In contrast, Plant argues that it is necessary to consider the moral implications of property ownership and to consider whether the 'property titles that have led to existing inequalities are . . . just' (1992: 96). Essentially what is at issue here are the competing claims of the 'free' market and appeals to social justice for a political allocation of resources to improve the lot of the socially excluded or poor.

The defence of market outcomes as 'unintended' and therefore invulnerable to the court of social justice is also open to question. If consideration is given to the extent and frequency of monopolistic practices directed towards price control and demand manipulation exercised through the media of marketing, advertising and branding (Klein 2001), then the idea that outcomes of market processes are unintended is, to say the least, debatable. But even if it is accepted that outcomes are unintended, it does not follow that they are immune to criticism in terms of social justice criteria. Plant contends that in so far as the outcomes of market processes are foreseeable ('those who enter the market with least are likely to leave it with least') then participants have some responsibility for distributive outcomes, even if they are unintended. In short,

> [T]he foreseeable consequences of markets lie at the heart of the case for markets and also lie at the heart of the possibility of a critique of their outcomes and of asserting our collective moral responsibility for them.
>
> (Plant 1992: 98)

Finally, there has been a critical response to the view that we lack a public morality and any agreed sense of social justice. In particular, analysts have responded critically to the emphasis placed upon individualism and self-interest. It has been argued that, notwithstanding the 'privatization of morality' and the 'reduction of morality to self-interest', a vestige of civic culture and a commitment to the idea of the community and the public good remain an important part of contemporary social life (Plant 1992; Bellah *et al.* 1996). Indeed, Plant suggests that the case for moral pluralism has been overstated. First, in the sense already addressed above – that the market itself is predicated upon particular shared moral assumptions, which in turn suggests the existence of some form of civic culture. Consideration might be given here to Coleman's (1988) identification of the importance of 'social capital' in processes of economic exchange which are shown to be regulated by a variety of civic forms of life, including networks, norms and relations of trust. The clear implication being that economic actions, including market exchange processes, are necessarily embedded in social practices and cultural norms, not to mention institutional structures, internalized rules and knowledges, and legal and political frameworks (Brown *et al.* 2000: 195; Slater and Tonkiss 2001: 101). However, it is also important to emphasize that the relations of trust and the norms and networks vital to community life have been impaired by the development of a radically reorganized global free-market capitalism (Putnam 1995; Brown *et al.* 2000).

There is a second respect in which the significance of moral pluralism can be considered as exaggerated and the case for a public or civic culture appealing to a notion of distributive justice can be advanced. This is in terms of the idea that there are a range of fundamental needs that all members of a society require access to in order to be able to participate in social life. Can the market mechanism be relied upon to provide the necessary means to meet basic needs in respect of food, shelter, health and education? Plant's answer is that fundamental goods such as these,

> and the capacity to live a relatively free and autonomous life . . . cannot be secured to individuals as of right, never mind with some degree of fairness or equality, by the market; and there is a role for an appeal to distributive justice in terms of these necessary conditions of human fulfilment.
>
> (1992: 98)

In short, the equation of free markets with 'freedom' is called into question by a realistic assessment of the impact markets have on individuals and social relations. But what kind of appeal to distributive justice is implied? The assumption intrinsic to free-market philosophy is that all goods may be regarded as commensurable in terms of criteria of utility or monetary value, that a common measure of market value can be achieved that does not do violence to the specificity of any good. In contrast, Walzer (1983) argues that modern societies are highly differentiated and that the different spheres of social life display different forms of social relationships, different codes of acceptable and unacceptable conduct and different rules for the distribution of associated social goods. By implication, the mechanisms and rules that may be appropriate for the distribution of social goods such as money and wealth cannot be assumed to be appropriate for the distribution of other social goods such as health and security. In other words, as I have already noted above, boundaries to the extension of market forces are necessary if a potentially destructive colonization of non-market spheres is to be avoided.

The extension of market relations

The effects of the market extend beyond the particular spheres and domains in which market forces are directly operational. The culture of the market respects no boundaries. Money is an insidious means that has become an end in a society that has succumbed to the culture of the market. As Simmel was moved to comment on the subject of capitalist modernity, the 'concrete values of life' have been reduced to the 'mediating value of money' (1990: 255). Market relations encroach on more and more areas of modern life and as they do so they transform more and more social goods into commodities. However, the issue of the increased reach of market culture, its expansion and extension, is not exhausted by a consideration of the formal process of commodification to which an increasing range of social goods have been exposed. Concern over the colonizing consequences of the market extends beyond the question of commodification in the specific sense of what might be bought and sold, or what it is appropriate to buy and sell (Keat 1993). The impact of the market, and its colonizing consequences in particular, include subtle processes of cultural transformation affecting 'the character of . . . institutions themselves . . . [and] the kinds of commitments and attitudes that may be encouraged in their participants' (Keat 1993: 14). What is at issue here is the potential for people and social goods to be treated as though they are commodities, even though they have not literally become commodities in the sense of formally purchasable items. It is a matter of how conduct towards people, as well as the social meaning of relationships and social goods, have been transformed by the expansion of the culture of the market and the colonizing consequences of an associated process of commodification.

The extent to which we are living within the culture of the market is exemplified not only by the dominance of the market exchange process, but also by the respects in which there is, as Keat contends, an 'illegitimate extension' of the social meanings and norms of the market 'to other institutions and activities, without these being straightforwardly (re-)located within the market' (1993: 15). That there has been an extension of market meanings and norms to non-market domains is not in doubt. However, the illegitimate status attributed to the idea of an extension of the meanings and norms of the market to other, non-market, contexts warrants consideration.

A significant feature of free-market philosophy is the assumption that human beings are motivated by self-interest in both market and non-market domains. This view is clearly articulated in the 'public choice' approach to economic analysis which recognizes no grounds for limits or boundaries to an extension of the meanings and norms of the market to non-market domains. The implication is that whatever the institutional setting the motivation of individuals remains the same – namely, rational self-interest. From this perspective institutions in the public sector are no different from those in the private sector. Workers in health care, education and welfare are considered to be motivated not by a public service ethos, but in precisely the same way as those in the private sector – that is, they seek to maximize their utilities. In consequence an extension of market meanings and norms to non-market domains is regarded as perfectly legitimate (Plant 1992; O'Neill 1998). Such a diagnosis has contributed to the reconsideration of the relationship between the private and public sectors and the introduction within the latter of market principles.

There are a number of important issues at stake in the discussion that has developed around public choice theory (O'Neill 1998). However, it is the assumption of the universality of rational self-interested behaviour that is most questionable. The assumption that self-interested behaviour manifested in the market domain can be extrapolated to non-market domains is unwarranted. It is not legitimate simply to assume that 'utility maximisation is the basic form of human behaviour' (Plant 1992: 93), or that the interests of the individual can be reduced to 'that narrow set of preferences exhibited in the market place' (O'Neill 1998: 169). There are other possible motivations and interests that individuals may and do exhibit in appropriate institutional settings. Individual preferences and interests are not independent of institutional settings, they are not given – on the contrary, they are defined and fostered in specific institutional contexts. However, as the culture of the market has expanded and intruded into more and more domains of everyday life, 'egoism' or 'self-interested behaviour' has been fostered and has become more prominent. Signs of a change are particularly evident in some areas of public service provision where the service ethos is being undermined by the increasing employment of market principles. Plant (1992: 94) observes that in these circumstances

> there is a danger that people whose self-understanding is that they are offering a service, but are being constrained to behave as if they were in a market or quasi-market, might then only act within the terms of the contract.

In short, called upon to embrace market principles and relations, how are public sector workers likely to respond? Will they conclude that it is in their self-interest to do what their contracts require and nothing more? If that should prove to be the case the prospects for maintaining a public sector service ethos will be bleak indeed.

The 'wholesale conversion to neo-liberalism' identified by Bourdieu, a conversion that has gathered momentum since the 1970s, has led to the association of private enterprise with 'efficiency and modernity' and the public sector with 'archaism and inefficiency' (Bourdieu et al. 1999: 182). In the current context the market is extolled for its greater effectiveness in delivering goods and services and the exercise of self-interest, expression of consumer preferences and pursuit of associated forms of satisfaction are represented as though they are self-evidently virtuous and require absolutely no justification at all. The neo-liberal nurturing of a 'market society' has legitimated the pursuit of self-interest and has lent weight to an already well-established calculating orientation to contemporary social life (Simmel

1990; Callon 1998). As public sector institutions have become more and more exposed to market principles and practices they have had to evaluate their operational effectiveness in terms of market criteria of economic efficiency and profitability. Increasingly they have been required to 'discharge . . . business according to calculable rules' (Weber 1970: 215) and to submit to an audit culture (Power 1997). The extension of market principles and practices to such non-market institutional spheres has transformed priorities and working practices. The increased emphasis placed upon market norms and meanings compromises, if it does not undermine entirely, the ethical consideration or regard for persons that is both appropriate and necessary in relation to public service provision in a civilized society.

Notes

1 Consider Emile Durkheim's (1957, 1984) accounts of the non-contractual elements in contract relations.
2 For a comprehensive discussion of monetary analysis and the nature of money from a sociological standpoint see Nigel Dodd's book *The Sociology of Money* (1994).
3 In a context where economic restructuring has transformed productive processes and neo-liberal economic policies have sought to liberate market forces, those in and those seeking employment have had to accommodate to a brave new world of work (Gorz 1999; Beck 2000) in which employment is becoming precarious and part-time, casual, temporary forms of work, or 'McJobs', are becoming increasingly common. In such circumstances, rather than being protected from employer coercion *by* the market, those in work and those seeking work have increasingly found themselves subject to the coercion *of* the market. This is particularly apparent in the case of those working in the export processing zones (EPZs) in countries such as Sri Lanka, Indonesia, Southern China and the Philippines. Here in the unheralded productive underbelly of a globally extensive consumer capitalist economic system, where multinational companies such as Nike, Adidas, Gap, IBM, Ralph Lauren and other celebrated 'brands' increasingly source their products, the market provides little or no protection to workers who are both very poorly paid and very badly treated (Klein 2001).

CHAPTER 5

AFFLUENCE AND SQUALOR: THE PRIVATE AND PUBLIC SECTORS

Introduction: the public-private distinction

Distinctions between 'public' and 'private' have been present in some form in western thought since classical antiquity (Hohendahl 1974). Analyses of 'public' and 'private' have become a particularly prominent feature of contemporary social, economic and political thought. The question of relationships between public and private sectors and associated interests has become a particularly significant issue in contemporary debates over political and economic policy (Habermas 1974, 1989; Galbraith 1975; Hayek 1979; Weintraub 1997; Wolfe 1997).

Drawing a distinction between public and private is by no means an easy task, as several social analysts have noted (Weintraub and Kumar 1997). From the outset it is important to recognize that a number of distinctions between public and private are present in modern social, economic and political thought. Weintraub (1997) outlines four prominent forms in which such a distinction currently appears in analytic discourse. These forms can be described in the following terms:

- liberal-economistic
- republican virtue
- modes of sociability
- feminist

The 'liberal-economistic' version of the distinction between public and private is particularly prominent in contemporary public policy discourse. In this instance the distinction drawn is generally between a 'public sector', including the realm of state administration and governmental activity, and a 'private sector', including the market economy and non-governmental activity. On the one hand there is the 'public authority' of the state, on the

other 'private' individuals and organizations 'rationally' engaging in voluntary contractual relations in pursuit of their self-interests through the market.
The key preoccupation in this context, as Weintraub observes, has been
the relationship between the two, the jurisdictional boundary to be drawn
between public and private:

> The questions of jurisdiction tend predominantly to boil down
> to disputes about whether particular activities or services should
> be left to the market or be subject to government 'intervention'
> usually conceived in terms of administrative regulation backed
> by coercive force.
>
> (1997: 8)

In a sense it comes down to a matter of proportion or balance between
state and market. A question of what goods and services can, and perhaps
should, be financed and/or administered by the state and what might be
more appropriately left to the forces of the market (Hayek 1979: 41–64).
It is this sense of public and private sectors that informs discussion in this
chapter.

The 'republican virtue' form of the distinction is of a different order. The
public realm is equated with political community and citizenship and is
differentiated from both the state and the market. In this instance the politics of public life is not the institutional form of the administrative state,
but the active participatory process of discussion and collective decision
making (Habermas 1974, 1989). These two different senses of the 'public'
– namely, 'politics as sovereignty' exercised by a state apparatus that governs
private individuals and 'politics as citizenship' in which individuals participate in collective self-determination, have their roots in classical antiquity
and both are prominent in contemporary social and political discourse.

Behind the modern attempt to realize, institutionalize and combine the
two different senses of the public realm lie three historical transformations.
These are the development of modern civil society, the recovery of the idea
of sovereignty and the recovery of the idea of citizenship. Civil society
constitutes the world of 'self-interested individualism, competition, impersonality and contractual relationships – centred on the market' (Weintraub
1997: 13). The philosophy of civil society is liberalism and its tendency, as
Weintraub observes, is to 'reduce society to civil society' and to 'collapse . . .
politics and community into the market' (1997: 13). Retrieval of the notion
of sovereignty is articulated with the idea of the atomistic liberal individual.
The abstraction of the sovereign state is a corollary of modern times; it
emerges with the abstraction of private life. As Sayer observes, a 'clear
separation of "public" and "private"' is fundamental to the modern state
(1991: 75; see also Giddens 1991: 151). With the development of a modern
capitalist social formation, political rule is exercised not through person-
alized relations but through impersonal forms. Both the rule of law and

representative democracy 'presume a civil society of abstractly equal free individuals' (Sayer 1991: 74). Simultaneously, the distinctive features and activities of a person's life became matters merely of individual significance, concerns of the 'private' individual.

Recovery of the notion of citizenship took a different course to that of sovereignty and is traced by Weintraub to the re-emergence of the 'self-governing city in the later Middle Ages' (1997: 14). It is argued that the logic of the associated idea of the public realm as 'participatory self-determination' or active citizenship is distinct from both the state and civil society. Such a conception of the 'public realm' (Arendt 1958) or 'public sphere' (Habermas 1974, 1989) as active citizenship effectively calls into question the analytic adequacy of an over-generalized public/private distinction (Weintraub 1997: 15).

In addition to the two different notions of the public and private implied above, a further form of the distinction involving modes of sociability has been identified. What is at issue here is not the purposeful assembly of citizens contemplating and engaging in collective action in public, but the multiplicity of diverse encounters in which individuals and groups routinely and mundanely engage in everyday social life. 'Public' in this context is equivalent to a form of sociability found in Mediterranean cities, present to a degree in all cosmopolitan modern cities, and held, more generally, to be typical of the form of social life associated with a premodern era. It constitutes a form of social life 'lived in public'. Typically, in its premodern form, it was where a sharp differentiation of family life and intimate personal relations (what with the development of modern conditions would come to be identified as 'private') had yet to be differentiated from 'public' life.

Contemporary experiences and understandings of 'public' and 'private' have been influenced substantially by the development of distinctively modern modes of sociability. Modernity constitutes a social configuration in which there is a plurality of life-worlds. Modern social life is characterized by diversity and segmentation, and in particular by a marked 'differentiation between the public and private domains' (Giddens 1991: 83). With the emergence of modernity, relations of personal dependency began to be transformed and impersonal forms of life began to emerge in which social relations were increasingly mediated by things (Simmel 1990). As modern sociality developed, the process of differentiation led to the formation of distinctive orders of social life. For example, it is with the development of modern sociality that 'economy' came to refer to a distinctive sphere of public human activity concerned with the production, distribution and consumption of goods and services. The notion of human beings as individuals with private lives and the experience of individualism also have their roots in the formation of modernity.

This modern process of development precipitated a 'breakdown of the older "public" realm of polymorphous sociability' (Weintraub 1997: 20).

In turn the advent of modernity led to an increasingly marked differentiation of social life

> between an increasingly impersonal 'public' realm (of the market, the modern state, and bureaucratic organisation) and a 'private' realm of increasingly intense intimacy and emotionality (the modern family, romantic love, and so forth).
>
> (Weintraub 1997: 20)

In this instance the modern public/private distinction corresponds to a contrast between the impersonal and the personal, between abstract and formal institutional forms of social life on the one hand and intimate, emotional primary group forms of social life on the other. But there remains a residual sense of the public realm that is not encompassed by the contrast between impersonal and personal, notably the vitality of public life that has been identified with cosmopolitan modern cities. The domain in which this form of public life is to be found is 'the public space of street, park, and plaza – but also . . . neighbourhood, bar, and café', and Weintraub (1997: 23) argues that its articulation with other forms of public life, in particular political community, needs to be analysed.

The final form of the public/private distinction to be considered here is that to be found in feminist analyses. Whereas in the first and second forms it is the public domain and its boundaries that is analytically more prominent, in this instance emphasis has tended to be placed on the private sphere, generally equated with the family and domestic life. In some cases the very distinction between public and private has been criticized as 'gender linked'. The feminist view is that the distinction has inadvertently served to assign men and women to different domains of social life, to consign domestic life to the analytic margins. By designating the family and domestic life as 'private', it is argued that the distinction has effectively concealed what goes on within from public view. But this criticism of the public/private distinction has itself been subject to a process of critical review (Helly and Reverby 1992).

In contrast to the conception of the public/private distinction as equivalent to a distinction between state and civil society, typically within a feminist perspective a contrast has been drawn between a 'private' realm of domestic life and a 'public' realm of civil society (Pateman 1989). In so far as the equation of public/private with state/civil society led to an analytic neglect of family and domestic life, and an associated marginalization of women's role in society, an unqualified distinction between public and private is to be regarded as ambiguous, if not misleading. The problem with the alternative contrast between domestic and public life is that the latter ends up as an 'undifferentiated or . . . residual category' (Weintraub 1997: 32).

Ultimately what emerges from a consideration of the public/private distinction is that no single conception of the dichotomy can provide a basis from which to develop a comprehensive understanding of the complexity of contemporary social life. Indeed, as Weintraub cautions, the particular formulation of the distinction tends to determine what is allocated to the respective public and private realms. For example, the market economy is located in the private realm in the liberal-economistic formulation of the distinction, but it is in the public realm, along with the sense of public politics as citizenship, in feminist formulations.

As the capitalist market economy has become an increasingly central feature of modern social life, so the liberal-economistic version of the distinction between public and private has gained in prominence. The sense in which it is appropriate to describe the market economy, 'a large-scale and impersonal system of interdependence' (Weintraub 1997: 35), as 'private' is that it is constituted through relations of production, distribution and consumption that are capitalist. On one side there is the public realm of the administrative state and on the other the private realm of the market, including civil society predicated on the market. It is a contrast between 'the use of legitimate coercion and the authoritative direction of collective outcomes, as opposed to formally voluntary contract and spontaneous order' associated with the expression of 'competitive and self-interested individualism' in the market (Weintraub 1997: 36, 38).

The relationship between public and private sectors, conceptualized broadly in terms of state and market economy, has been an important focus of social, economic and political analysis. On what has conventionally been described as 'the left' of the political spectrum the preference has been for the public sphere, for greater state involvement in social and economic life, for more centralized forms of regulation and planning and for a greater degree of accountability and democracy in public life. From this standpoint, private ownership of the means of production and the associated accumulation of private wealth and power have been regarded as problematic. In contrast, on what has been regarded as 'the right' of the political spectrum it is the private sphere that has been accorded emphasis. The argument articulated by advocates has been that centralized power constitutes a threat to both freedom and capitalism.

Reflecting on the 'dismal record' of state intervention Milton Friedman (1982: 200) asks,

> Is it an accident that so many of the governmental reforms of recent decades have gone awry, that the bright hopes have turned to ashes? Is it simply because the programs are faulty in detail?
>
> I believe the answer is clearly in the negative. The central defect of these measures is that they seek through government to force people to act against their own immediate interests in order to promote a supposedly general interest.

Reflecting on the conditions of existence experienced by people in modern capitalist societies Friedman finds many signs of improvement or progress. These include citizens being better fed, clothed and housed; a narrowing of class and other social distinctions; minorities being less subject to disadvantage; and the quality of popular culture being raised. All of these are attributed by Friedman to 'the initiative and drive of individuals co-operating through the free market' (1982: 200). Government measures are regarded as merely serving to hamper the process. From this standpoint, one exemplified by the advocates of a neo-liberal free-market perspective, the problem with the public sector is that

> society is so complex that no comprehensive public authority can guide all acts to their appropriate destination. Under such circumstances, we are far better off allowing private individuals to make private decisions, especially if we have faith that markets can guide those decisions toward an unplanned, but nonetheless harmonious equilibrium.
>
> (Wolfe 1997: 189)

Essentially the contrast outlined above is between what Giddens (1998) has termed 'classical social democracy' and 'neo-liberalism'. Classical social democracy has favoured extensive state intervention in social and economic life, Keynesian demand management, market regulation and a comprehensive programme of welfare provision. In contrast, neo-liberalism advocates a minimal role for government, the freeing of market forces from regulation and far more modest welfare provision to provide a safety net (Giddens 1998: 7–8). However, in practice the available alternatives are not simply between state and market, as a number of analysts have recognized (O'Neill 1998; Brown *et al.* 2000). Alongside the institutions that are conventionally associated with economic activity, namely state and market, and to a lesser extent household and firm, there are a 'variety of economic and non-economic associations that are directly or indirectly central to economic life' (O'Neill 1998: 2). With the process of 'marketization' – that is, a reduction of state responsibility and the introduction of market forces in the public sector, the significance of voluntary associations has grown and they now constitute a 'third sector' alongside the state and the market economy (Brown *et al.* 2000: 3).[1]

The decline and regeneration of market economy

In his analysis of the social and economic origins of western European societies, Karl Polanyi described a period of transformation extending from the late eighteenth century through to the mid-twentieth century. It is a period in which it is possible to chart the rise and fall of the market economy. In the closing decades of the nineteenth century the institution of a self-regulating market began to be regarded as a threat to the social fabric and a 'deep-seated movement sprang into being to resist the pernicious effects of a market-controlled economy' (Polanyi 1968: 76). In the opening decades of the twentieth century the prestige of economic liberalism continued to decline as its tenets were called into question. As the Second World War was drawing to a close, Polanyi confidently confirmed the 'end of the self-regulating market' (1968: 142).

Reflecting on the disintegration of the market economy and the emergence of a variety of new societies in the mid-twentieth century, Polanyi (1968: 256) observed that

> regulation and control can achieve freedom not only for the few, but for all. Freedom not as an appurtenance of privilege, tainted at the source, but as a prescriptive right extending far beyond the narrow confines of the political sphere into the intimate organization of society itself.

At the time, social relations were no longer considered to be 'embedded in the economic system' and the primacy of society over the economic system seemed secure. However, Polanyi was forced to acknowledge the continuing presence of economic liberalism and its opposition to state regulation, planning and control because of the threat they were perceived to pose to freedom. Within approximately three decades of the publication of *The Great Transformation* the economic policy agenda was, once more, beginning to be radically transformed by the increasing prominence accorded to a neo-liberal economic discourse and political programme favouring the free market (Bourdieu 1998).

The period following the economic depression of the 1930s and, in particular, the post-1945 emergence of a Fordist-Keynesian configuration, was marked by an increase in the regulatory role of the state in various aspects of economic life. The state took on a range of obligations as it sought to assist in the creation of relatively stable demand conditions by moderating business cycles through a combination of fiscal and monetary policies. State intervention in economic life assumed a number of forms including

> public investment – in sectors like transportation, public utilities, etc. – that were vital to the growth of both mass production and mass consumption, and which would also guarantee relatively full employment. Governments also moved to provide a strong underpinning to the social wage through expenditure covering social security, health care, education, housing, and the like. In addition, state power was deployed, either directly or indirectly, to affect wage agreements and the rights of workers in production.
>
> (Harvey 1989: 135)

Towards the end of the 1960s the Fordist-Keynesian configuration, with its emphasis upon mass production, mass consumption and state intervention, began to encounter difficulties. In the period 1965–73 it became increasingly apparent that the system of capital accumulation based on Fordism and Keynesianism was proving to be too rigid. Long-term, large-scale programmes of fixed capital investment in mass-production systems 'precluded much flexibility of design' (Harvey 1989: 142) and were unable to cope with the increasing unpredictability and diversity of consumer markets. Rigidities in labour markets represented another source of problems. And rigidities associated with state commitments proved to be particularly problematic as 'entitlement programmes (social security, pension rights, etc.) grew under pressure to keep legitimacy at a time when rigidities in production *restricted any expansion in the fiscal basis for state expenditure*' (Harvey 1989: 142, emphasis added). It is as a consequence of this implicit imbalance between expenditure and revenue that welfare states began to encounter a fiscal crisis (O'Connor 1973; Bell 1976; Habermas 1976; Offe 1985). Towards the end of the 1970s the welfare state was being described as a burden on the development of a vibrant capitalist economy. Critics began to extol the virtues of the free market, market forces and market principles as the means necessary to regenerate economic life and enhance private freedoms (Brown *et al.* 2000).

As the Fordist-Keynesian configuration of capital accumulation began to be displaced during the late 1970s by a more flexible form of capital accumulation involving greater flexibility in labour processes, markets, products and patterns of consumption, so the fiscal crisis confronting welfare states deepened. In turn this led to a reconsideration of the relationship between public and private sectors. The fiscal crisis encountered was a product of a complex range of factors. These included the increasing difficulty of realizing appropriate levels of capital accumulation through the Fordist-Keynesian configuration and the consequential constraints placed on any expansion of the fiscal foundations of state expenditure. There were significant political pressures on the liberal democratic state, in particular in respect of increased demand for welfare provision. In response to the fiscal crisis there was an expansion of the state and state intervention, on the one hand to bolster economic activity, on the other to meet 'the claims of all groups in the society – claims for protections and rights – in short for entitlements' (Bell 1976: 233). Such developments led to large, inflexible welfare bureaucracies that were deemed 'inefficient and unresponsive to client needs' (Brown *et al.* 2000: 25). By the end of the 1970s state expenditure, the public sector and the welfare state in particular were regarded by neo-liberal advocates of greater market freedom as responsible for the deterioration in economic performance, as having undermined 'free enterprise'.

Throughout the 1980s governments were not only reluctant to embark on programmes that required *additional* levels of investment in the public sector – there was also an increasing emphasis on the need to *reduce* public expenditure and 'roll back the state'. The promise and delivery of reductions in levels of personal and company taxation were increasingly regarded as important to electoral success. Likewise, the threat of increases in levels of direct taxation was regarded as likely to precipitate electoral failure. Where possible, governments began to withdraw from areas of public sector provision requiring a high level of investment, or sought private sector partnerships to provide capital. Services under public control that had proven to be too costly, and/or were deemed 'inefficient', began to be sold off or 'privatized'.

The neo-liberal and managerialist response to changing economic circumstances, most clearly articulated by Republican, Conservative and Labour administrations in America, Britain and New Zealand respectively in the course of the 1980s, was to promote the private sector. In this period increasing emphasis was placed upon the virtues of the free market and various measures were introduced 'to shift responsibility from the state to the individual' (Elliott and Atkinson 1999: 87). In short, there was a movement away from the economic policies of Keynes, in particular state intervention to manage the economic cycle and maintain full employment, and an increasing endorsement of alternative neo-liberal policies. These included

> the privatization of state utilities, reduction in centralized welfare provision and the removal of trade restrictions such as import duties and quotas. There was also an attempt to create internal markets or quasi-markets to discipline welfare services and increase the efficiency of public utilities.
>
> (Brown *et al.* 2000: 28)

Changing the relationship and the balance between public and private sectors was central to the 'market revolution' engineered in the course of the late twentieth century.

Concern about the relationship between public and private sectors, and how best to reconcile or balance public and private interest, was a recurring feature of modern social thought during the twentieth century. In this chapter consideration will be given to the way in which the relationship between public and private sectors has been addressed in the respective works of Joseph Schumpeter (1954a), J.K. Galbraith (1963, 1969, 1975, 1993), F.A. Hayek (1979) and Daniel Bell (1976).

Fiscal sociology and the question of the public finances

In a generally neglected paper, originally presented as a lecture in 1918, Joseph Schumpeter (1954a) addresses the fiscal problems confronting the 'tax state' in the immediate aftermath of the First World War. At the time, as Schumpeter notes, doubts were being expressed about the prevailing economic order. Would capitalism survive the 'war burden'? How would the state respond? In some instances the response was to call for greater economic freedom, while in contrast other voices demanded a more regulated or 'administered economy' to resolve fiscal difficulties. At the centre of Schumpeter's discussion is the 'tax state', its emergence, nature and fate.

Schumpeter remarks that the 'public finances are one of the best starting points for an investigation of society' (1954a: 7). The budget is described as 'the skeleton of the state', as revealing its inner reality. Fiscal history is argued to constitute a vital part of the history of a people, 'the economic bleeding which the needs of the state necessitates' (p. 7) representing a significant influence on the development of the economy and everyday social life in general. Fiscal measures are recognized by Schumpeter to have contributed to the transformation of the economy as a whole and, in turn, to the 'modern spirit'. By the latter Schumpeter means the culture and social structure of a people, as well as other broader consequences of fiscal policy – 'all this and more is written in its fiscal history' (p. 7). In short, Schumpeter argues that there is a distinctive field of inquiry with its own order of facts and problems and its own distinctive approach – 'fiscal sociology'. However, while the importance of an analysis of fiscal history for an understanding of social life is emphasized, it is simultaneously argued that the state's influence on the economy must not be overestimated. As Schumpeter comments, 'never has the state been able to create something lasting which the free economy would not have created' (p. 7, Note 2).

The crisis of the modern tax state is approached by Schumpeter through a consideration of 'the feudal relationship'. Reflecting on the nature of premodern conditions at the close of the Middle Ages (fourteenth to sixteenth centuries), Schumpeter notes that while there were several sources of revenue open to rulers there was 'no general right to "taxes"' (1954a: 12). Rulers got into increasingly difficult financial straits because of mismanagement of their affairs, the cost of maintaining court officials and the growing expense of warfare. Such difficulties precipitated a crisis of the fiscal system that ultimately led rulers to turn to the estates for support. Schumpeter describes how rulers, facing insolvency, were able to convince the estates that the difficult financial straits they encountered were a 'common exigency' rather than a personal matter. When the estates finally accepted this, circumstances were radically transformed:

> the old forms were dead ... the individual economy of each family had become the centre of its existence; and ... thereby a private sphere was created which was now to be confronted by the public sphere as a distinguishable element. Out of the 'common exigency' the state was born.
>
> (1954a: 15)

From such developments in the course of the sixteenth century 'the idea and the machinery' of the tax state, including the notion of tax liability 'on the basis of a majority decision' (Schumpeter 1954a: 16, 15) was destined to emerge everywhere in Europe. The implication is clear: financial need and tax demands as its method of satisfaction played a significant part in the formation of the modern state, as did the associated disintegration of medieval forms of life. As Schumpeter observes,

> Taxes not only helped to create the state. They helped to form it . . . Tax bill in hand, the state penetrated the private economies and won increasing dominion over them. The tax brings money and calculating spirit into corners in which they do not dwell as yet, and thus becomes a formative factor in the very organism which has developed it. The kind and level of taxes are determined by the social structure, but once taxes exist they become a handle . . . which social powers can grip in order to change this structure.
>
> (1954a: 17)

Elaborating further on the formation of the tax state, Schumpeter emphasizes the importance of the 'stream of productive revolutions' that contributed to the break-up of medieval forms of life into individuals and families and the associated emergence of the 'individual economy' and the personal sphere.

For Schumpeter, the role of the economy in the processes of transformation identified is pivotal – it is, as he remarks, 'of the essence' (1954a: 18). With the development of the individual economy – that is, with the emergence of a form of life in which 'meaning lies in the individual and his personal sphere, where the fulfilment of the personality is its own end' (p. 18), individual self-interest becomes an economic reality. It is in this context, where the narrow horizons of self-interest shape the conduct of individuals, that fiscal demands represent in Schumpeter's view the 'first sign of life of the modern state' (p. 19). But if common need and the associated necessity of collecting taxes partly formed the modern state, it is clear that subsequently such financial means have been developed considerably and that they now extend 'deep into the flesh of the private economy' (p. 19).

However, there are limits to the potential fiscal reach of any state. Schumpeter (1954a) identifies a number of factors as setting limits to the fiscal potential of the state. These include the level of wealth or poverty of the nation concerned, its social structure and the nature of its wealth ('new, active and growing wealth' in contrast to 'old wealth'). Other factors identified include the costs of military activity, 'the power and morality of its bureaucracy, and . . . the intensity of the "state-consciousness" of its people' (p. 20). The 'tax state', operating within the parameters of a modern capitalist economy, is described by Schumpeter as 'something alien to the proper purpose of the private economy' (p. 20), as possessing relatively few means and as dependent on what it can extract from the private sphere. The economic capacity of the tax state is affected by the fact that

> What is produced is produced for the purposes of the private economic subjects. The driving force is individual interest . . . In this world the state lives as an economic parasite. It can withdraw from the private economy only as much as is consistent with the continued existence of this individual interest in every particular socio-psychological situation.
>
> (1954a: 20)

In short, the level of taxation must not undermine people's financial interest in productive activity and thereby reduce their motivation to work to the best of their ability. Precisely what level this will be is likely to vary according to the particular historical circumstances in which tax demands are being made on people. For example, Schumpeter comments that at 'times of patriotic fervour tax payments are consistent with extreme productive adaptation of strength which *normally* would make production cease altogether' (1954a: 20).

Elaborating on the limits to which the fiscal capacity of the tax state is subject, Schumpeter (1954a) distinguishes between indirect and direct taxation as potential sources of revenue. Indirect taxes are identified as shifting and curtailing consumption in various ways, but Schumpeter remarks that it is not the effect such taxes have first on 'the economy, then the way of life, and thus finally the cultural level' (p. 21) that is of immediate analytic interest. Rather it is the fact that indirect taxes are 'an indispensable' if not 'the most important element of the mechanism of the tax state' to which attention is drawn. In turn, Schumpeter cautions that care needs to be taken in setting levels of indirect tax, for there is a level beyond which such taxes must not rise if the tax yield is not to decline. Determining the precise level at which maximum revenue is achieved is made difficult, if not impossible, by the fact that the introduction of indirect tax measures generally leads to wider, frequently unpredictable, changes. For example, 'technical and commercial changes in the productive apparatus' (p. 21) generally follow in the wake of the introduction of significant forms of indirect tax. In addition, the situation in which tax measures are imposed is inclined to change in other respects as a consequence of 'disturbances' which may differentially affect the impact on consumers and producers. The key point is that there is a limit to the indirect tax revenue-raising capacity of the state and as Schumpeter notes, '[n]o need for more funds can push it further out' (p. 21).

In the case of direct taxes the focus falls on individual categories of income accruing from 'entrepreneurial profit, monopoly profit, interest, rent and wages' (Schumpeter 1954a: 21). The prospect of entrepreneurial profit constitutes the inner dynamic of the capitalist economy, it represents 'the premium capitalism attaches to innovation', and Schumpeter adds that it is 'by far the most important individual motive for work towards industrial progress' (p. 22). Caution needs to be exercised in respect of taxation on entrepreneurial profit for the risk is that the pace of industrial development may be slowed. By implication the incentive to invest and to innovate has to be protected from 'excessive' tax pressure. In short, it is argued that there is a 'limit to the taxation of entrepreneurial profit beyond which tax pressure cannot go without first damaging and then destroying the tax object' (p. 22).

Turning to monopoly profit and ground rent, and 'windfall profits which are not the result of special economic activities', Schumpeter (1954a: 22) observes that there are few risks that taxation will damage the tax object. These forms of income constitute ideal tax objects because the 'tax never reflects back on the productive process' (p. 22). However, in the case of interest and wages the situation is rather different and potential tax yields are subject to more limitations. In considering the tax limits on such forms of income, Schumpeter comments that all states face a similar problem and that it is a 'problem of the system and not of a particular state'. What Schumpeter draws attention to is the way in which an inappropriate level of taxation may restrict the growth of production, paralyse capital formation and, where it affects labour incomes adversely, discourage 'all above-average effort where the effort is not its own end' (p. 23). The suggestion is that there is a significant relationship between level(s) of taxation and the reproduction of conditions necessary to maintain the forces that drive the economy.

The key point to which Schumpeter (1954a) directs attention is that the 'fiscal capacity of the state has its limits' (p. 24) and this has significant implications for the public sector. In a prescient footnote that anticipates aspects of the neo-liberal argument that developed in the late 1970s in Britain and the USA, Schumpeter cautions that as the tax state approaches these limits, more and more bureaucrats are needed to enforce an ever more intrusive taxation system. In these circumstances the tax state encounters resistance and the general impression that emerges is of an 'absurd waste of energy'. Schumpeter adds that the rationale of the tax state, its meaning and organization, is bound up with the 'autonomy of the private economy and of private life' and that this is threatened when the state 'can no longer respect this autonomy' (p. 24, Note 21). In so far as the free-market competitive capitalist economy is the complement of the tax state then the relationship and balance between the private economy and the public economy is pivotal, indeed critical. Outlining a possible crisis to which the tax state might be vulnerable in the future, Schumpeter (p. 24) speculates that

> If the will of the people demands higher and higher public expenditures, if more and more means are used for purposes for which private individuals have not produced them, if more and more power stands behind this will, and if finally all parts of the people are gripped by entirely new ideas about private property

and the forms of life – then the tax state will have run its course and society will have to depend on other motive forces for its economy than self-interest.

The aftermath of the October Revolution and the fiscal and reconstruction problems that had to be addressed following the First World War constitute the immediate context in which Schumpeter's analysis of the crisis confronting the tax state is located. In the conclusion to his analysis he remarks that '[s]ociety is growing beyond private enterprise and tax state' (1954a: 38). Subsequent historical developments, including the collapse of 'actually existing socialism' (Bahro 1978; Fukuyama 1992) and the adoption of capitalist economic principles and practices in formerly opposed countries such as Russia and China (Gray 1999), suggest otherwise. Capitalist economic development shows little sign of slowing down. In sum, paraphrasing Schumpeter, the hour still belongs to private enterprise and the tax state, and the complex relationship between private and public sectors remains a pivotal, if not critical, issue.

The public and private sector – Hayek's conception

Writing towards the close of the Second World War, Hayek expressed concern that life in modern western capitalist societies was becoming subject to a growing army of state bureaucrats; that these societies were heading, as the title of one of his influential texts suggests, down *The Road to Serfdom* (1944). For Hayek the answer was to limit government and to free the market economy from intrusive and unnecessary regulation. In the period from the end of the Second World War through to the late 1970s advocates of a free-market economy fought Keynesianism and the collectivism they considered an inevitable corollary. Throughout this period the targets remained the same – namely excessive growth of the state, extensive and intrusive regulation of the economy and erosion of individual freedom.

The question of the limits that a free society needs to place on government power is at the centre of Hayek's (1979) discussion of the public and private sectors. Notwithstanding his preference for the market, Hayek acknowledges that in an advanced society government will need to 'use its power of raising funds by taxation to provide a number of services which for various reasons cannot be provided, or cannot be provided adequately, by the market' (p. 41). In outlining a range of activities that government may legitimately undertake, Hayek distinguishes between two categories. The first includes the spheres of law, defence and 'the levying of taxes to finance its activities' (p. 42). It is this category to which governmental authority is held properly to belong and to which 'coercive activities and the monopoly of government' (p. 42) are to be limited. The second includes services currently organized by government because it is thought to represent 'the most expedient way of providing them' (p. 42). Hayek argues that his intention is not to limit government activity as a whole to the spheres of law, defence and taxation, but to prevent inappropriate extension of coercive authority to the domain of utilitarian service provision. The objective is to counter the implied tendency for legitimate use of coercive or monopoly powers to obtain the means necessary to provide particular services being illegitimately extended to the supply and organization of the same. As Hayek argues, while it might be necessary for government to use coercive powers to raise the means to provide services, it by no means follows that 'those services ought also to be organised by government' (p. 42). On the contrary, his argument is that it is often more effective to leave service delivery – that is, matters of organization and management, to competitive enterprise.

The key issue is to determine which goods and services are the responsibility of government. To that end Hayek (1979) turns his attention to collective goods and the parameters of the public sector. Within the order of the market, commodities are produced for sale to individual consumers who will purchase them and benefit from them. The benefits of commodities (and harms associated with them) are generally conferred on and confined to those willing and able to pay for them, and withheld from those unwilling and/or unable to do so. Such material commodities designated for private possession and use may have 'external effects' – for example, pollution of air or water – which extend beyond the individual owner or user, thereby creating a form of 'collective good (or collective nuisance)' (p. 46). There are clearly categories of goods and services that it would either prove 'technically impossible' or 'prohibitively costly' to provide through the market to individuals. Such goods and services can only be, or are more economically and effectively, provided for all; they are not going to be provided through the market because they would 'bring no gain'. Examples given include 'protection against violence, epidemics, or such natural forces as floods or avalanches', as well as the wide range of amenities and facilities 'which make life in modern cities tolerable' (p. 44). These are described as 'collective or public goods proper' for which production and sale to individual users would not be practical, viable or effective.

Turning directly to the question of the parameters of the public sector, Hayek (1979) comments that the distinction between public and private sectors is 'sometimes erroneously taken to mean that some services beyond the enforcement of rules of just conduct should be reserved to government by law' (p. 47). Criticizing such an understanding, Hayek argues that services currently provided by government should remain open to potential private sector providers who may be able to find new methods for providing a particular service without recourse to coercive powers. Alternatively, new methods may be uncovered that will make a service saleable by making it possible to confine it to those willing to pay for it, thereby opening up the service to market forces and relations. This constitutes an argument for replacing the notion of the public sector as a set of functions, services or institutions monopolized by government with an alternative. The alternative proposed by Hayek is that the public sector should be regarded as 'a circumscribed amount of material means placed at the disposal of government for the rendering of services it has been asked to perform' (p. 47).

Rather than viewing the public sector in terms of purposes or functions over which government has a monopoly, Hayek contends that it should be regarded as a 'range of needs' government is currently meeting because, thus far, the needs concerned cannot be satisfied in other, better ways. It may be necessary for government to provide a service where either the market has failed to do so or where currently the public sector constitutes the most effective way of delivering collective goods. However, Hayek urges us to remember that before government entered the arenas concerned, many collective needs were met by other means. What Hayek has in mind is an independent or voluntary sector of public-spirited individuals and groups: the churches, and 'foundations and endowments, private associations . . . private charities and welfare agencies' (1979: 50). Indeed, the contribution of this independent sector to social life leads Hayek to describe the conventional distinction between public and private sectors as misleading. In contrast to Galbraith (1963), who contends that there is really no alternative to public management in many instances, Hayek argues that a third 'independent' sector between a public 'governmental' sector and a private 'commercial' sector contributes significantly to the development of a healthy society. This third sector is described by Hayek as having the potential to be able to take over much that is currently considered to be the province of government and thereby is able to 'ward off the danger of complete domination of social life by government' (1979: 51).

In considering the parameters of the public sector, as Schumpeter reveals, the additional critical factor of taxation needs to be considered. Hayek's (1979) view is that 'the decision on the level of taxation . . . should determine the total size of the public sector' (p. 51), but that the practice of public finance has taken a different course. Rather than agreement on the level of resources to be entrusted to government determining the parameters of the public sector, there has been no 'rational limitation of the volume of public expenditure' (p. 52). On the contrary, instead of limiting the volume of public expenditure, Hayek contends that the main aim of public finance seems from the outset to have been raising 'the largest sums with the least resistance' (p. 52). From this perspective the problem is that there are no democratic checks on total public expenditure. Hayek argues that while there continues to be a belief that the cost of public expenditure can be shifted to others, who will carry the tax burden, then public expenditure will continue to grow. As a result, rather than expenditure being 'adjusted to available means . . . means will be . . . [continually sought] to meet an expenditure which is determined without regard to costs' (p. 52). What is necessary from this standpoint is that those who argue for and consent to levels of public expenditure realize that they will have to pay for it.

Writing at the close of the 1970s, Hayek expressed concern that in Britain the share of national income controlled by government had grown to more than 50 per cent. Evidence of the continuing growth of government expenditure, and with it the 'machinery of government', represents a significant process of transformation in which more and more of the spontaneous ordering of the market, that attempts to provide for the varying needs of individuals, is displaced by

> an organisation which can serve only a particular set of ends determined by the majority – or increasingly, since this organisation is becoming too complex to be understood by voters, by the bureaucracy in whose hands the administration of means is placed.
> (Hayek 1979: 53)

Once again the concern articulated is about an accelerating growth of government and the public sector, and parallel erosion of the private sector and individual liberty.

It is worth emphasizing that Hayek is not outlining an argument for a 'minimal state'. The necessary role of the state in relation to a number of key areas of social life is freely acknowledged. For example, in respect of 'security' the need for governmental action is readily recognized and accepted. Whether it is the threat posed by potential external enemies, the risk of natural disasters or the more personal problems represented by ill-health, old age or physical and mental incapacity afflicting those unable to make adequate individual provision for their own care, governmental action will be necessary. In addition to considering different aspects of security provided by government, the main proviso being that they do not undermine market order or erode individual liberty, Hayek makes reference to the issue of provision of information and education at public expense. The argument outlined is that while information and education may lend themselves to sale in the market, potential purchasers, those who are without either, may not realize that it is in their interests to acquire them. It may also be to the benefit of others that such individuals should possess information and education. In support of such ideas Hayek observes how individuals must possess a certain stock of knowledge if they are to be law-abiding and capable of participating as citizens in the democratic process. Moreover, while the market may constitute an efficient means for distributing information, Hayek acknowledges that it will 'function more effectively if the access to certain kinds of information is free' (1979: 60).

On the specific subject of education, Hayek's main argument for public provision is that children cannot be expected to know what they need.

Moreover, children do not have control over the resources necessary to secure acquisition of knowledge, and their parents may not recognize the need, or be able, or prepared, to invest resources in education. Hayek suggests that there is a case for extending the logic of this argument to adults. Exposure to education may alert individuals to interests, capacities and potentials of which they are unaware and in respect of which therefore they are not in any position to be able to exercise choice. But once again, Hayek's line is that while there is perhaps a case for government finance of general education it does not follow that delivery – that is, organization and management – should be a government monopoly.

In his discussion of the public and private sector, Hayek also offers consideration of additional areas of legitimate government activity. For example, certification and licensing of goods and services, including such matters as building regulations; food laws; restrictions on the sale of dangerous goods (e.g. drugs, armaments, etc.); professional competence; and safety and health measures as they apply to productive activity and leisure pursuits. Reflecting on these, Hayek remarks that they assist in the making of intelligent choices. Notwithstanding recognition of the necessity of state responsibility for the provision of some collective goods, Hayek is critical of analysts who have sought to argue that the problem is not that the public sector is too large, but that it is lacking in resources necessary to operate effectively. In short, the response is that if there is public squalor it is not because of 'an insufficient provision for the public sector' or because 'the aggregate of government expenditure is too small' (Hayek 1979: 53). Rather the contention is that government has taken on too many tasks and in consequence is falling short in important areas. The defects of the existing order will not be remedied in Hayek's view by more public expenditure, a more extensive public sector or an increase in state organization and intervention. Hayek argues that the one permanent interest shared by all individuals in society is 'interest in the continuous adaptation to unpredictable changes' and that to this end it is necessary to remove impediments to strictly economic decisions, to preserve 'the spontaneous order of the market' (p. 94). While for Hayek the 'spontaneous' ordering potential of impersonal market forces constitutes the basis of a solution to the defects of the existing social order, for Galbraith 'unregulated' market forces represent a prominent source of significant social difficulties.

Squalor amidst affluence: public services and private goods

Writing towards the close of the 1950s, the American social economist J.K. Galbraith noted how social ideas could acquire the status of a 'conventional wisdom' – that through familiarity they could achieve acceptability and stability. Since the nineteenth century there have been prolonged periods in which the conventional wisdom in respect of economic activity has favoured freeing market forces because of their assumed economic and social benefits. The idea that social and economic life is best left in the invisible hands of a self-regulating market acquired the status of conventional wisdom. But the economic crisis of the 1930s and the publication of Keynes's *General Theory of Employment, Interest and Money* (1936) produced a significant change in economic thought and policy. The economic system 'was no longer assumed to be self-regulating' and it was argued that '[o]nly active intervention by the state . . . would keep the economy at or near full employment and ensure its steady growth' (Galbraith 1975: 27–8). But by the close of the 1970s this conventional wisdom, in turn, appeared discredited by events, notably the crisis of organized capitalism, a subsequent far-reaching process of economic restructuring and an associated neo-liberal promotion of the necessity of freeing market forces to regenerate economic growth and restore individual freedom.

In his analysis of *The Affluent Society* Galbraith comments that the central tradition within economic thought has tended to picture the economic system as perilous, as offering little prospect of economic security for the ordinary individual. The idea of the competitive market economy, and its reality in the nineteenth and early twentieth centuries, exposed individuals to a 'remarkable measure of uncertainty' (Galbraith 1963: 43). The idea that economic processes are cyclical and self-correcting, and that intervention would only impede the process of adjustment and recovery, if not lead to new forms of maladjustment, was part of economic orthodoxy until the economic crisis of the 1930s. Such views did nothing to alleviate feelings of insecurity and uneasiness about economic conditions.

What was to be done about the weak and vulnerable? What was to happen to workers who lost their jobs, to investors who lost their savings and businessmen who went bankrupt? Galbraith remarks that such concerns ultimately led people to seek measures from government to make life more secure and that during the course of the 1930s the 'Keynesian Revolution' ensured that governments would deploy increased expenditure, not covered by general taxes, to compensate for deficiencies in aggregate economic demand. By acting to raise the level of aggregate demand governments believed that they could likewise exert an upward influence on the level of production and in consequence on the level of employment. The benefits of increasing aggregate demand and thereby production were recognized to be substantial. Simultaneously, or so it seemed, it was possible to 'ameliorate unemployment, agricultural insecurity, the threat of bankruptcy to the small businessman, the risks of investors, the financial troubles of the states and cities . . . Scarcely a single social problem was left untouched' (Galbraith 1963: 159) by the attainment of increased production.

The objective of increased production – that is, increased aggregate output – quickly became identified as the key to political success and was embraced by both Democratic and Republican political parties in the USA and Labour and Conservative parties in the UK. But while on both sides of the Atlantic the economic creed became 'more production', questions concerning what was being produced and how produced goods and services were being distributed among social groups were at best of secondary concern, if not entirely marginal to political debate. Keynes directed political attention to the importance of production, but there is a significant difference between increases in production that are directed towards the reduction of widespread unemployment and increases in production that simply involve adding to 'an already opulent supply of goods . . . that add to affluence' (Galbraith 1963: 161). While production continues to be important for the economic security it brings, Galbraith argues that increases in the quantity and range of goods produced are at best 'incidental' and 'no longer very urgent' (p. 165).

Focusing on American and European societies in the late 1950s (i.e. developing affluent societies), Galbraith recognizes that production is of paramount importance – its growth is regarded as the yardstick of progress. Specifically, it is privately produced production that is valued and its increase is considered to be synonymous with increased national wealth, and, thereby, enhanced national well-being. In contrast, public services are regarded as a 'burden' which must be borne by private production (Galbraith 1963: 116).

Contrasting social attitudes towards private goods and wealth and public services and expenditure are exemplified in numerous ways. We value our cars, but resent paying road and fuel taxes that are necessary to maintain roads and fund forms of public transport that might ease traffic congestion. We value our homes and continually add to our material possessions, but we prefer tax cuts to increases in public expenditure to improve the protection of persons and security of property afforded by police and fire services.

Galbraith (1963) identifies a strong suspicion of government among citizen-taxpayers that extends to political philosophers, economists and the discourse of modern economics itself. For nineteenth-century economic liberalism, a key objective was a state which provided 'order reliably and inexpensively and which did as little as possible else. Even Marx intended that the state should wither away' (p. 117). However, with increases in the production of basic and essential goods, 'all of which so fortuitously lend themselves to private production, purchase, and sale' (p. 117), there arose a demand for other things that had to be provided collectively if they were to be provided at all. For example, the requirements of modern urban life – streets, law enforcement, mass literacy, sanitation and various measures to protect populations from epidemics and external threats. Despite the desirability, indeed necessity, of such public services and the fact that in modern societies economic growth and an expanding public sector have been closely connected, growth in public services has continued to be regarded with suspicion. Increases in public spending, with the notable exception of defence expenditure, tended to be regarded, particularly at the height of the Cold War (1945–89), as manifestations of a creeping socialism. In a related manner the funding of public services through redistributive taxation has been regarded, in some respects at least, as a response to the problem of inequality and in consequence has attracted criticism from those required to pay more, those who oppose the levelling tendencies of such tax measures.

Consumer demand and social imbalance

A corollary of the paramount position occupied by private production of goods and services has been the significance accorded to private consumption. Consumer demand is crucial: it is as Galbraith remarks, an imperative. Relatively few, if any, judgements are made about the necessity or importance of what is consumed. What matters is that the wanting of consumers is continually regenerated, that consumer desires remain strong, that satisfaction proves perpetually temporary and vulnerable to the promise that its achievement lies waiting in the seductive arms of the next purchase. In short, demand continually has to be managed, it has to be perpetually orchestrated and provoked, and this represents in Galbraith's (1969) view one of the most important consequences of increasing affluence. If consumers were to reach a point where they had acquired a sufficiency of goods then 'there would be limits on the expansion of the system. Growth could not then remain a goal' (p. 214). It is in this context that the arts of consumer seduction – advertising, marketing and branding – have found their place, helping to constitute consumer subjects ever ready to spend their income and incur debt to obtain more goods and services, the felt need for which is continually regenerated. Contrary to economic orthodoxy which depicts the consumer as sovereign and presents the flow of influence as being from 'consumer to market to producer', Galbraith (p. 216) emphasizes the ways in which producers seek to control markets, as well as to manage market behaviour and influence the attitudes of consumers.

As I have noted above there is a general reticence to question what gets produced in affluent societies. There is a general disinclination to consider whether particular goods and services are necessary or unnecessary, important or unimportant. From the standpoint of conventional economics such judgements seem inappropriate, for what gets produced simply reflects the choices of supposedly sovereign consumer subjects expressed in and through the impersonal mechanism of the market. The conventional narrative is that producers simply produce what it is that consumers demand, but this particular narrative has little credibility.

Why is it, Galbraith asks, that there is a profusion of some things and a dearth of others? The answer given is that the disparity identified between plenty and poverty follows a fault line 'which divides privately produced and marketed goods and services from publicly rendered services' (1963: 206). Moreover, it is the wealth of privately produced goods and services that is, 'to a marked degree' responsible for the critical condition of the public services. In short, there is a social imbalance between the stock and flow of private and public goods. To illustrate the point, Galbraith observes how in America after the end of the Second World War (post-1945) there was increasing wealth in privately produced goods, gross national product was rising, retail sales and personal income were also rising, and yet elementary municipal and metropolitan public services were deficient. Revisiting these concerns nearly a quarter of a century after the publication of *The Affluent Society* Galbraith (1985: xxii) remarked that the imbalance had worsened:

> By any possible test the balance between our private consumption and our public services is far worse now . . . The condition of the large cities is a compelling case. Private living standards have continued to improve, having risen to unprecedented heights for unprecedented numbers . . . By contrast the urban public services have grown steadily worse.

Just as a close relationship is necessary between the production of various kinds of goods in the private sector (steel, machine tools, cars), so there is a necessary relationship between the supply of privately produced goods and services and those of the public sector. The consumption of private means of transport like the car requires roads, motorways, traffic regulation, parking areas, as well as police, fire and hospital services. Where public provision of services has not kept pace with increases in the consumption of private goods, Galbraith suggests there will be 'an atmosphere of private opulence and public squalor . . . [and that] private goods [will] have full sway' (1963: 209).

Alongside the argument for a degree of social balance between public services and private goods, on the grounds that imbalance may lead to 'social disorder', or even the impairment of economic performance, Galbraith provides a more positive statement. The suggestion is that more needs to be made of the potential benefits, both collective and personal, that might follow from enhanced public sector provision. While we have an abundance of private goods and allow no restrictions on the pursuit of further satisfactions promised by private production, in respect of public goods and services the situation is quite different. The public services continually lag behind private production, because while the latter benefits from advertising, marketing and branding, not to mention the effects of emulation, which serve to create and manage demand, nothing comparable 'operates on behalf of the non-merchantable services of the state' (Galbraith 1963: 213). This represents one of the key factors that has led to social imbalance between the public and private sectors. The other two factors identified by Galbraith are the constraints to which tax revenues to fund public services are subject and the impact of inflation on public service provision.

The perennial problem with the public services is how to fund them. Galbraith remarks that in the USA a large proportion of federal tax revenue has been directed towards defence expenditure. This, along with public pressure to cut taxation from what were regarded as artificially high Second World War levels, reduced the possibility of improving the social balance between public and private sectors. Moreover, when there is persistent inflation the problem of funding the public sector is aggravated. In the private sector there can be an immediate adjustment in prices and incomes to accommodate inflationary movement. In the public sector there is no automatic adjustment or increase in revenue to meet the rising cost of services, or to compensate public sector employees for a relative decline in the purchasing power of their wages and salaries. In consequence inflation has tended to lead to deterioration in public services.

Contentment versus concern

In the period after the end of the Second World War doubts began to be expressed about the way in which public services and the public sector were expanding. In many respects the worries expressed reflected the range of criticisms outlined by Hayek (1944). Galbraith notes how public services were regarded as 'inflated and excessive' and how the costs of the public sector were considered to be a 'burden on private production'. Private wants, where individuals are supposedly free to choose, came to be regarded as inherently superior to all public desires 'which must be paid for by taxation and with an inevitable component of compulsion (Galbraith 1963: 218). An expanding public sector and an associated increased role for government was considered to represent a threat to individual liberty (Hayek 1944).

Not only is there a social imbalance between consumption of private goods and consumption of public services, there is also a related imbalance between investment in 'material capital' and investment in what Galbraith describes as the 'personal capital of the country' (1963: 220). While investment in material capital occurs predominantly through the market, with the increasing development of productive forces there is a requirement for more investment in individuals, in particular investment in education and training, and virtually all of this has remained outside of the market system and within the public sector. With the accelerating pace of developments in science and technology, investment in the education of individuals is argued to have become increasingly essential. But as this has occurred there has not been a commensurate recognition of the need to reallocate appropriate resources from material to human investment – on the contrary, there tends to be 'active discrimination' against investment in the public sector (Galbraith 1963: 223).

The existence of discrimination against the public sector is reaffirmed in Galbraith's analysis of *The New Industrial State* (1969). At the heart of this study is an analysis of the emergence of what is described as a new industrial system. Galbraith places emphasis on the impact of technological innovations in production, the rise to economic dominance of the large corporation and the growth of state economic activity. An additional key factor is the increasing prominence of 'the technostructure', effectively a form of organization – 'a collective and imperfectly defined entity . . . [that] embraces all who bring specialised knowledge, talent or experience to group decision making' (p. 80). Other significant developments identified by Galbraith include advances in techniques of consumer demand management; a decline in trade union membership; and 'a large expansion in enrolment for higher education together with a somewhat more modest increase in the means for providing it' (p. 15).

Reflecting on the range of changes to which 'economic society' has been subject, Galbraith argues that large-scale organization has become imperative. Increasingly, only the large corporation is in a position to make the advance commitment of capital and organization that product research, design and planning, and the inevitable lapse of time between product conception and eventual marketing and sale, necessitates. Moreover, heavy investment in increasingly costly technological developments in both methods of production and in products themselves serve to make consumer demand management even more significant. In this context, where a lack of consumer demand for a product may prove very costly, Galbraith notes that the state may play a crucial role by covering the cost of 'more exalted technological development' as well as by guaranteeing a 'market for the technically advanced product' (1969: 17). Significant practical manifestations of the continuing role of the state in this respect are particularly evident in the area of defence procurement (Harvey 1989; Castells 1996).

If modern technology led to an increasing role for the state in respect of overall demand management, in the sense that having been persuaded to purchase a product people need to be in possession of the means to do so, affluence, in its turn, presents comparable problems. In an affluent community consumption is less reliable than in a poor community. When life is lived closer to subsistence, consumption does little more than reproduce existence – there is little or no scope for abstaining from consumption to save, other than in the sense of harbouring resources for future rounds of consumption necessary to reproduce existence. In contrast, in an affluent society consumption of goods and services extends far beyond the level required to reproduce existence and as a result there is considerable scope for those with discretionary spending power to abstain from forms of consumption. Addressing the impact of affluence, Galbraith remarks that spending and demand 'lose their reliability precisely when high costs and the long period of gestation imposed by modern technology require greater certainty of markets' (1969: 17). In consequence, instead of economic activities being subject to the mechanism of the market, Galbraith observes that in the heartland of the modern economy, occupied by a 'few hundred technically dynamic, massively capitalised and highly organized corporations' (p. 21), industrial planning and particular state services occupy an increasingly prominent place.

The objective of industrial planning is enhanced control and a reduction of market uncertainties. Given the unreliability of the market, planning becomes essential within the industrial system. In addition there are particular state services that are closely related to the needs of the industrial system. Such services and functions as national security and defence, support for research and technological development, and provision of appropriate communication, transport and education infrastructures, reflect the needs of the industrial system. In contrast, state services that are not considered to be so directly related to the requirements of the industrial system are viewed less favourably – consider, for example, the generally poor standard of public service provision offered to the elderly, the infirm and the disabled. Such services are increasingly in competition for resources with more exotic wants and desires cultivated through 'aggressive management of the consumer by the industrial system' (Galbraith 1969: 348).

Notwithstanding the mid-1970s break-up of the Fordist-Keynesian configuration and emergence of a global neo-liberal capitalist economy, important aspects of Galbraith's analysis continue to be relevant to present economic conditions. The subsequent shift in economic policy and the strategy of 'rolling back the state' have merely served to further increase the disparity between private goods and public services. In that respect alone Galbraith's critical observations on the imbalance between private affluence and public squalor continue to resonate with contemporary experiences.

Much has rightly been made of the development since the 1970s of more flexible or reflexive forms of capital accumulation and of changes in corporate organizational forms to cope with conditions of increasing unpredictability (Harvey 1989; Lash and Urry 1994; Castells 1996). Undoubtedly these developments reflect significant processes of economic transformation, but evidence also indicates the continuing centrality, if not increased dominance, of the large corporation in economic life (Donald and Hutton 2001; Klein 2001). The large corporation has undoubtedly changed its organizational form in significant respects. There has been a shift from a 'vertical' more bureaucratic form to a 'horizontal', more flexible 'network' organizational strategy (Castells 1996: 164–5). But the economic landscape continues to be moulded by the large corporation, if now through 'strategic alliances' with other comparably influential organizations (Castells 1996: 162). Moreover, rather than signalling the end of 'the technostructure', such changes signify its metamorphosis. Managerial and supervisory employment has at least remained steady, if it has not increased, and 'state-corporate networks' remain prominent and influential (Keaney 2001: 71, 84).

Discrimination against the public sector has been compounded by the growth of a culture of contentment. The emergence of an electoral majority who view favourably any political constituency that promises not to disturb or disrupt their immediate comfort and contentment has had significant consequences for the role of government, especially in relation to public service provision. There is now a sizeable economically and socially fortunate constituency, representing a majority of the voting electorate. As diverse as this constituency is by income and occupational criteria, they share a pronounced sense of 'self-regard'. Their main concern is to protect their present condition of well-being and to ensure as far as possible that their future prospects remain secure. The primary threat to their condition of contentment arises 'when government and the seemingly less deserving intrude or threaten to intrude their needs or demands. This is especially so if such action suggests higher taxes' (Galbraith 1993: 17). Taxation is not only resisted by the relatively affluent, it is argued that beyond a modest level it acts as a disincentive to wealth creation and thereby threatens to damage the economic prospects of the community as a whole. While the prevailing assumption is that the already wealthy need the incentive of additional good income, it is held that 'the poor are deserving of their poverty' (Galbraith 1993: 145) and that in so far as this is the case economies in public provision may be warranted. It is difficult to avoid the conclusion that increasing indifference towards the poor appears to be a corollary of growing affluence.

While the poorer sections of the community needs must rely on public sector provision, Galbraith (1985) observes that the more fortunate are able to pay for private education, private health care, private security, private transport and other private facilities and services – for example, membership of private leisure and recreation clubs. Those who proceed in this manner are effectively paying both for public and private provision and this has further contributed to the general attitude towards taxation, notably that it is to be 'urgently, even righteously resisted' (Galbraith 1993: 47). At the very heart of the public services there is an asymmetry: 'The fortunate pay, the less fortunate receive. The fortunate have political voice, the less fortunate do not' (Galbraith 1993: 46). In consequence it is no surprise to find that the state, the public sector and taxation have come to be regarded as a burden by the contented majority.

A corollary of the culture of contentment has been an economic accommodation exemplified by the emergence of a 'new overriding commitment to laissez faire and the market' (Galbraith 1993: 62). There is now a wide-ranging acceptance of the assumption that state intervention in the economy is to be limited to a minimum. Private organizations allowed to operate freely in the market are regarded as 'efficient and dynamic'. In contrast, the state and public organizations are regarded as 'bureaucratic', a synonym for inefficiency, incompetence, impersonality and remoteness. Uninhibited pursuit of personal wealth and individual material well-being has become not simply accepted but socially valued, if not the object of reverence. And high regard for wealth is accompanied by disdain, if not contempt, for those unable to escape the constraints of relative impoverishment. As Galbraith (1985: xxx) comments:

> concern for the poor in both the United States and the rest of the affluent world has diminished; assistance, far from keeping pace with the growing capacity to provide it, has, in fact, levelled off or, in some categories, decreased.

In a sense the poor, the 'flawed consumers' (Bauman 1998b: 38), are held responsible for the defective and deficient conditions they encounter – they are regarded as 'architects of their own fate' (Galbraith 1993: 97) and thereby a reduced sense of public responsibility for the poor seems perfectly justified. In such circumstances the contented majority are able to continue enjoying their private wealth undisturbed by any feelings of unease or guilt about the public squalor to which the less fortunate are consigned. The poor conditions of the less fortunate are considered to be a direct consequence of their unwillingness to act responsibly to take advantage of available opportunities. Their predicament is widely regarded as compounded by the bureaucratic inefficiency attributed to the public sector.

Galbraith argues that the contented and self-approving now represent a majority of those who vote in America and in other comparable modern societies (e.g. Great Britain, France, Germany, Canada, Australia). There is in these societies a politics of contentment that reduces the scope for taking difficult, potentially unpopular, yet necessary long-term measures. Emphasis increasingly tends to be placed upon electorally attractive 'short-run economic policies of contentment' (1993: 157).

There now appears to be no viable alternative to a global capitalist market economy. But while recognizing the prominence of the neo-liberal economic and political programme, 'which holds that all possible economic activity should be returned to the market', Galbraith (1998: 19–20) remains a critic. On the specific issue in question, namely the relationship between private and public sectors, it is argued that policy decisions should be taken on the merits of the particular case rather than on the basis of abstract theoretical grounds or blind faith in 'privatization'. The case for a viable public sector and for effective forms of public intervention is held to emerge irresistibly from a consideration of the evidence of 'continuing flaws, inequities, and cruelties in the market system' (1998: 20).

Market performance is unreliable and both willing and unwilling particip-ants in market processes are affected by the consequences. In such circum-stances public intervention is deemed necessary to ameliorate the damaging effect on the vulnerable of speculative and depressive economic excesses. In good economic times the 'public budget – taxes and expenditure – must be a restraining force' (Galbraith 1998: 21), in particular to guard against corporate excesses. In more difficult economic circumstances a broadly Keynesian policy is proposed to tackle 'the social waste' of enforced idle-ness (Galbraith 1998: 22). The capitalist market system produces very wide disparities of income, the prevailing rationale seemingly being that the rich will not work if they have too little income and the poor will not work if they have too much. In response to the evidence of increasing disparities, Galbraith proposes that the tax system must be utilized to achieve a 'socially defensible distribution of income' (1998: 25). However, Galbraith's iden-tity as an 'economist with a public purpose' (Keaney 2001) is perhaps most closely associated with his consistently critical response to a further flaw of the market system, notably the continuing imbalance in the allocation of resources to public and private services and functions. As Galbraith (1998: 25) observes:

> In the United States, private television is richly financed; urban public schools are badly starved. Private dwellings are clean, tolerable, and pleasant; public housing and public streets are filthy. Libraries, public recreational facilities, basic social ser-vices – all needed more by the poor than by the rich – are seen as a burden. The private living standard, in contrast, is good, sacrosanct.

While these observations reflect American experience they also apply to Britain and they are no less relevant to other societies increasingly subject to the market-based disparities and material contradictions intrinsic to contemporary capitalist economic life.

Private wants/public needs: fiscal sociology and the contradictions of capitalism

An explicitly sociological response to the problem of reconciling private interests and public sector provision emerged in the 1970s. Responding to Schumpeter's identification of the potential analytic benefits to be derived from a 'fiscal sociology', Daniel Bell embarked on an analysis of the contra-dictions besetting contemporary capitalism. Central problems and tensions affecting contemporary capitalism are deemed to be a product of 'the unravelling of the threads which once held the culture and the economy together', as well as the 'influence of hedonism which has become the prevailing value in our society' (Bell 1976: xi). In particular, it is suggested that economic, political and cultural forms of life are governed by contrary principles – namely efficiency, equality and self-realization/self-gratification respectively.

It is the tensions and social conflicts that are a consequence of a lack of fit between economy, polity and culture that are of primary concern to Bell (1976), and this is especially evident in his discussion of the problem of the 'public household'. This term is introduced to describe the problem of 'common living', in particular the 'management of state revenues and expenditures' (p. 221) required for public needs and public wants. The central concern of the public household is with the 'good condition of human beings' (p. 278), with social purposes, rather than with the stimulation and satisfaction of private economic appetites. The notion of the public household reaffirms the need to reconnect and coordinate the economy with the polity, to regenerate a sense of common purpose and promote the public good. The critical issue for Bell is how the momentum behind economic (neo-)liberalism is to be countered, for by the mid-1970s it had already become 'in corporate structure, economic oligopoly, and, in the pursuit of private wants, a hedonism that is destructive of social needs' (p. 277).

Bell begins by noting that there is no integrated theory of public finance and no sociology of the 'structural conflicts between classes and social groups on the decisive question of taxation' (1976: 221). To redress matters Bell outlines a sociological analysis of the constraints on the public household or public sector subject to capitalist market conditions, a culture of individualism and a liberal democratic polity. The central problem confronting the capitalist state is how to nurture the conditions appropriate and necessary for an effective process of capital accumulation, while simultaneously maintaining legitimacy through meeting the social needs and demands of the population as a whole. With the development of consumer capitalism, unlimited and seemingly insatiable desires have replaced more basic needs and as consumer expectations have risen there has been a growing demand for protections and rights. In short, with the advent of a consumer society the problems confronting the modern state have increased significantly.

In addition to providing goods and services that do not lend themselves to individual purchase through the market, for military and defence purposes, transport infrastructure and so on, Bell (1976) argues that since the 1930s the state has taken on three major additional commitments. These are involvement in the direction and management of the economy; a substantial stake in science and technology policy and research and development expenditure; and a commitment to 'normative social policy . . . to redress the impact of social and economic inequalities' (pp. 225–6) respectively. These commitments have undoubtedly created 'new and deep dilemmas' (p. 226). The state assumed a range of obligations in respect of economic life after 1945, but by the mid-1970s it was becoming increasingly apparent that Fordism and Keynesianism could not manage the problems to which capitalism was becoming more and more exposed. Because the state had promoted the idea that it had responsibility for the economy, questions of growth, direction, priority and policy became matters of public debate. In turn, the public household became the domain in which not only public needs but also private wants were increasingly expressed.

It is in this context that Bell identifies two key problems for the public household. The first of these is the prospect of the political system being unable to cope with the increasing range and growing complexity of the issues confronting it. Noting the threat of issue 'overload' facing the political system, Bell describes the 'virtue of the market', specifically its capacity to disperse 'responsibility for decisions and effects', unlike the public household which 'concentrates decisions and makes the consequences visible' (1976: 235). The second problem identified concerns the financial implications of the rising demand for entitlements, specifically growing state expenditure at both local and national levels and a subsequent requirement for increases in tax revenue to meet the increasing cost of services. Both problems constitute, Bell suggests, prescriptions for an increase in political instability.

The growth of entitlement programmes (social security, health care, pension rights, etc.) in circumstances where rigidities in production are restricting expansion in the fiscal basis for expenditure is critical for the state. How are demands for rising entitlements to be met? How are claims on the community, on the public household, for educational, health and welfare services and resources to be funded? Bell anticipates an 'enormous expansion' in such services, but notes that their labour intensive character and slower rate of increase in productivity, compared to manufacturing industry and other commercial sectors, represent a major problem. Wage costs constitute the most significant part of the cost of such services and in so far as that is the case, wage increases, other things being equal, will lead to a significant increase in unit costs. Moreover, if gains in productivity are lower than the rate of increase in wages then an inflationary gap is likely to develop.

The central dilemma identified by Bell (1976: 248–9) remains, for we continue

> to combine . . . appetites which resist curbs on acquisitiveness, either morally or by taxation; a democratic polity which increasingly demands more and more social services as entitlements;

and an individualist ethos which at best defends the idea of personal liberty, and at worst evades the necessary social responsibilities and social sacrifices which a communal society demands.

Moreover, we still lack a normative commitment to the public good that might help us to deal with private conflicts. But perceptive as the analysis is, it inadvertently reveals the volatility of social and economic processes and the potential perils of trying to anticipate how such processes might develop in the future.

Within modern capitalist societies, economic growth has become a virtually unquestioned objective, a virtuous common purpose around which members of society can be mobilized. Among other things, economic growth has been identified as a potential 'political solvent', in so far as it may provide the additional resources necessary to meet the increased expectations it has helped to promote, without politically contentious changes to the tax system. Economic growth may provide funds for increased welfare, health and education expenditure without the introduction of potentially politically divisive redistributive taxation measures. However, Bell suggests that the expectation of economic growth and the benefits that are deemed to be associated with it may be 'the source of a distinctive "contradiction" of capitalism', perhaps even 'the cause of its economic undoing' (1976: 238). During the 1970s, western governments sought to deal with the growing inability of Fordism and Keynesianism to cope with the contradictions of capitalism by employing monetary policy to keep the economy growing. One consequence was an increasing acceleration in the rate of inflation. Reflecting on the way in which economic growth seemed to have become 'inextricably linked with inflation' Bell (1976: 238) noted that democratic governments were leaving themselves little room for manoeuvre.

Economic growth had set in train a seemingly irreversible process through which economic expectations were being continually raised. With the adoption of Keynesian economic policies, full employment and increasing levels of consumption had become core, increasingly taken for granted objectives of economic growth. In such circumstances Bell believed it had become difficult for governments to contemplate resorting to traditional methods of economic restraint to deal with problems of inflation – for example, dampening down demand; allowing unemployment to increase; and/or reducing state expenditure. To emphasize, the way things appeared to have changed since the economic turmoil of the 1930s, Bell comments, 'where workers once feared losing a job . . . they now expect a job and a rising standard of living. *And no government can deny that expectation*' (1976: 239, emphasis added).

A great deal has changed in the intervening quarter of a century. Democratically elected governments in many societies with capitalist economic systems have turned to forms of economic policy Bell regarded as unavailable to them, because of the potential social and political costs. Furthermore, the shift Bell detected, 'slowly away from the economising mode' (1976: 269) – that is, away from the financial discipline of concise calculation of monetary costs and benefits, and market forces and principles – has proven, with the benefit of hindsight, to have been totally misconceived. The economizing mode has grown in importance and has extended its reach as more and more areas of social life have become subject to financial discipline, monetary calculation and market forces.

Contrary to Bell's expectations, the balance has not shifted from an economizing mode to 'social criteria of non-economic values'. There has not been an inevitable movement 'from . . . laissez faire to negotiated decisions' (Bell 1976: 269, 270). With the implementation of neo-liberal economic and political policies towards the end of the 1970s, the debate over the relationship between public and private sectors and interests has been radically recast. The objective of constructing a normative framework for the public domain has been displaced by increased promotion of market forces, the private sector and the interests of the individual, generally configured as a consumer whose freedom of choice is represented as of paramount importance. There has also been a related promotion of the private sector in general and designation of a growing role for the private sector within the public domain through private finance initiatives (PFIs) and public-private partnerships (PPPs). Such initiatives are justified on the grounds that the introduction of market forces and principles will inevitably produce 'efficiency' gains and that the latter will translate into improvements in the quality of the services delivered and received.

Some features of Bell's work on processes of social and economic transformation have proven to be misguided, but the dilemma he identified at the heart of a liberal democratic society – namely how and where to strike a balance between public and private spheres – remains unresolved. We continue to live with a serious imbalance between affluence in private goods (an affluence that is increasing for a substantial contented majority) and poverty in public provision. Moreover, we appear to be no closer to finding a means of redressing the imbalance between the two. While Bell's expectations have not been realized, the concerns he has raised remain relevant. The promotion of private interests and vices has led to a 'loss of *civitas*', an erosion of respect for the rights of others and a frequent unwillingness to 'compromise private ends for the public interest' (Bell 1976: 245). It continues to be difficult to convince people that more of their personal income needs to go into the purchase of public goods rather than into private consumption. It remains the case that private consumption is regarded as an expression of freedom of choice, whereas contributions to public consumption are generally experienced as a curtailment of freedom. In the end, as Bell (p. 250) recognized, any society is a moral order that has to justify . . . its allocative principles and the balances of freedoms and coercions necessary to facilitate or enforce such rules. The problem, inevitably, is the relation between self-interest and the public interest, between personal impulses and community requirements. Without a public philosophy, explicitly stated, we lack the fundamental condition whereby a modern polity can live by consensus . . . and justice.

What Bell did not foresee was that in response to the central dilemma identified, democratic governments would seek to reduce the overload of issues confronting them. Subsequently, democratic governments have sought to limit, and in some instances remove, responsibility for policy decisions and their effects in respect of a range of public services. This they have attempted by extolling the virtues, as well as encouraging the introduction, of processes of 'privatization' and 'marketization' of public services (Galbraith 1996). Encouragement of private enterprise and entrepreneurial activity has been accompanied by a relative withdrawal of the democratic state from a number of sectors of social life and a diminution of its role as 'guardian of the public interest' (Bourdieu 1998: 2). But if what Bourdieu describes as the 'left hand of the state' – that is, the public sector spending ministries – have been in retreat, the technocratic, financial and managerial 'right hand of the state' has been simultaneously on the advance within civil society (1998: 2; see also O'Neill 1998: 175).

On the de(con)struction of the public sector

At the end of the 1960s the Fordist-Keynesian configuration was approaching a crisis that subsequently led to a sustained period of economic restructuring. With the development of an increasingly competitive global economy there was a requirement for nation states to be more entrepreneurial and ready to overcome rigidities in respect of labour markets and state commitments in order to create the conditions necessary for more flexible forms of capital accumulation. In the face of a rising demand for public sector services, the funding of which had become increasingly problematic given fiscal limits on state expenditure, recourse was made to forms of restructuring under the banner of 'modernization'.

In consequence the public sector has been subject to a number of initiatives, including the imposition of a market philosophy and the selective employment of mechanisms that replicate particular market practices – for example, the introduction of performance indicators and 'centralised specification of financial targets' (Lash and Urry 1994: 209). There has been an associated increased emphasis on regulation and managerialism, exemplified by the introduction of strata of non-professional managers within public service organizations (Lash and Urry 1994). In turn, this development has been accompanied by the 'imposition of auditing schemes and accounting techniques' (Brown *et al.* 2000: 28), ostensibly to determine the extent to which contractual responsibilities are being met in practice.

Without doubt the imposition of a market philosophy within the public sector has created tensions and contradictions. Services originally designed to be delivered in a manner that prioritizes an *ethical* regard for the needs of persons are increasingly being required to accommodate to an *economic* agenda that is relatively independent of the needs of persons, if it does not demonstrate a disregard for the same. The creation of internal markets has been justified as a means to regulate or discipline service provision, as well as to enhance 'efficiency', but it is far from clear that all parties involved in public sector service provision have benefited from the measures imposed. As far as the question of increasing the 'efficiency' of public services is concerned there is no necessary correspondence between the perspectives and interests of taxpaying agencies, public sector professional providers of services and those requiring and receiving public services.

The distinctive features of publicly provided services mean that there is only limited scope for restructuring the public sector. In a discussion of some of the more important distinguishing features Lash and Urry (1994) note that in most cases profit maximization cannot be the objective of public sector activity for a number of reasons. To begin with there is an obligation to provide an appropriate range of services on a roughly comparable basis to all people in the areas where they are living. This means that a number of private sector strategies (e.g. spatial relocation) are difficult to pursue in the public sector, in so far as educational, health and welfare services need to be delivered to those requiring them in their local environment. A number of other distinctive features can be identified. There are a disproportionately high number of professional groups working within the public sector in comparison to the private sector. It follows that delivery or practice tends to be guided by professional ethics and this, in turn, leads to a greater uniformity of service delivery than would otherwise be the case. In addition, public service goods are said to be distinctively experiential in character and this means that users 'have to take the service "on trust"' (Lash and Urry 1994: 208). Such distinctive features mean that potential restructuring strategies, involving technical changes, reorganizations of production and product transformations, are of relatively limited value.

Given these circumstances Lash and Urry identify the strategies that are most likely to be employed to transform the public sector. There is likely to be a heightened specification of organizational objectives; a commodification of services and an emulation of market procedures; and a concentration of power, involving 'the relevant minister and/or "outsiders" to the service being much better placed to "manage" it' (Lash and Urry 1994: 209). Finally, given that 'the main possibilities of cost-saving arise from reductions in the quality of the service-product' (p. 209) there is likely to be a 'domestication' of some aspects of service provision. 'Domestication' is all about reducing public sector provision through a transfer of responsibility for the provision of a service to unpaid volunteers, frequently family members and generally women. In short, domestication means offloading responsibility onto the community to compensate for any unmet needs.[2]

Public service provision is widely recognized to be in difficulty, if not in crisis. Funding of provision, organizational and management issues, recruitment and performance of staff, and quantity and quality of services provided have each in turn been identified as problematic. The most pressing of these difficulties however has been the first – the fiscal problem arising from a continuing growth of demand for public services, a need for matching increases in public expenditure and a recognition of potential limitations to the state's revenue-raising capacity (Gamble 1987). In particular, evidence of growing opposition to increases in taxation on the part of the corporate sector and the electorate in general has aroused concern that the 'tax state' is approaching, or indeed has reached, the limits of its fiscal capacity (Schumpeter 1954a; O'Connor 1973; Castells 1997). It is in this context in particular that the scale, organization and method of delivery of public sector provision and the scope of the 'welfare state' have been called into question.

While notions of public interest and collective responsibility at the heart of the welfare state have been steadily questioned, if not undermined, pursuit of private interest has been encouraged and the virtues of private enterprise have continued to be extolled. A cultural climate that focuses 'relentlessly on the idea that individuals are self-interest maximizers' (Bellah *et al.* 1991: 50), preoccupied with the pursuit of private accumulation and private pleasures, has served to further undermine the idea of a public ethos and erode provision of public goods and services. As the idea of the welfare state and public provision has been called into question, so 'charity' has been accorded greater prominence and an increased emphasis has been placed on '[s]elf help (personal provision) and individual responsibility . . . over communal (or corporate) provision for the economic and social security of families' (Donald and Hutton 2001: 203).

The crisis in public service provision associated with the restructuring of the global capitalist economy has led a number of analysts to place emphasis on the potentially compensatory role of the voluntary sector. It is argued that voluntary associations have the potential to make a significant contribution to the provision of welfare, the regeneration of civic life and the achievement of democratic governance and that, in turn, significant economic benefits may follow (Hirst 1994; Putnam 1995; Brown *et al.* 2000). It has been argued that the stock of 'social capital' in consumer capitalist societies is low. In other words, that an erosion of trust, loss of mutuality and an undermining of norms of reciprocity – in short an erosion of community life – are a consequence of the culture of free-market capitalism. It is to this dominant culture and its social consequences, one that has placed a high premium on a competitive self-interested individualism and an associated pursuit of material wealth through uncontrolled markets, that voluntary associations have been identified as a potential counter-force.

Voluntary associations have been recognized to possess the potential to 'provide for a strong civil society that counterweights the tendencies towards domination of the state and market forces' (Brown *et al.* 2000: 59). However, such potential has yet to be realized and significant doubts have been raised about the independence of voluntary organizations from both state and market. As Brown *et al.* note, 'markets and state can be regarded as equal threats to voluntary associations' (2000: 61). Given a process of increasing 'marketization' and 'professionalization' it is not clear what part voluntary associations will play in the provision of public services in the future. It has been suggested that 'we stand at a point in time where a choice must be made between associationalist structures of welfare or mass welfare production and consumption within a thoroughly marketized environment' (Brown *et al.* 2000: 208). Notwithstanding neo-liberal rhetoric about the sovereign consumer and choice, the suspicion must be that this is one choice that will not be offered to the citizen-consumer, for the culture of the market and a culture of consumption are already well-entrenched features of contemporary social life (Jameson 1991).

The public sector has been subjected to a range of market influences and quasi-market forces. A wide-ranging process of restructuring and the introduction of various auditory and accounting mechanisms have significantly transformed organizational and managerial structures and practices. But such initiatives have done nothing to alter the general pattern of allocation of resources between public and private services and functions. On the contrary, the continuing promotion of the market system has meant that the allocation of income between public and private sectors has continued to favour the latter (Galbraith 1998). The new political economy of insecurity associated with neo-liberalism has merely served to exacerbate the flawed relationship between public and private sectors. With the development of a neo-liberal global capitalist economic order there has been a marked acceleration in affluence in private goods and this has been paralleled by a rapid deterioration in public services and an erosion of 'traditional institutions which protected people against the market' (Sennett 1999: 14–15).

But the erosion of public service provision and the undermining of a public service ethos is not inevitable. Recognition of the 'involution of the state' does not mean that a reduction in its 'social functions' in respect of education, health and welfare simply have to be accepted (Bourdieu 1998: 34). On the contrary, it is the very assumption of 'inevitability' attributed to neo-liberalism that, as Bourdieu argues, 'gives the dominant discourse its strength' (1998: 29) and needs to be challenged.

Notes

1 The question of alternatives to a contrast between the state and the market is a complex one. It is one to which a number of analysts advocating a 'third way' (Giddens 1998), 'communitarianism' (Etzioni 1994), 'associations and non-market orders' (O'Neill 1998) or associationalism and active citizenship (Hirst 1994; Brown et al. 2000) have sought to provide an answer.
2 The proposal made in the UK by the Chancellor of the Exchequer, Gordon Brown, for a massive volunteer army to take over some tasks of health workers, teachers and other public sector workers, constitutes an example of this type of strategy (Nicholson 2001; Webster 2001).

CHAPTER 6

CONCLUSION: NEW ECONOMIC CONDITIONS AND THEIR SOCIAL AND POLITICAL CONSEQUENCES

Introduction: the transformation of economic life

Significant changes have been taking place in the structure and organization of economic life during the past three decades. While there are evident differences of conceptualization, there is a broad degree of agreement among social analysts on a number of important aspects of the processes of transformation to which economic life has been exposed in this period. The economic contradictions to which the Fordist-Keynesian configuration became increasingly subject from the late 1960s lent credence to the neo-liberal claim that the market had been impaired by excessive state intervention in economic life and led to wide-ranging processes of economic restructuring (Offe 1985; Lash and Urry 1987, 1994; Harvey 1989; Castells 1996). The subsequent transformation of economic life has involved the implementation of flexible forms of capital accumulation, accomplished by means of the introduction of new organizational forms and the deployment of information technology in production processes. Organizational changes, such as subcontracting and outsourcing, along with ' "just-in-time" delivery of intermediate goods and materials' (Lash and Urry 1994: 56), have reduced stock inventories and these, with the benefits of new information technologies and small batch production, have led to reductions in turnover times. In turn, work, the labour process, has become subject to increasing intensification as well as to acceleration in the transformation of required skills.

The restructuring process and deployment of neo-liberal economic policies has radically transformed the nature of work and employment and has led to the development of a 'political economy of insecurity' (Beck 2000). Specifically, it has been suggested that the work-based society is coming to an end and that the idea of a job for life has largely disappeared for all but a privileged few. With the increasing deployment of 'smart technologies' (Beck 2000) more and more people are being ousted from their jobs, or fear the same, and in consequence are experiencing insecurity. In a comparable manner Gorz (1999: 53) remarks that

> *Each* of us is aware, emotionally and intellectually, that we are potentially unemployed, potentially under-employed, potentially insecure or temporary workers, potential 'part-timers'. But what *each* of us knows *individually* has yet to become . . . a *common* awareness of our *common* condition: that is to say, an awareness, publicly formulated and accepted, of the fact that the central figure of our society – and the 'normal' condition within that society – is no longer (or is tending no longer to be) that of the 'worker'. It is becoming, rather, the figure of the insecure worker, who at times 'works' and at times does not 'work', practises many different trades without any of them actually being a trade, has no identifiable profession . . . and cannot therefore identify with his/her work.

Without doubt the neo-liberal programme to deregulate economic life and to free market forces has produced an increase in temporary and insecure forms of employment. For a growing number of people work or employment is becoming increasingly insecure, and in turn, as Beck notes, the prospect of secure 'highly skilled and well-paid full-time employment' (2000: 2) is declining in significance. Instead of having a job an increasing number of people are now finding that they are involved in a combination of various work-related activities in precarious conditions (small-scale retailing, craft-work, personal services, casual and temporary work) (Gorz 1989). Citing the experience of workers in Germany, where the proportion of those engaged in insecure forms of work rose from 10 per cent in the 1960s to over 30 per cent by the late 1990s, Beck argues that 'flexibility' and 'deregulation' have led to insecurity prevailing in nearly all positions within society. With the development of a new political economy 'even in the apparently prosperous middle layers, . . . basic existence and lifeworld will be marked by endemic insecurity' (2000: 3).

Informational capitalism

The effect of economic restructuring and in particular the impact of information technology on the transformation of work and employment is a key part of Castells's (1996) discussion of the development of an informational economy and the emergence of a 'network society'. Reflecting on the specific question of the impact of new information technologies on employment, Castells remarks that, notwithstanding fears about 'a jobless society', a convincing clear-cut answer has yet to emerge. It is evident that information technologies and socioeconomic restructuring have brought about a 'fundamental transformation of work, workers, and working organisations in our societies' (Castells 1996: 272). But does this process of fundamental transformation to which work has been subject signify the 'end of work' (Rifkin 1995)? As jobs in manufacturing disappeared with the rapid de-industrialization of the economy in countries like Britain, America and Italy in the period 1970–90, there was a compensatory increase in both service jobs (in production, distribution, and personal and social services) and information-processing forms of employment. Evidence such as this leads Castells to argue that while most traditional manufacturing jobs seem destined to disappear, sharing the same fate that befell agricultural jobs in the past, it is important to recognize that 'new jobs are being created, and will be created, in high technology manufacturing and, more significantly, in "services"' (1996: 252).

Undoubtedly there is evidence of new jobs being created. For example, between 1993 and 1996, as Castells notes, over 8 million new jobs were created in the USA alone. However, it is also necessary to acknowledge that the *quality* of the new jobs and the *levels of pay* are frequently a 'different matter', the clear implication being that a significant proportion of the 'new' jobs are temporary, part-time, casual or insecure and, in turn, poorly remunerated (Castells 1996: 259, Note 78). Reflecting on the enormous number of new jobs created in the USA in the period in question, Ritzer has observed that 'unfortunately' the majority of them are in service industries that have been 'McDonaldized' (1998). In other words, the new jobs, or 'McJobs' as Ritzer calls them, reflect the increasing rationalization of the labour process. 'McJobs' require little or no skill, they are frequently part-time and they are low-paid, 'with many earning the minimum wage, or slightly more' (Ritzer 1998: 59).

The American style 'jobs miracle' has largely been a product of deregulation, especially a deregulated labour market. Deregulation increases the flexibility and adaptability of labour, effectively enforces or imposes it through the governance of the market and simultaneously enhances the mobility and profitability of capital. The combination of a deregulation of markets coupled with the deployment of new information technologies provided the appropriate conditions within which capital could become globally both more mobile and extensive, opening up and taking advantage of the economic opportunities represented by new locations and new markets. Reflecting on the consequences of deregulated labour markets in contemporary Europe, Beck notes an accumulation of evidence of a 'shift from normal to non-normal work situations' (2000: 104) and an increase in social exclusion. Unemployment, underemployment and intermittent forms of part-time and poorly paid work effectively lead to a growing number of people being excluded from mainstream society. These are the 'new poor', those Bauman has described as having 'no access' to normal life in a consumer society, those who are defined and increasingly define themselves as 'inadequate' or 'flawed' consumers (1998b: 38). Lacking the capacity to respond, in the only terms that matter, to the seductive wares and ways of the consumer society – that is, spending existing income or increasing indebtedness through the use of credit cards (Ritzer 1998: 69) – the poor come to be regarded as a 'liability' (Bauman 1998b: 90–1). In an earlier industrial era society engaged its members primarily as producers and the poor and unemployed would have constituted a reserve army of labour. Now the economy does not need a reserve army of labour, ready to be 'called back into active service as producers' (Bauman 1998b: 77). In a context where technological innovations make it possible for increases in production to be achieved with reductions in labour it is primarily as consumers that members are engaged in contemporary society: 'only secondarily, and partly, does it engage them as producers' (Bauman 1998b: 90). While production (lean, labour-saving, and cost-effective) undoubtedly remains a necessity for the capitalist economic system, it is consumption that is imperative.[1]

The new information-based global economy has been closely associated with wide-ranging and diverse forms of deterioration in the working and living conditions of labour (Gorz 1999; Beck 2000; Klein 2001). Examples include

> the rise of structural unemployment in Europe; declining real wages, increasing inequality, and job instability in the United States; underemployment and stepped-up segmentation of the labour force in Japan; informalisation and downgrading of newly incorporated urban labour in industrialising countries; and increasing marginalisation of the agricultural labour force in stagnant, underdeveloped economies.
>
> (Castells 1996: 273)

Such forms of deterioration are recognized to be a direct consequence of the restructuring of capital-labour relationships associated with the neo-liberalization of an increasingly 'informational' and 'global' capitalism.

The economy is *informational* in so far as the productivity and competitiveness of enterprises are bound up with the 'capacity to generate, process, and apply efficiently knowledge-based information' and it is *global* because production, consumption and circulation are increasingly 'organised on a global scale' (Castells 1996: 66). The liberalization of economic markets, achieved through deregulation and privatization, 'helped by the powerful tools provided by new information technologies' (Castells 1996: 273) and associated new flexible and more adaptable organizational forms, has dramatically transformed relations between capital and labour. On one side there is the powerful threat of the mobility of capital, possessing 'the ability to assemble and disperse labour on specific projects and tasks anywhere, any time' (Castells 1996: 278); literally able to make the 'virtual enterprise' a reality through the global reach of information technology. On the other side there is the rigidity of labour, challenged 'under the potential threat of virtualisation' (Castells 1996: 278) to concede to demands for greater flexibility and adaptability in order to promote the prospect of enhanced productivity and profitability for capital. While capital is mobile and able to flow freely around the globe to take advantage of lower production costs and deregulated working conditions (Klein 2001), disadvantaged labour is 'highly constrained, and will be for the foreseeable future, by institutions, culture, borders, police and xenophobia' (Castells 1996: 232). In short, capital can move quickly and easily, it can withdraw investment and reinvest elsewhere, and it does. As John Gray notes, '[w]hen capital is as mobile as it is today, it will tend, other things being equal, to gravitate to countries where workers have the lowest absolute wages' (1999: 83).

The overall effect of the move towards less regulated, if not unregulated global free trade, particularly when combined with the labour-cost saving impact of information technologies, has been a decline in the bargaining power of workers and a tendency for wages to be driven down. Examining the consequences of economic restructuring and the move towards a more flexible labour market on wages and living conditions in the USA during the 1980s and 1990s, Castells notes that 'family income . . . plummeted' and that from '1989 to 1993 the typical American household lost 7 per cent in annual income' (1996: 275). Considering the possibility that the USA may represent a more extreme case, Castells counters that its labour market flexibility has become a model to be emulated for many European nations and firms, and that other labour forces are destined to become vulnerable to the consequences of unrestrained labour market flexibility.

This process of economic restructuring, Castells suggests, is, on the surface at least, creating a 'dual society'.[2] The emerging dual society is one in which there is a relatively privileged 'core labour force' (information-based workers and symbol analysts) and a substantial and growing 'disposable labour force that can be automated and/or hired/fired/offshored, depending upon market demand and labour costs' (Castells 1996: 272). In such circumstances labour has little institutional protection. Economic restructuring of firms and organizations made necessary by global competition and made possible by information technology undoubtedly has transformed work. Management is increasingly decentralized, work has become more and more individualized, markets have been customized and societies are becoming increasingly fragmented. Through the use of subcontracting, outsourcing, the movement of productive activity to offshore locations and customizing, production has become increasingly 'lean' (Castells 1996; Klein

2001). In turn, the pursuit of flexibility, adaptability and an ever-leaner production profile has led to temporary and part-time forms of employment being the fastest growing categories of work in the new political economy of insecurity (Gorz 1989, 1999; Beck 2000).

Capitalism: production for a culture of consumption

Acceleration of production turnover time has been accompanied by comparable accelerations in both exchange and consumption (Harvey 1989; Lash and Urry 1994). Improvements in communication and information technologies, along with changes in distribution techniques, 'have made it possible to circulate commodities through the market system with greater speed' (Harvey 1989: 285). In a comparable manner, information technology has made possible increases in the speed of money transactions and other financial services and forms of market trading. In respect of consumption, acceleration in the pace or speed with which things are consumed through the market system has been achieved by the deployment of advertising, marketing and branding techniques and strategies. The objective of these is both to promote different, and forever changing, fashions and styles in relation to virtually all goods and services and, no less significantly, to reproduce consumers ever eager to believe that their fantasies can be fulfilled.

The crucial trick for producers, retailers and advertisers is to keep perpetually alive and strong the belief that fantasy can achieve fulfilment through consumption. Notwithstanding increasing consumer awareness and experience of the harsh but necessary reality of capitalist consumer life, namely that today's desirable/fashionable/state-of-the-art good is tomorrow destined to be obsolete and/or in the discount bin, the fantasy-like life of consumption, in particular the illusion that dreams can be fulfilled through consumption, must be maintained. Capitalism needs to continually replenish its supply of consumers and to that end its culture of consumption is perpetually working to produce 'new', 'improved', 'better designed', more contemporary or 'fashionable' and appealing goods. Just as today's goods displaced those of yesterday, so those of tomorrow will surely in their turn displace those of today. What remains constant is the cultural imperative to consume.

An additional factor that has contributed to the increased pace of consumption is the prominent place occupied by the consumption of services within contemporary social life. The 'life' of a manufactured good within a system of capitalist commodity production is ultimately a consequence of the vagaries of use, the whims of fashion and/or the impact of innovative design. Products tend to be replaced when they are no longer working effectively, or when they are deemed to be 'unfashionable' as a consequence of the production of new 'fashionable' alternatives (themselves destined in turn to become unfashionable), or when innovations in design lead to improved products. In the case of services, 'life' tends to be far shorter, as it is bound up with the duration of the immediate 'service' experience and any subsequent impact or effect. In so far as there may be 'limits to the accumulation and turnover of physical goods', Harvey argues that it 'makes sense for capitalists to turn to the provision of very ephemeral services in consumption' (1989: 385). The growth in 'personal, business, educational and health services' identified by Harvey, along with evidence of growth in other sectors such as entertainment, leisure, sport and tourism testify to the increasing significance of services in consumption.

Consumption has undoubtedly increased in significance in present-day society. A number of analysts contend that within a 'late-modern' or 'postmodern' capitalist context there has been a 'shift in focus from production to consumption' (Ritzer 1998: 118; see also Gorz 1989; Harvey 1989; Bauman 1992, 1998b). In comparable terms it has been suggested that 'the consumption of goods and services has become *the* structural basis of western societies' (Lash and Urry 1994: 296). Subject to a globally extensive capitalist market economy it seems there is no prospect of escape from the 'inner dynamic of the culture of consumption' (Jameson 1991: 206). While the designation of our society as a 'consumer society' is understandable, and in some respects appropriate, it is important to remember that a corollary of the dynamism of the capitalist culture of consumption is the production of forms of social exclusion (Bauman 1997, 1998b; Young 1999).

One form of exclusion is that experienced by those living in a consumer society who lack the means (capital, disposable income and/or creditworthiness) to fulfil the duties or responsibilities of the consumer by buying the goods and services on offer in the market (Bauman 1997: 41–2, 1998b: 38–9, 90–1). In the absence of a demand for their labour, the new poor, without work, income or credit facility, find themselves excluded from the mainstream society of consumption. However, there is another, in many respects less visible, form of exclusion. It is a form that the analytic focus on consumer life in the consumer society inadvertently helps to occlude.

With the development of global capitalism the relationship between the production and consumption of goods has been significantly transformed. The goods made available in retail stores and online, the goods promoted by advertising, marketing and branding agencies and sought and purchased by consumers in rich countries around the world, are increasingly being made in those countries with the lowest labour costs and least restrictive labour laws (Gray 1999; Klein 2001). In some instances this arises as a consequence of capital migrating to countries that offer lower costs of production. In other instances it is a result of companies deciding to move out of manufacturing altogether and devote themselves to 'brand management, marketing and product design' (Klein 2001: 195), with product manufacture being transferred to contractors throughout the world. The countries to which capital has migrated to take advantage of lower labour costs to produce goods, or to which companies have turned to source products from contractors in 'free trade zones' or 'export processing zones' (EPZs) are 'rarely . . . the countries in which such goods are consumed' (Gray 1999: 87). The 'local' EPZ producers are not the consumers of the goods produced for the global market-place and they rarely have any knowledge of the economic value or cultural significance that the products they have produced will acquire through the marketing-branding-retailing process.

Increasingly it is from countries such as Indonesia, China, Mexico, Vietnam and the Philippines that brand-name multinationals like Levi, Nike, Champion, Wal-Mart, Reebok, Gap, IBM and General Motors source their products (Klein 2001). It is in countries such as these, where labour costs are very low, that workers are employed to assemble finished products for brand-name multinational companies. Typically products are made in 'labour warehouses' anonymously located in high security, gated and fenced, tax-free zones or compounds where workers present ID cards to armed guards to gain entrance. Klein notes that illustrious multinational companies deliberately have no profile in such military-like locations; there are no names or logos on factory façades and rival company products are frequently produced on adjacent production lines, literally 'side by side in the same factories' (2001: 203).

It is in these distant locations, far removed from exotic shopping malls and retail emporia that another category of the excluded is to be found. It is in the unheralded and unsavoury EPZs that we find those whose exclusion is the invisible price paid for the 'logo life' of branded trainers, jeans, casual clothing, personal computers and other similar goods increasingly equated with full membership rights in the consumer society. As Klein (2001: 205–6) observes,

> Regardless of where the EPZs are located, the workers' stories have a certain mesmerising sameness: the workday is long – fourteen hours in Sri Lanka, twelve hours in Indonesia, sixteen in Southern China, twelve in the Philippines. The vast majority of the workers are women, always young, always working for contractors or subcontractors from Korea, Taiwan or Hong Kong. The contractors are usually filling orders for companies based in the US, Britain, Japan, Germany, or Canada. The management is military-style, the supervisors often abusive, the wages below subsistence and the work low-skill and tedious . . . These pockets of pure industry hide behind a cloak of transience: the

contracts come and go with little notice. Fear pervades the zones. The governments are afraid of losing their foreign factories; the factories are afraid of losing their brand-name buyers; and the workers are afraid of losing their unstable jobs.

There is no prospective shopping spree to compensate these workers, they are the expendable drones in a devalued manufacturing process.

Taking stock of the increase in the free trade zone industry at the close of the twentieth century, Klein notes that the International Labour Organization reported 'at least 850 EPZs in the world . . . spread through seventy countries and employing roughly 27 million workers' (2001: 205). More and more multinationals have concluded that 'there is no value in making things anymore . . . value is added by careful research, by innovation, and by marketing' (Katz 1994: 204). As the number of EPZs around the world has continued to grow, so multinational companies have sought to significantly increase the mark-up between factory and retail price. Klein (2001) notes that the pursuit by companies of significant increases in the mark-up between factory cost and retail price, increasing from 100 to 400 per cent in some instances, has had inevitable consequences for wages. There is always a country that will bid lower, that will offer better 'tax holidays' and other incentives to potential companies looking to set up factories. As the report of the 1997 United Nations Conference on Trade and Economic Development recorded, wages as a proportion of manufacturing costs have fallen below the level of the 1970s and early 1980s (cited in Klein 2001: 197).

Brand-name multinationals are no longer producers with factories and goods-producing employees. Rather multinational companies like Wal-Mart, Ralph Lauren, Esprit, Kmart, Nike, Adidas and so on have become more like corporate consumers, literally shopping in the global market-place for the best bargain. In this instance the best bargain means the lowest price for factory product achievable from the ranks of the various contractors and subcontractors in the EPZs clustered around the world. The complex network of connections between multinationals, contractors, subcontractors and factory workers, and perhaps home-workers, means that the conditions in which products are produced, the terms on which workers are hired and the rates of pay that workers receive, may remain conveniently unknown to multinational companies interested only in the quality and purchase price of their finished product.[3]

Work in such zones is casual and temporary in nature, contracts of employment are at best short-term, a matter of months, and many workers are hired through employment agencies. Wages are low and workers 'cannot dream of affording the consumer goods they produce' (Klein 2001: 210, see also 218). It is a case of production for consumption elsewhere, elsewhere being largely the consumer societies of North America and Europe. Klein describes the export processing zones as global capitalism's 'dirty little secret' and observes that,

> the planet remains sharply divided between producers and consumers, and the enormous profits raked in by the superbrands are premised upon these worlds remaining as separate from each other as possible . . . for the system to function smoothly, workers must know little of the marketed lives of the products they produce and consumers must remain sheltered from the production lives of the brands they buy.
>
> (2001: 347)

A sense of the transience of work is not confined to economic production zones alone, as analysts who have drawn attention to the emergence of a wider-ranging 'political economy of insecurity' have recognized (Gorz 1999; Beck 2000). The 'casualization' of work, an increase in temporary, part-time and insecure forms of work, is now a prominent feature of economic life around the world. More and more corporations want to reduce their permanent workforces to a minimal core, to 'travel light' and take advantage, as and when necessary, in line with market fluctuations, of the possibility of drawing on part-time, temporary and freelance workers to reduce the cost of overheads. The objective is to facilitate a speedier, more flexible response to changing market conditions. As Klein remarks, instead of being 'one component of a healthy operation, labour is increasingly treated by the corporate sector as an unavoidable burden' (2001: 262).

The developments identified above in respect of relations of production, distribution and consumption are analysed further by Castells (1998). In the course of a discussion focused on the growth of inequality and social exclusion within an informational and global capitalism, Castells notes that relations of production are becoming increasingly unregulated, and that as work has become 'individually contracted' so it has become more precarious (the 'individualization of work'). In turn, there is evidence of increasing 'over-exploitation' of workers, by which Castells means 'working arrangements that allow capital to systematically withhold payment/resource allocation, or impose harsher working conditions, on certain types of workers' (p. 72). Finally, a lack of availability of regular work, the primary source of income, is deemed to be the 'key mechanism' in the process of social exclusion within an informational and global capitalism. In respect of 'relationships of distribution/consumption or differential appropriation of the wealth generated by collective effort', Castells (p. 71) documents accumulating evidence of rising inequality, a growing global polarization of income and wealth distribution, and increases in poverty and social exclusion.

Reflecting further on the impact of an informational capitalism on social and economic life, Castells (1998) argues that effects are extremely uneven. Global capitalism, complemented by an informational mode of development, leads to 'simultaneous economic development and underdevelopment, social inclusion and social exclusion' (p. 82). Informationalism and globalization not only contribute significantly to the growing disparity in wealth *between* countries, but also to inequality and polarization *within* countries. The informational mode of development leads to distinctions being made between 'valuable and non-valuable people' and locations. In turn, the process of globalization leads to selective inclusion and exclusion of 'segments of economies and societies, in and out of the networks of information, wealth, and power, that characterise the new, dominant system' (p. 162). The process of capitalist restructuring and increased emphasis on economic competitiveness, exemplified by the global development of informational capitalism and associated emphasis placed on the necessity of deregulating market forces, has led to substantial increases in social inequality and social exclusion. The combination of a global informational capitalism operating in terms of a virtually 'unrestricted market logic' has produced forms of social exclusion and associated social imbalances, as Castells (p. 162) illustrates through a detailed analysis of the 'dehumanisation of Africa' and the 'new American dilemma'.[4]

Evidence of a complex 'widespread and multiform' pattern of rising inequality and social exclusion around the world leads Castells to argue that 'segments of societies, of areas of cities, of regions, and of entire countries' (1998: 337, see also 162–5) have become increasingly marginal, if not structurally irrelevant, to informational capitalism. These spaces of social exclusion – the 'black holes of informational capitalism' – are now to be found all around the planet (Castells 1998: 164). They signify, notwithstanding the process of globalization, that the world is not one, but remains sharply divided.

Virtually everyone is now living inside the culture of the market, in the sense that hardly anyone's life is unaffected by the direct or indirect consequences of the global diffusion of capitalist forms of economic life. But with the development of a global informational capitalism, lives are being affected in radically different ways. Increasingly the world is becoming divided between those who are beneficiaries of economic restructuring, including those who have yet to suffer adverse consequences and who are still able to continue living the 'consuming life' (Bauman 2001b), and those who find that they have been effectively excluded (Castells 1998; Gray 1999; Klein 2001). On one side there are the economically and socially fortunate, the 'increasingly global and extraterritorial elites' who are becoming steadily wealthier (Bauman 1998b: 3). On the other there are a growing number of people who experience economic insecurity and social exclusion. Feelings of insecurity are proliferating as the 'great non-class of the excluded is becoming ever larger', but comparable feelings are increasingly present even among those at the very heart of society, 'where hierarchies still persist in terms of education and income' (Beck 2000: 118–19).

State and economy

The recent process of economic restructuring, involving what has been termed a 'recapitalization of capitalism' (Castells 1998: 129), has been paralleled by a regeneration of neo-liberal economic philosophy. Economic concepts and ideas are integral to what economic life is all about and in that sense it becomes virtually 'meaningless to distinguish between an existing reality (economy) and the analytical discourse explaining it' (Callon 1998: 29). Neo-liberal economic discourse is not simply 'theory' – it has been transformed into a political programme that continues to guide the economic choices and actions of influential economic agents and institutions (Bourdieu 1998). It is clear that 'economic representations are at work whenever an economic action is performed' (Steiner 2001: 445) and with regard to the matter in hand, it is evident that neo-liberal representations of economic processes and practices have contributed powerfully to the reshaping of economic life.[5]

One of the central tenets of neo-liberal 'free market' economic philosophy has been that the scope of government must be limited if economic freedom and political freedom are to be enhanced. The market is argued to be both economically more efficient and politically more desirable in so far as it enhances the possibility of human freedom. The capacity of the market to handle and respond to a multiplicity of complex data sets led analysts such as Hayek and Friedman to argue that it is more efficient and beneficial than alternatives involving state intervention – alternatives that simply serve to distort market performance. The consequences of the articulation of neo-liberal ideas and courses of economic and political action directed towards a deregulation of markets have been identified to include increasing exploitation and a marked increase in insecurity, suffering and stress (Bourdieu 1998; Gorz 1999; Beck 2000). But whereas neo-liberal economic philosophy has tended to place emphasis on the need for a *reduced* role for the state, in practice the state has not so much been shrinking in influence as changing in form (Bourdieu 1998; Bourdieu *et al.* 1999).

Towards the close of the 1960s a 'new industrial state' (Galbraith 1969) was identified as emerging from the continuing transformation of economic life, a state marked by an increased role for industrial planning and control of markets by large corporations. The new economy was argued to be dominated by 'technically dynamic, massively capitalised and highly organised corporations' (Galbraith 1969: 21). The research and development costs and time frames involved in the process of technological innovation, along with recognition of the unreliability of markets, made industrial planning seem logical and necessary. The constraints of capital, time, scale and control led inexorably to planning and to forms of government intervention. In so far as economic production increasingly involved the deployment of sophisticated technology, then there were substantial research and development costs, high capital investment was required, and there was likely to be a long lead-time before benefits were realized in production. In circumstances such as these, especially

> in the development and supply of modern weapons, in the exploration of space and in the development of a growing range of modern civilian products or services, including transport planes, high speed ground transport and various applied uses of nuclear energy . . . the state guarantees a price sufficient, with suitable margin, to cover costs. And it undertakes to buy what is produced or to compensate fully in the case of contract cancellation. Thus, effectively, it suspends the market with all associated uncertainty.
>
> (Galbraith 1969: 41)

In short, the industrial system, characterized by large corporations, was argued to be 'inextricably associated with the state' (Galbraith 1969: 300).

Reflecting briefly on the changing relationship between state and economy, Galbraith (1969) notes how at the close of the nineteenth century the corporation was the paramount power and '[b]usiness control of the state was the thing to fear' (p. 301). As the twentieth century developed, worries about the power of business were matched and then 'replaced by the fear that the state would dominate business' (p. 304). By the close of the twentieth century, after a further period of significant economic transformation, analysts were once again expressing concern about the regeneration of corporate power and drawing attention to the growing impact corporations were having on the state and social life (Monbiot 2000; Hertz 2001; Klein 2001).

In the closing decades of the twentieth century, free markets were being engineered through 'artifice, design and political coercion' (Gray 1999: 17) and in this process the state was playing an active role. The state began to withdraw from forms of direct ownership and administration of particular industries, through programmes of 'privatization' that effectively transferred ownership of nationalized industries to the private sector. But at the same time, as the state was engaged in privatizing publicly-owned assets, the important influence it exercised over economic life continued, if it did not increase, through its growing involvement in regulatory and managerial activity (Bourdieu 1998).

With the development of a post-Fordist, more flexible and globally extensive form of capital accumulation, an increased responsibility has been placed on the nation state to maintain a conducive environment for business and entrepreneurial activity. While a neo-liberal line of non-intervention in economic life that would leave matters in the hands of the market has grown in prominence, the state has repeatedly found it necessary to intervene in the economy to deal with internal and external indebtedness and other manifestations of financial instability. Indeed, it has been suggested that notwithstanding the 'age of deregulation' the economic role of the state remains pivotal, especially in fostering appropriate developmental strategies for business, and further that as a lender of last resort its role may have become even more crucial (Harvey 1989; Castells 1996).

Information technology and the state

There is an additional and related respect in which the state has played, and indeed continues to play, a significant role in economic life and that is through military and defence related expenditures and associated research and development initiatives. While there is evidence of significant forms of change or discontinuity between different periods, there are also examples of important forms of continuity between different economic eras.

Worthy of note in the current context is the evidence of consistently high levels of defence expenditure by the US government throughout the Fordist era, levels of expenditure that have not only continued into the present, but have increased substantially over time. In the late 1960s US defence expenditure was running at $60 billion a year, leading the US government, through the Department of Defence, to be identified as supporting 'the most highly developed planning in the industrial system' (Galbraith 1969: 314). Since then, US defence expenditure has continued to constitute a large part of the federal budget and subsequently it has been identified as 'fundamental to whatever economic growth ... [occurred] in world capitalism in the 1980s' (Harvey 1989: 170). Furthermore, given the percentage increases in US defence expenditure planned for the twenty-first century, the potential future impact on economic growth is likely to be no less significant. Military and defence related expenditure has tended to be exempted from pleas for public sector economies and thereby has contributed indirectly to the regulation, stabilization and stimulation of aggregate demand. It has also continued to contribute to technological innovation by underwriting research and development costs in a number of fields with direct/indirect and actual/potential military and defence related relevance.

The impact of the development of an informational and global capitalism, favouring enterprise, flexibility, innovation and the freeing of markets from regulation has been a prominent part of my analysis of contemporary conditions. A vital element in the development of informational capitalism has been a broad range of innovations in information technology. What is frequently termed the 'information technology revolution' has a complex history. The new information technology employed to overcome rigidities and to accelerate turnover time has its roots in initiatives developed from the 1940s within a 'military-industrial complex' that has been particularly prominent in the USA (Smart 1992). Recent studies have demonstrated that state funding, particularly of military contracts and defence related initiatives, was vital for the development of the electronics industry in the 1950s and 1960s. Federal government expenditure in the USA has continued to play a decisive role in the subsequent development of information technology (Noble 1983, 1984; Roszak 1986; Lyon 1988; Robins and Webster 1989; Castells 1996).

Military and defence related research programmes have provided a number of fundamental breakthroughs, 'from 1940s computers to optoelectronics and artificial intelligence technologies of the 1980s', to the more recent 'design and initial funding of the Internet' (Castells 1996: 59). While during the 1980s administrations in the USA and Britain were extolling a free-market philosophy, they were simultaneously providing substantial funding support for information technology companies. As Castells notes, a substantial slice of the funding that allowed European information technology companies to keep up with competitors came from the state. In America the federal government provided funding for high cost research and development programmes in electronics manufacturing and, in turn, assisted major companies in the field of microelectronics 'for reasons of national security' (Castells 1996: 59). The weight of evidence points to an inexorable conclusion – namely that the state has played a pivotal role in the development of information technology by underwriting research and development costs and by providing guaranteed markets for products.

The prospect of a 'new world order', heralded by US President George Bush following the end of the Cold War, very briefly opened up the possibility of cuts in the military and defence budget. But evidence of instability and disorder in international affairs, exemplified by the Gulf War, soon put paid to such optimism. Fears about security became an increasingly prominent feature of international affairs and everyday life in the 1990s (Ahmed 1992). The attacks of 11 September 2001 on the USA and the city of New York in particular, have been interpreted as providing dramatic confirmation of the continuing need for vigilant national defence and security. The subsequent declaration of a 'war on terrorism' led another US president, George W. Bush, to submit a budget to Congress requesting an 11.6 per cent increase in defence expenditure. In 2002, before the budget, military expenditure in the USA was reported to be already greater than the combined total of the next 15 highest military spending countries. The proposed 11.6 per cent increase in federal government expenditure promises to raise defence spending from $330.8 billion in 2002 to $369.3 billion in 2003, rising to $451 billion in 2007. By way of comparison, Britain's annual defence budget in 2002 was reported to be £24 billion. The significance of defence related expenditure in the US federal government budget can be gauged from the following comparative data.

In the period 2002–3 the US federal government was requesting additional increases in expenditure of 1 per cent for education (from $49.8bn to

$50.3bn), 4.7 per cent for energy ($21.0bn to $21.9bn), 9.1 per cent for health and human services ($59.8bn to $65.3bn) and 6.7 per cent for housing and urban development ($29.5bn to $31.5bn). It was proposed that in the same period expenditure on environmental protection would *fall* by 3.7 per cent (8.0bn to 7.7bn) (Maddox 2002). These proposed increases in expenditure follow a $40 billion emergency spending bill, a $15 billion package to support the airline industry and other measures taken to restore consumer confidence, stimulate the economy and avert the threat of a global recession in the wake of 11 September. Such signs of increased federal government expenditure have led commentators to speculate that perhaps we may be witnessing a turning of 'the free market tide' (Elliott 2001). The events of 11 September seem to have led to a reassessment of a number of assumptions that have guided policy. The conventional wisdom of the 1980s was that 'Government isn't the solution. Government is the problem'. One possible implication of the aftermath of 11 September is that a different view of the role of the state may now be emerging. However, at this point it is premature to consider this as anything more than conjecture.[6]

Throughout the modern era, as a number of analysts have demonstrated, the state has been in a functionally symbiotic relationship with the capitalist economic system (Polanyi 1968; Harvey 1989; Block 1994; Castells 1996). The inextricable association between the state and the mature corporations of the industrial system identified by Galbraith (1969) has continued, albeit in a rather different form, to be an important feature of an informational and global capitalist system. Increasingly, the state is serving as regulator, 'legitimising the new regime whilst facilitating accumulation' (Keaney 2001: 71). Meanwhile the corporate sector continues to acquire ownership or administration of public assets and access to the benefits of any income or profits that might follow, while reducing exposure to risk by achieving a simultaneous socialization of a substantial part of the costs of production (Monbiot 2002). It has been suggested that such developments indicate an 'ever-deepening entwining of the state and monopoly sectors' (Keaney 2001: 71). To some extent this process is exemplified by a raft of related initiatives involving PPPs and PFIs in a number of areas of the public sector, including health, education and transport. However, such changes are taking place on terms that are increasingly being set by the continuing transformation, or modernization, of global capitalism.

This process of modernization has undoubtedly had a significant impact on the state. Public sector provision of goods and services, predicated on a notion of 'collective responsibility', is being subjected to a logic of commodity production that is steadily commodifying 'that which was previously regarded as part of the commons' (Keaney 2001: 71). What this demonstrates is an ongoing process of accommodation, if not submission, to the values of capitalist economic life (Bourdieu 1998). It represents, in short, the impact of an ongoing process of capitalist modernization.

With the development of an informational, free-market oriented global capitalism, nation states are encountering a radical reduction in their sovereignty. The continuing 'technical, economic, political and cultural development of global capitalism' is stripping away at the nation state (Beck 2001: 267). New technologies are transforming economic life around the world and market forces are increasingly operating relatively free of regulation or constraint. With the growth of a global, flexible and deregulated capitalist economy, nation states are finding it increasingly difficult to exercise political sovereignty over their own national economies. The growing influence of transnational corporations, foreign trade, global financial markets, private international banks and agencies such as the International Monetary Fund, have reduced the level of control states are able to exercise over their economies (Martinelli and Smelser 1990). Democratic governments now face great difficulties as they try to cope with the consequences of a global market economy. As John Gray (1999: 213–14) observes:

> Global bond markets will not allow social democracies to borrow heavily. Keynesian policies are not effective when in open economies from which capital can exit at will. Worldwide mobility of production allows enterprises to locate where regulatory and tax burdens are least onerous . . . in general terms the contradiction between social democracy and global free markets seems irreconcilable.

It is in the context of assessments of contemporary economic life such as this that the question of alternatives has been addressed.

The question of alternatives

In a postscript to his discussion of the delusions of global capitalism John Gray (1999) notes that our time is marked by a disconnection of economic efficiency from any sense of human well-being. The continuing endorsement of the 'Anglo-Saxon free market . . . [as] the model for economic reform everywhere' (p. 234) has meant that the organization of social life has become, in many respects, subject to the logic of the market. The idea of a single universal market and economic civilization embodying western values, increasingly informed, if not dominated, by American values, constitutes a legacy of the modern 'Enlightenment ideal of a universal civilisation' (p. 234). But rather than bringing closer the realization of such a conception, Gray argues that the globalization of capitalism is producing more diversity and new forms of difference. Instead of a single economic civilization predicated on western values, the development of a global informational capitalism is making 'a plural world irreversible' (p. 235). But it remains a world that is in thrall to the USA, whose dominant economic, military and political influence allows it to treat its particular national sovereign interest as universal. The fact that the USA is able 'to combine an absolutist insistence on its own national sovereignty with a universalist claim to worldwide jurisdiction' leaves Gray sounding pessimistic about the immediate prospects for a change in economic policy away from 'global *laissez-faire*' (p. 235).

Gray asks, 'Can anything be done?' The answer that emerges is to wait for the crises and fluctuations, to which global markets are vulnerable, to become so unacceptable that other nation states begin to act unilaterally to protect their own sovereign interests. The expectation is that when/if that happens 'global *laissez-faire* will begin to crumble' (Gray 1999: 235) and by implication greater emphasis will be placed upon the need for forms of economic regulation. Currently there seems to be no serious alternative to the global free market, although there are a variety of social movements expressing opposition and offering resistance to the 'new global order' and its social, economic, political and environmental consequences (Castells 1997; Klein 2001).

In a series of related critical reflections on the way in which neo-liberalism has come to be seen as part of the natural order of things, as 'an inevitability', Bourdieu lists a series of presuppositions that have become a central part of the culture of our economic life:

> it is taken for granted that maximum growth, and therefore productivity and competitiveness, are the ultimate and sole goal of human action; or that economic forces cannot be resisted. Or again – a presupposition which is the basis of all the presuppositions of economics – a radical separation is made between the economic and the social, which is left to one side, abandoned to sociologists, as a kind of reject.
>
> (1998: 31)

The very language in which we are informed about transformations to economic life, the terms in which economic conditions and processes are explained, tend to present the neo-liberal programme and its impact as positive and beneficial. Rationalization, restructuring, modernization, flexibility and deregulation may be employed, as Bourdieu suggests, to 'imply that the neo-liberal message is a universalist message of liberation' (1998: 31), but the reality is radically different. Processes of 'rationalization' or 'restructuring', when applied to production, generally mean reductions in numbers employed, i.e. workers losing jobs. 'Modernization' in practice is frequently a code 'for political accommodation to the reinforcement of privilege' that is presented as necessary, if not unavoidable, and as 'self-evidently desirable' (Donald and Hutton 2001: 211). Those who oppose such a notion of 'modernization' are often portrayed as 'wreckers'.

'Flexibility' in relation to economic activity means a number of things, but most importantly for employers it has meant a transformation in the patterns of work and employment. On the one hand, a reduction in 'costly' full-time permanent employees with job security, pension rights and other benefit entitlements, and on the other an increase in part-time, casual, fixed contract, temporary and subcontracted employees who have little job security and few, if any, rights or entitlements. The aggregate effects of flexible employment arrangements, 'when looked at from the standpoint of insurance coverage and pension rights, as well as wage levels and job security, by no means appear positive from the standpoint of the working population as a whole' (Harvey 1989: 151; see also Bourdieu 1998: 34). The same holds for 'deregulation', where the benefits of free markets accrue to employers and corporations, not to employees and workers, who end up with less protection and are more vulnerable to exploitation.[7]

The objective of Bourdieu's analytic narrative is to expose neo-liberalism to criticism, to counter the idea that the global free market leads to economic and political liberation and reveal the reality of its impact. In particular Bourdieu notes how in Europe the mechanism of the global free-market economy has led to deterioration in the working conditions of workers and has eroded the gains associated with the welfare state. The mobility of capital, and the existence of countries with no minimum wage, long working hours, limited statutory regulation of the work-place environment and no trade unions, to which production might be exported, have made European workers feel vulnerable to job loss, to the export of jobs. This is the context in which flexible working practices (night work, weekend work, irregular working hours) have been imposed (Bourdieu 1998: 34).

The neo-liberal globalization of economic life, particularly with regard to the development of financial markets, has led to the return of an 'unrestrained', 'unfettered' or 'cynical' capitalism.[8] The globalization of finance markets has brought into being a form of 'casino capitalism' (Beck 2000: 62) in which achievement of wealth is increasingly the measure of virtue. In a market-driven society it is market values that determine what matters. Non-market values are increasingly marginalized and devalued, if not discredited, by the 'glorification of earnings, productivity, and competitiveness, or just plain profit, [that] tends to undermine the very foundation of functions that depend on a certain professional disinterestedness often associated with militant devotion' (Bourdieu et al. 1999: 183–4). In such circumstances the prospects for the welfare state, for public sector services and for a public sector ethos, seem poor indeed. It is against this 'withering' of the state and the public sector that Bourdieu argues critical analysis needs to be directed.

The call for a more critical and engaged form of social analysis that questions the inevitability ascribed to neo-liberalism is implicitly endorsed in arguments advanced by Gorz (1999), Beck (2000) and Galbraith (1996,

1998). Noting the respects in which the nation state is undermined both from without and within – by external global financial forces and flows and by their 'inside . . . accomplices . . . the financiers, bankers and finance ministry officials' – Bourdieu (1998: 41–2) argues that there is a need to create a 'genuine critical internationalism'. By this he means European institutions able to protect social gains and counter the influence exerted by global financial markets. In a comparable manner, in the course of outlining a 'vision of the future', Beck affirms the need for transnational institutions – civil movements and political parties – capable of matching the reach and influence of global corporations and able to respond to their impact. More broadly there is a call for a 'European cosmopolitan movement' that will be able to contribute to the development of appropriate institutions to deal with the consequences of 'postnational' forms of economic, political and social life.

In the course of elaborating his vision of a possible 'postnational civil society', Beck notes the difficulties that might arise both nationally and transnationally and cites, as an example, the ongoing difficulty of bridging 'discord between the United States of America and the European Union' (Beck 2000: 177). This is an uneven contest. The USA has come to be regarded as the model of western modernization. Its global economic influence is unrivalled and its cultural forms have penetrated every corner of the globe. Moreover, since the end of the Cold War and the collapse of the Soviet Union it is the only remaining 'superpower' (Castells 1998). But the USA does not provide an appropriate model to emulate for, as analysts have noted, there are increasing signs of trouble in the free market 'paradise' (Bourdieu 1998; Castells 1998; Gray 1999; Beck 2000).

In the USA a growing disparity exists between the privileged wealthy section of the community and a growing constituency confined, literally as far as the large prison population is concerned, within a system of social exclusion that is an expression of rising insecurity, inequality and poverty (Bourdieu 1998; Castells 1998). Deregulation of markets and flexibility in the organization and management of production may have contributed to the USA's 'jobs miracle', but they have simultaneously contributed to the development of a divided country (Gray 1998). A considerable number of the new jobs that have been created are in service sectors with low productivity, requiring little or no skill, where job security is virtually non-existent and where rates of pay are very poor (Ritzer 1998; Beck 2000). In addition, since the 1970s, economic restructuring and the deployment of neo-liberal economic policies have exacerbated the problem of inequality. Over the past 30 years the proportion of national income going to those in the top 5 per cent has increased from *ten times* that of those in the bottom 5 per cent to *almost fifty times* as much (Beck 2000). Such evidence of the way in which the domination of unrestricted market forces has increased inequality and social fragmentation leads Galbraith to offer further criticism of the consequences of the market system and the leading role played by the USA within the world economy.

Acknowledgement of the inescapable prominence of economic factors is a long-standing feature of Galbraith's work, as is critical recognition of the fact that left unregulated 'economic forces do not work out for the best except perhaps for the powerful' (1975: 3). The continuing salience of this cautionary observation receives confirmation from evidence of the impact the development of a global free-market capitalist system has had on income distribution and resource allocation patterns. The global free market is producing an increasingly more unequal distribution of income, both within and between societies, with the USA exercising 'an adverse world leadership' (1998: 24), and it has contributed significantly to the deteriorating imbalance in the allocation of resources between public and private services and functions. The associated relative 'downsizing' of the public sector has led analysts to refer to its 'pauperization' and to note its increasing inability to 'fulfill its minimum function as provider of collective goods such as safety, health, education, housing, and justice' (Wacquant 1999: 136; see also Galbraith 1996, 1998).

The pace and scale of social and economic transformation has led some analysts to argue that existing conditions cannot be analysed effectively 'without scenarios of possible futures' (Gorz 1982, 1985, 1999; Beck 2000). For others the passing of socialism and the discrediting of old-style social democracy, coupled with concern about the social consequences of neo-liberal free-market fundamentalism, has persuaded them to formulate programmatic statements of possible 'third ways' to the achievement of a better society (Giddens 1998, 2000). But there is another alternative, one that involves deliberately abstaining from the formulation of such a programme. It is precisely this order of analytic response that is exemplified by the work of Castells (1997: 358–9) and in a related way by that of Bourdieu (1998: 56, 1999).

The primary task of intellectual inquiry outlined by Castells is to provide a rigorous, relevant and accurate account of the world. The appropriate use of theory and research is not to try to frame political practice. Rather, the objective is to develop the tools necessary to expose the myths and deconstruct the doctrines and policies that have acquired the status of self-evidence and, in turn, to reinterpret and promote understanding of the world in which we live. And in so far as it is now widely recognized that 'the ineluctable fact about any society . . . is that there is no escape from "economics"' (Bell 1976: 254), then the tools provided must contribute to the development of an effective understanding of economic life.

To achieve a critical understanding of the rhetoric and reality of economic life it is necessary to recognize the close articulation of the economic and the social, and the negative consequences that have followed from their analytic separation. The various orders of facts studied by the different disciplines do not constitute independent worlds – on the contrary, they are in reality closely interrelated. An 'unjustifiable' analytic separation of the economic and the social has been a feature of economic discourse in general and neo-liberalism in particular (Bourdieu 1998: 31, 51). This has contributed to the regeneration of the 'market economy' and the transformation of society into 'an accessory of the economic system' (Polanyi 1968: 75; see also Gorz 1989: 187). It is important to understand the respects in which an economizing logic has intruded into and shaped more and more areas of modern social life. To that end it is necessary to nurture the return of an analytic interest in economic life within contemporary sociology, for 'few of the economic processes and institutions are actually explored through the theoretical lenses of orthodox economics' (Beckert and Swedberg 2001: 382).

In a series of critical observations on social science, economics and social movements, Bourdieu (1998) argues that it is necessary to take issue with the complacent interpretation of economic tendencies as 'destiny'. Neo-liberalism and the associated idea of a global free-market economy have acquired a predetermined and self-evident character for policy makers, analysts and commentators. It is one of the more important tasks of social theory to expose both the fragile foundations of such a conception of economic life and the harmful social consequences that have followed from its policy implementation. To that end an 'economic (re)turn' within contemporary social theory is both necessary and to be welcomed.

Notes

1 In his discussion of the consequences of the restructuring of capitalism and the rationalization of the labour process in particular, Ritzer (1998: 69) notes that

> Capitalism has found that it is imperative for people to consume far beyond their cash in hand . . . Capitalism can only grow so far by getting us to spend everything we have, so it has found a way through credit cards and other types of readily available loans to get us to spend money we have not yet even earned. Capitalist growth is dependent on the finding of ever new and more refined ways of getting us to spend money that is not to be earned until farther and farther into the future.

2 In a comparable manner it has been argued by Andre Gorz (1989: 65) that what is emerging as a consequence of the restructuring of contemporary capitalism is indeed a 'dual society' comprising a 'privileged stratum of permanent workers' at the top of the social hierarchy and a 'growing mass of casual labourers, temporary workers, the unemployed and "odd jobbers"' at the bottom (see also Castells 1998: 130 on the emergence of a dual society in the USA).

In response to the continuing transformation of capitalism, Beck outlines a somewhat different scenario, which suggests that if what he terms the

'Brazilianization of the West' (2000: 106) continues, then in western societies there are likely to be *four* groups:

- those who have gained from globalization, especially the 'owners of globally active capital';
- 'precarious employees at the top of the skills ladder';
- the 'working poor' – low-skilled and unskilled workers whose jobs are increasingly at risk from automation and/or transfer of production to another lower-cost, less regulated supplier in another country;
- the 'localized poor', those who have come to be regarded as a 'liability' (Bauman 1998b: 91).

3 Citing a 1998 study of Chinese special economic zones where goods are manufactured for prominent brand-name multinationals, Klein notes that although approximately US87 cents an hour was recognized to be necessary for a living wage, workers were in fact only being paid a fraction of that sum and some were being paid 'as little as 13 cents an hour' (2001: 212, 474).

4 Specifically Castells considers the interrelationship between the development of a global informational capitalism and economic, political and social problems in Africa and, in turn, the impact structural and organizational transformations associated with informational capitalism have had on social inequality, polarization, poverty and social exclusion in the USA.

5 There is a wider issue here of the way in which economic decisions and actions are shaped by expectations and understandings informed by interpretations of information. For a consideration of the role of information in economic action see Nigel Dodd's *The Sociology of Money* (1994).

6 The expansion in the role of the US government exemplified by various economic packages to stimulate the economy, a redefined role in relation to the education system, the introduction of various security measures, along with a significantly increased commitment to military and defence expenditure, has been regarded as signifying the return of 'big government' (Fletcher 2001; Stelzer 2002).

7 See Klein (2001), especially Chapters 9 and 10, for a discussion of the consequences of deregulated global markets for workers.

8 Consider as an example the events associated with the bankruptcy of the Enron energy group. Enron overstated its profits by nearly $600 million and understated its debt by $2.6 billion over four years. Much of its debt was concealed in complex off-balance-sheet partnerships and was only revealed after an inquiry by the Securities and Exchange Commission (SEC). A major international accountancy firm, Andersen, the energy group's former auditor, was found guilty of trying to sabotage the inquiry by destroying thousands of key financial documents. Senior managers of Enron were paid nearly $845 million in cash and stock in the year before the energy group's bankruptcy on 2 December 2001. In addition, other Enron managers received about $99 million in 'other bonuses' in November 2001 as the group headed for meltdown. During the year when the $845 million was paid out the company's stock fell in value from $80 to under 10 cents, leaving investors with losses of over $60 billion (*The Times*, Business, 18 June: 23).

FURTHER READING

Baudrillard, J. (1998) *The Consumer Society: Myths and Structures*. London: Sage.

Beck, U. (2000) *The Brave New World of Work*. Cambridge: Polity Press.

Bourdieu, P. (1998) *Acts of Resistance – Against the New Myths of Our Time*. Cambridge: Polity Press.

Brown, K.M., Kenny, S., Turner, B.S. with Prince, J.K. (2000) *Rhetorics of Welfare: Uncertainty, Choice and Voluntary Associations*. Basingstoke: Macmillan.

Castells, M. (1996) *The Rise of the Network Society*, vol. 1 of *The Information Age: Economy, Society and Culture*. Oxford: Blackwell.

Castells, M. (1997) *The Power of Identity*, vol. 2 of *The Information Age: Economy, Society and Culture*. Oxford: Blackwell.

Castells, M. (1998) *End of Millenium*, vol. 3 of *The Information Age: Economy, Society and Culture*. Oxford: Blackwell.

Dodd, N. (1994) *The Sociology of Money: Economics, Reason & Contemporary Society*. Cambridge: Polity Press.

Galbraith, J.K. (1985) *The Affluent Society*, 4th edn with a new introduction. London: Andre Deutsch.

Gorz, A. (1999) *Reclaiming Work – Beyond the Wage-Based Society*. Cambridge: Polity Press.

Gray, J. (1999) *False Dawn – The Delusions of Global Capitalism*. London: Granta Books.

Klein, M. (2001) *No Logo*. London: Flamingo.

O'Neill, J. (1998) *The Market – Ethics, Knowledge and Politics*. London: Routledge.

Slater, D. and Tonkiss, F. (2001) *Market Society – Markets and Modern Social Theory*. Cambridge: Polity.

REFERENCES

Ackerlof, G.A. (1990) Interview in R. Swedberg (ed.) *Economics and Sociology: Redefining their Boundaries: Conversations with Economists and Sociologists*. Princeton, NJ: Princeton University Press.

Ahmed, A. (1992) *Postmodernism and Islam: Predicament and Promise*. London: Routledge.

Arendt, H. (1958) *The Human Condition*. Chicago: University of Chicago Press.

Arnason, J. (1993) *The Future that Failed: The Challenge and Collapse of the Soviet Model*. London: Routledge.

Bahro, R. (1978) *The Alternative in Eastern Europe*. London: New Left Books.

Baudrillard, J. (1975) *The Mirror of Production*. St Louis: Telos Press.

Baudrillard, J. ([1970] 1998) *The Consumer Society: Myths and Structures*. London: Sage.

Bauman, Z. (1992) *Intimations of Postmodernity*. London: Routledge.

Bauman, Z. (1997) *Postmodernity and its Discontents*. New York: New York University Press.

Bauman, Z. (1998a) *Globalization: The Human Consequences*. Cambridge: Polity Press.

Bauman, Z. (1998b) *Work, Consumerism and The New Poor*. Buckingham: Open University Press.

Bauman, Z. (2001a) *The Bauman Reader*, edited by Peter Beilharz. Oxford: Blackwell.

Bauman, Z. (2001b) Consuming Life, *Journal of Consumer Culture*, 1(1): 9–29.

Beck, U. (1992) *Risk Society: Towards a New Modernity*. London: Sage.

Beck, U. (1994) The reinvention of politics: towards a theory of reflexive modernization, in U. Beck, A. Giddens and S. Lash (eds) *Reflexive Modernization – Politics, Tradition and Aesthetics in the Modern Social Order*. Cambridge: Polity Press.

Beck, U. (1998) *Democracy without Enemies*. Cambridge: Polity Press.

Beck, U. (2000) *The Brave New World of Work*. Cambridge: Polity Press.

Beck, U. (2001) Interview, *Journal of Consumer Culture*, 1(2): 261–77.

Beckert, J. and Swedberg, R. (2001) Introduction to symposium: the return of economic sociology in Europe, *European Journal of Social Theory*, 4(4): 379–86.

Bell, D. (1976) *The Cultural Contradictions of Capitalism*. New York: Basic Books.

Bell, D. (1990) Interview, in R. Swedberg (ed.) *Economics and Sociology – Redefining their Boundaries: Conversations with Economists and Sociologists*. Princeton, NJ: Princeton University Press.

Bellah, R.N., Madsen, R., Sullivan, W.M., Swidler, A. and Tipton, S.M. (1991) *The Good Society*. New York: Alfred A. Knopf.

Bellah, R.N., Madsen, R., Sullivan, W.M., Swidler, A. and Tipton, S.M. (1996) *Habits of the Heart – Individualism and Commitment in American Life*. London: University of California.

Berman, M. (1983) *All That Is Solid Melts Into Air – The Experience of Modernity*. London: Verso.

Block, F. (1994) The roles of the state in the economy, in N.J. Smelser and R. Swedberg (eds) *The Handbook of Economic Sociology*. Princeton, NJ: Princeton University Press.

Bottomore, T. (1979) Marxism and sociology, in T. Bottomore and R. Nisbet (eds) *A History of Sociological Analysis*. London: Heinemann.

Bourdieu, P. (1984) *Distinction: A Social Critique of the Judgement of Taste*. London: Routledge & Kegan Paul.

Bourdieu, P. (1990) *In Other Words – Essays Towards A Reflexive Sociology*. Cambridge: Polity Press.

Bourdieu, P. (1993) *Sociology in Question*. London: Sage.

Bourdieu, P. (1998) *Acts of Resistance – Against the New Myths of Our Time*. Cambridge: Polity Press.

Bourdieu, P. et al. (1999) *The Weight of the World: Social Suffering in Contemporary Society*. Cambridge: Polity Press.

Boyer, R. (1990) *The Regulation School: A Critical Approach*. New York: Columbia University Press.

Brown, K.M., Kenny, S. and Turner, B.S. with Prince, J.K. (2000) *Rhetorics of Welfare: Uncertainty, Choice and Voluntary Associations*. Basingstoke: Macmillan.

Callon, M. (1998) Introduction: the embeddedness of economic markets in economics, in M. Callon (ed.) *The Laws of the Markets*. Oxford: Blackwell.

Castells, M. (1992) The beginning of history, *Socialism of the Future*, 1(1): 86–96.

Castells, M. (1996) *The Rise of the Network Society*, vol. 1 of *The Information Age: Economy, Society and Culture*. Oxford: Blackwell.

Castells, M. (1997) *The Power of Identity*, vol. 2 of *The Information Age: Economy, Society and Culture*. Oxford: Blackwell.

Castells, M. (1998) *End of Millenium*, vol. 3 of *The Information Age: Economy, Society and Culture*. Oxford: Blackwell.

Castoriadis, C. (1997) The crisis of western societies, in D. Ames Curtis (ed.) *The Castoriadis Reader*, Oxford: Blackwell.

Coleman, J. (1988) Social capital in the creation of human capital, *American Journal of Sociology*, 94: 95–120.

Davern, M.E. and Eitzen, D.S. (1995) Economic sociology: an examination of intellectual exchange, *American Journal of Economics and Sociology*, 51(1): 78–88.

Derrida, J. (1994) *Specters of Marx: The State of the Debt, the Work of Mourning and the New International*. London: Routledge.

Dodd, N. (1994) *The Sociology of Money: Economics, Reason & Contemporary Society*. Cambridge: Polity Press.

Donald, D. and Hutton, A. (2001) Galbraith, globalism and the good life: making the best of the capitalist predicament, in M. Keaney (ed.) *Economist with a Public Purpose: Essays in Honour of John Kenneth Galbraith*, pp. 199–218. London: Routledge.

Durkheim, E. (1957) *Professional Ethics and Civic Morals*. London: Routledge & Kegan Paul.

Durkheim, E. (1959) *Socialism and Saint-Simon*, edited with an introduction by A.W. Gouldner. London: Routledge & Kegan Paul.

Durkheim, E. (1978) *Emile Durkheim On Institutional Analysis*, edited, translated and with an introduction by M. Traugott. London: University of Chicago Press.

Durkheim, E. (1982) *The Rules of Sociological Method and Selected Texts on Sociology and its Method*, edited with an introduction by S. Lukes, translated by W.D. Halls. London: Macmillan.

Durkheim, E. (1984) *The Division of Labour in Society*. London: Macmillan.

Elliott, L. (2001) The free market tide has turned, *The Guardian*, 20 September: 15.

Elliott, L. and Atkinson, D. (1999) *The Age of Insecurity*. London: Verso.

Etzioni, A. (1994) *The Spirit of Community – The Reinvention of American Society*. London: Simon & Schuster.

Featherstone, M. (1991) *Consumer Culture and Postmodernism*. London: Sage.

Fletcher, M. (2001) Bush drafts legions of big government to fight war, *The Times*, 2 October: 4.

Foucault, M. (1973) *The Order of Things: An Archaeology of the Human Sciences*. New York: Vintage Books.

Friedman, M. (1980) *Free to Choose*. Harmondsworth: Pelican.

Friedman, M. ([1962] 1982) *Capitalism and Freedom*. Chicago: University of Chicago Press.

Frisby, D. (1984) *Georg Simmel*. London: Tavistock.

Frisby, D. (1987) The ambiguity of modernity: Georg Simmel and Max Weber, in W.J. Mommsen and J. Osterhammel (eds) *Max Weber and his Contemporaries*. London: Allen & Unwin.

Frisby, D. (1990) Preface to the second edition of G. Simmel, *The Philosophy Of Money*. London: Routledge.

Frisby, D. (1997) Introduction to the texts, in D. Frisby and M. Featherstone (eds) *Simmel on Culture*. London: Sage.

Fukuyama, F. (1992) *The End of History and the Last Man*. New York: The Free Press.

Galbraith, J.K. (1963) *The Affluent Society*. Harmondsworth: Penguin.

Galbraith, J.K. (1969) *The New Industrial State*. Harmondsworth: Penguin.

Galbraith, J.K. (1975) *Economics and the Public Purpose*. Harmondsworth: Penguin.

Galbraith, J.K. (1985) *The Affluent Society*, 4th edn with a new introduction. London: Andre Deutsch.

Galbraith, J.K. (1993) *The Culture of Contentment*. Harmondsworth: Penguin.

Galbraith, J.K. (1996) *The Good Society: The Humane Agenda*. MA: Houghton Mifflin.

Galbraith, J.K. (1998) *The Socially Concerned Today*. Toronto: University of Toronto Press.

Galbraith, J.K. and Salinger, N. (1981) *Almost Everyone's Guide to Economics.* Harmondsworth: Penguin.

Gamble, A. (1987) The weakening of social democracy, in M. Loney (ed.) *The State or the Market: Politics and Welfare in Contemporary Britain,* pp. 189–202. London: Sage.

Giddens, A. (1987) *Social Theory and Modern Sociology.* Cambridge: Polity.

Giddens, A. (1990) *The Consequences of Modernity.* Cambridge: Polity Press.

Giddens, A. (1991) *Modernity & Self-Identity.* Cambridge: Polity Press.

Giddens, A. (1994) *Beyond Left and Right.* Cambridge: Polity Press.

Giddens, A. (1998) *The Third Way: The Renewal of Social Democracy.* Cambridge: Polity Press.

Giddens, A. (2000) *The Third Way and its Critics.* Cambridge: Polity Press.

Gorz, A. (1982) *Farewell to the Working Class: An Essay on Post-Industrial Socialism.* London: Pluto Press.

Gorz, A. (1985) *Paths to Paradise: On the Liberation from Work.* London: Pluto Press.

Gorz, A. (1989) *Critique of Economic Reason.* London: Verso.

Gorz, A. (1999) *Reclaiming Work – Beyond the Wage-Based Society.* Cambridge: Polity Press.

Gray, J. (1999) *False Dawn – The Delusions of Global Capitalism.* London: Granta Books.

Habermas, J. (1974) The public sphere: an encyclopedia article, *New German Critique,* 3 (Fall): 49–55.

Habermas, J. (1976) *Legitimation Crisis.* London: Heinemann.

Habermas, J. (1989) *The Structural Transformation of the Public Sphere.* Cambridge: Polity Press.

Hall, S. (1996) Introduction: who needs 'identity'?, in S. Hall and P. du Gay (eds) *Questions of Cultural Identity.* London: Sage.

Harvey, D. (1989) *The Condition of Postmodernity.* Oxford: Blackwell.

Hayek, F.A. (1944) *The Road to Serfdom.* London: Routledge & Kegan Paul.

Hayek, F.A. (1949) *Individualism and Economic Order.* London: Routledge & Kegan Paul.

Hayek, F.A. (1960) *The Constitution of Liberty.* London: Routledge & Kegan Paul.

Hayek, F.A. (1976) *Law Legislation and Liberty,* vol. 2, *The Mirage of Social Justice.* London: Routledge & Kegan Paul.

Hayek, F.A. (1979) *Law Legislation and Liberty,* vol. 3, *The Political Order of a Free People.* London: Routledge & Kegan Paul.

Haug, W.F. (1986) *Critique of Commodity Aesthetics: Appearance, Sexuality and Advertising in Capitalist Society.* Cambridge: Polity Press.

Heelas, P. and Morris, P. (1992) Enterprise culture: its values and value, in P. Heelas and P. Morris (eds) *The Values of the Enterprise Culture – The Moral Debate.* London: Routledge.

Helly, D.O. and Reverby, S.M. (eds) (1992) *Gendered Domains: Rethinking Public and Private in Women's History.* Ithaca, NY: Cornell University Press.

Hennis, W. (1987) A science of man: Max Weber and the political economy of the German Historical School, in W.J. Mommsen and J. Osterhammel (eds) *Max Weber and His Contemporaries.* London: Allen & Unwin.

Hennis, W. (1988) *Max Weber – Essays in Reconstruction*. London: Allen & Unwin.

Hertz, N. (2001) *The Silent Takeover*. London: Heinemann.

Hirst, P.Q. (1994) *Associative Democracy: New Forms of Economic and Social Governance*. Cambridge: Polity Press.

Hodgson, G. (1994) *Economics and Evolution*. Cambridge: Polity Press.

Hohendahl, P. (1974) Jurgen Habermas: 'The public sphere', *New German Critique*, 3(Fall): 45–8.

Hutton, W. and Giddens, A. (eds) (2001) *On the Edge: Living with Global Capitalism*. London: Vintage.

Jameson, F. (1991) *Postmodernism or the Cultural Logic of Late Capitalism*. London: Verso.

Kalberg, S. (1979) The search for thematic orientations in a fragmented oeuvre: the discussion of Max Weber in recent German sociological literature, *Sociology*, (13): 127–39.

Katz, D. (1994) *Just Do It – The Nike Spirit in the Corporate World*. Holbrook: Adams Publishing.

Keaney, M. (2001) The role of the state in the good society, in M. Keaney (ed.) *Economist with a Public Purpose: Essays in Honour of John Kenneth Galbraith*. London: Routledge.

Keat, R. (1993) The moral boundaries of the market, in C. Crouch and D. Marquand (eds) *Ethics and Markets: Cooperation and Competition within Capitalist Economies*. Oxford: Blackwell.

Kellner, D. (1992) Popular culture and the construction of postmodern identities, in S. Lash and J. Friedman (eds) *Modernity & Identity*. Oxford: Blackwell.

Kellner, D. (1999) Theorizing/Resisting McDonaldization, in B. Smart (ed.) *Resisting McDonaldization*. London: Sage.

Keynes, J.M. (1936) *General Theory of Employment, Interest and Money*. London: Macmillan.

Klein, M. (2001) *No Logo*. London: Flamingo.

Krier, D. (1999) Assessing the new synthesis of economics and sociology: promising themes for contemporary analysts of economic life, *American Journal of Economics and Sociology*, 58(4): 669–96.

Lash, S. and Urry, J. (1987) *The End of Organized Capitalism*. Cambridge: Polity Press.

Lash, S. and Urry, J. (1994) *Economies of Signs and Space*. London: Sage.

Lipietz, A. (1987) *Mirages and Miracles: The Crises of Global Fordism*. London: Verso.

Lyon, D. (1988) *The Information Society: Issues and Illusions*. Cambridge: Polity.

Lyotard, J-F. (1986) *The Postmodern Condition: A Report on Knowledge*. Manchester: Manchester University Press.

Mackintosh, M., Brown, V., Costello, N. *et al.* (1996) *Economics and Changing Economies*. London: International Thomson Business Press.

Maddox, B. (2002) Foreign editor's briefing, *The Times*, 5 February: 12.

Mandel, E. (1975) *Late Capitalism*. London: New Left Books.

Marcuse, H. (1968) *One Dimensional Man*. London: Sphere Books.

Martinelli, A. and Smelser, N.J. (1990) Economic sociology: historical threads and analytic issues, *Current Sociology*, 38(2/3): 1–49.

Marx, K. (1973) *Grundrisse – Foundations of the Critique of Political Economy.* Harmondsworth: Penguin.

Marx, K. and Engels, F. ([1848] 1968) *The Communist Manifesto.* Harmondsworth: Penguin.

Marx, K. and Engels, F. (1953) *Selected Correspondence.* Mocow: Foreign Language Publishing House.

McDowell, L. (1997) *Capital Culture: Gender at Work in the City.* Oxford: Blackwell.

Monbiot, G. (2000) *The Captive State.* London: Pan.

Monbiot, G. (2002) Public fraud initiative, *The Guardian*, 18 June: 17.

Nicholson, H. (2001) National service, *The Times*, 16 January: 8.

Noble, D. (1983) Present tense technology, *Democracy*, 3(2–4).

Noble, D. (1984) *Forces of Production: A Social History of Industrial Automation.* New York: Knopf.

North, D. (1990) *Institutions, Institutional Change and Economic Performance.* Cambridge: Cambridge University Press.

O'Connor, J. (1973) *The Fiscal Crisis of the State.* New York: St Martin's Press.

O'Neill, J. (1998) *The Market – Ethics, Knowledge and Politics.* London: Routledge.

Offe, C. (1985) *Disorganized Capitalism: Contemporary Transformations of Work and Politics.* Cambridge: Polity Press.

Packard, V. (1957) *The Hidden Persuaders.* London: Longman.

Parsons, T. (1934) Some reflections on 'The nature and significance of economics', *Quarterly Journal of Economics*, 48: 511–45.

Parsons, T. (1935a) Sociological elements in economic thought, I: Historical, *Quarterly Journal of Economics*, 49: 414–53.

Parsons, T. (1935b) Sociological elements in economic thought, II: The analytical factor view, *Quarterly Journal of Economics*, 49: 646–67.

Parsons, T. and Smelser, N. (1956) *Economy and Society: A Study in the Integration of Economic and Social Theory.* Glencoe, IL: The Free Press.

Pateman, C. (1989) Feminist critiques of the public/private dichotomy, in *The Disorder of Women: Democracy, Feminism and Political Theory.* Stanford, CA: Stanford University Press.

Philo, G. and Miller, D. (eds) *2001 Market Killing: What the Free Market Does and What Social Scientists Can Do About It.* London: Longman.

Plant, R. (1992) Enterprise in its place: the moral limits of markets, in P. Heelas and P. Morris (eds) *The Values of the Enterprise Culture – The Moral Debate.* London: Routledge.

Polanyi, K. ([1944] 1968) *The Great Transformation: The Social and Economic Origins of Our Time.* Boston, MA: Beacon Press.

Power, M. (1997) *The Audit Society – Rituals of Verification.* Oxford: Oxford University Press.

Putnam, R.D. (1995) Bowling alone: America's declining social capital, *Journal of Democracy*, 6(1): 65–78.

Ray, L. and Sayer, A. (1999) (eds) *Culture and Economy – After the Cultural Turn.* London: Sage.

Rifkin, J. (1995) *The End of Work*, New York: Putnam.

Ritzer, G. (1995) *Expressing America: A Critique of the Global Credit Card Society.* Thousand Oaks, CA: Pine Forge Press.

Ritzer, G. (1998) *The McDonaldization Thesis*. London: Sage.

Robins, K. and Webster, F. (1989) *The Technical Fix: Education, Computers and Industry*. London: Macmillan.

Roszak, T. (1986) *The Cult of Information: The Folklore of Computers and the True Art of Thinking*. Cambridge: Lutterworth Press.

Sayer, A. (1999) Valuing culture and economy, in L. Ray and A. Sayer (eds) *Culture and Economy After the Cultural Turn*. London: Sage.

Sayer, D. (1991) *Capitalism & Modernity – An Excursus on Marx and Weber*. London: Routledge.

Schumpeter, J. (1949) The *Communist Manifesto* in sociology and economics, *Journal of Political Economy*, 57: 199–212.

Schumpeter, J. ([1918] 1954a) The crisis of the tax state, *International Economic Papers*, 4: 5–38.

Schumpeter, J. (1954b) *History of Economic Analysis*. London: Allen & Unwin.

Sennett, R. (1998) *The Corrosion of Character: The Personal Consequences of Work in the New Capitalism*. New York: W.W. Norton.

Sennett, R. (1999) Growth and failure: the new political economy and its culture, in M. Featherstone and S. Lash (eds) *Spaces of Culture – City, Nation, World*. London: Sage.

Sennett, R. (2001) Street and office: two sources of identity, in W. Hutton and A. Giddens (eds) *On the Edge: Living with Global Capitalism*. London: Vintage.

Simmel, G. (1990) *The Philosophy of Money*. London: Routledge.

Slater, D. and Tonkiss, F. (2001) *Market Society – Markets and Modern Social Theory*. Cambridge: Polity.

Smart, B. (1983) *Foucault, Marxism and Critique*. London: Routledge.

Smart, B. (1992) *Modern Conditions, Postmodern Controversies*. London: Routledge.

Smart, B. (1999) *Facing Modernity – Ambivalence, Reflexivity and Morality*. London: Sage.

Smart, B. (2000) A political economy of new times? Critical reflections on the network society and the ethos of informational capitalism, *European Journal of Social Theory*, 3(1): 51–65.

Smart, B. (2002) Accounting for anxiety: economic and cultural imperatives transforming university life, in D. Hayes and R. Wynyard (eds) *The McDonaldization of Higher Education*. London: Bergin & Garvey.

Smelser, N. (1990) Interview, in R. Swedberg (ed.) *Economics and Sociology – Redefining their Boundaries: Conversations with Economists and Sociologists*. Princeton, NJ: Princeton University Press.

Smelser, N. and Swedberg, R. (eds) (1994) *The Handbook of Economic Sociology*. Princeton, NJ: Princeton University Press.

Solow, R.M. (1990) Interview, in R. Swedberg R (ed.) *Economics and Sociology – Redefining their Boundaries: Conversations with Economists and Sociologists*. Princeton, NJ: Princeton University Press.

Soros, G. (1997) The capitalist threat, *The Atlantic Monthly*, 297(2): 45–58.

Soros, G. (1998) *The Crisis of Global Capitalism*. London: Little, Brown.

Steiner, P. (2001) The sociology of economic knowledge, *European Journal of Social Theory*, 4(4): 443–58.

Stelzer, I. (2002) Government: big is beautiful once again, *The Sunday Times*, 20 January: 6.

Swedberg, R. (ed.) (1990) *Economics and Sociology – Redefining their Boundaries: Conversations with Economists and Sociologists.* Princeton, NJ: Princeton University Press.

Swedberg, R. (1994) Markets as social structures, in N.J. Smelser and R. Swedberg (eds) *The Handbook of Economic Sociology.* Princeton, NJ: Princeton University Press.

Tenbruck, F.H. (1989) The problem of thematic unity in the works of Max Weber, in K. Tribe (ed.) *Reading Weber.* London: Routledge.

Thompson, E.P. (1967) Time, work-discipline and industrial capitalism, *Past and Present,* 38.

Tickell, A. and Peck, J.A. (1995) Social regulation after Fordism: regulation theory, neo-liberalism and the global-local nexus, *Economy and Society,* 24(3): 357–86.

Turner, B.S. (1999) *Classical Sociology.* London: Sage.

Velthuis, O. (1999) The changing relationship between sociology and institutional economics: from Talcott Parsons to Mark Granovetter, *American Journal of Economics and Sociology,* 58(4): 629–49.

Wacquant, L.J.D. (1999) America as social dystopia: the politics of urban disintegration, or the French uses of the 'American Model', in P. Bourdieu, *The Weight of the World: Social Suffering in Contemporary Society.* Cambridge: Polity Press.

Walzer, M. (1983) *Spheres of Justice.* London: Martin Robertson.

Weber, M. (1964) *The Theory of Social and Economic Organization.* London: Free Press.

Weber, M. (1970) *From Max Weber – Essays in Sociology,* edited with an introduction by H.H. Gerth and C. Wright. London: Mills, Routledge & Kegan Paul.

Weber, M. (1976) *The Protestant Ethic and the Spirit of Capitalism.* London: Allen & Unwin.

Weber, M. (1978a) Anticritical last word on *The Spirit of Capitalism, American Journal of Sociology,* 83(5): 1105–31.

Weber, M. (1978b) *Economy and Society – An Outline of Interpretive Sociology,* vols 1 & 2, edited by G. Roth and C. Wittich. London: University of California.

Weber, M. (1989) The national state and economic policy, in K. Tribe (ed.) *Reading Weber.* London: Routledge.

Webster, P. (2001) Brown seeks volunteers for hospitals, *The Times,* 11 January: 1.

Weintraub, J. (1997) The theory and politics of the public/private distinction, in J. Weintraub and K. Kumar (eds) *Public and Private in Thought and Practice – Perspectives on a Grand Dichotomy.* London: University of Chicago Press.

Weintraub, J. and Kumar, K. (eds) (1997) *Public and Private in Thought and Practice – Perspectives on a Grand Dichotomy.* London: University of Chicago Press.

Wolfe, A. (1997) Public and private in theory and practice: some implications of an uncertain boundary', in J. Weintraub and K. Kumar (eds) *Public and Private in Thought and Practice – Perspectives on a Grand Dichotomy.* London: University of Chicago Press.

Young, J. (1999) *The Exclusive Society – Social Exclusion, Crime and Difference in Late Modernity.* London: Sage.

Zafirovski, M. (1999) Economic sociology in retrospect and prospect: in search of its identity within economics and sociology, *American Journal of Economics and Sociology,* 58(4): 583–627.

INDEX

GENDER AND SOCIAL THEORY

Mary Evans

- What is the most significant aspect of current literature on gender?
- How does this literature engage with social theory?
- How does the recognition of gender shift the central arguments of social theory?

We know that gender defines and shapes our lives. The question addressed by *Gender and Social Theory* is that of exactly how this process occurs, and what the social consequences, and the consequences for social theory, might be. The emergence of feminist theory has enriched our understanding of the impact of gender on our individual lives and the contemporary social sciences all recognise gender differentiation in the social world. The issue, however, which this book discusses is the more complex question of the extent to which social theory is significantly disrupted, disturbed or devalued by the fuller recognition of gender difference. We know that gender matters, but Mary Evans examines whether social theory is as blind to gender as is sometimes argued and considers the extent to which a greater awareness of gender truly shifts the concerns and conclusions of social theory. Written by an author with an international reputation, this is an invaluable text for students and an essential reference in the field.

Contents
Introduction – Enter women – The meaning of work – The world of intimacy – The gendered self – The real world – Now you see it, now you don't – Notes – Bibliography – Index.

c.160pp   0 335 20864 9 (Paperback)   0 335 20865 7 (Hardback)

GENERATIONS, CULTURE AND SOCIETY

June Edmunds and Bryan S. Turner

... the most important statement since Mannheim's classic work. It establishes a traumatic events theory of generations, and elaborates a model of generational conflict ... All this is demonstrated through illuminating analyses ... For Edmunds and Turner, generations rather than classes have shaped much of the 20th century and beyond.

> Professor Randall Collins, University of Pennsylvania

... clearly establishes the relevance of generations as a key sociological concept for understanding cultural change today ... an excellent book that offers students and academics a lively and up-to-date text on the role and significance of generations, with comprehensive coverage of social scientific debates.

> Gerard Delanty, Professor of Sociology, University of Liverpool

- What is the role of generations in social, cultural and political change?
- How is generational consciousness formed?
- What is the significance of inter- and intra-generational conflict and continuity?

Despite the importance of the concept of generations in common sense or lay understanding of cultural change, the study of generations has not played a large part in the development of sociological theory. However, recent social developments, combined with the erosion of a strong class theory, mean that generations need to be reconsidered in relation to cultural change and politics. Moving beyond Karl Mannheim's classical contribution to generations, this book offers a theoretically innovative way of examining the role of generational consciousness in social, cultural and political change through a range of empirical illustrations. On the grounds that existing research on generations has neglected international generational divisions, the book also looks at the interactions between generations and other social categories, including gender and ethnicity, exploring both intra-generational conflict and continuity and considering the circumstances under which generational consciousness may become more salient. The result is a key text for undergraduate courses in social theory, cultural studies and social history, and an essential reference for researchers across these areas, as well as gender, race and ethnicity.

Contents

160pp   0 335 20851 7 (Paperback)   0 335 20852 5 (Hardback)

RISK

Roy Boyne

- Is risk always measurable?
- Why are some risks more important?
- Do we take a lot more risks now?
- On whom can we rely for advice?
- How critical is the sociology of risk for understanding contemporary society?

The term 'risk' occurs throughout contemporary social analysis and political commentary. It is now virtually a legal requirement that large organizations throughout the world establish formal risk assessment and risk management procedures. Increasingly dense communication and media networks alert huge numbers of people and organizations to a widening range of threats and possibilities. A basic understanding of the risks themselves may require specific technical knowledge of basic chemistry, or the psychology of motivation, or of contrasting interpretations of injustices deep within the past. However, at the same time as attending to specific risks, there are general questions such as those above which invite reflection.

This wide-ranging and concisely written text is devoted to these general questions, exploring issues such as the measurement of risk in its social context, the idea that the mass media or the political opposition always exaggerate risk, and the notion that the advice of the expert is the best we can get as far as risks are concerned. It asks if there are more risks now and whether a certain level of risk is inevitable or even desirable, and considers for example whether interference with nature has led us to a world which is just too full of risks. Each chapter in the book builds towards a basic picture of risk in the contemporary world, and of the place of the concept of risk within the social sciences today.

Contents
Acknowledgements – The limits of calculation – Risk in the media – Cultural variation or cultural rapture? – Risk-taking – Expert cultures – Risk society? – References – Index.

c.160pp   0 335 20829 0 (Paperback)   0 335 20830 4 (Hardback)

MAKING SENSE OF SOCIAL MOVEMENTS

Nick Crossley

... effectively demonstrates the enduring importance of 'classical' social movement theory ... and provides a cutting edge critical review of recent theoretical developments. This is one of the most important general theoretical texts on social movements for some years.

Paul Bagguley, University of Leeds

- Why and how do social movements emerge?
- In which ways are social movements analysed?
- Can our understanding be enhanced by new perspectives?

Making Sense of Social Movements offers a clear and comprehensive overview of the key sociological approaches to the study of social movements. The author argues that each of these approaches makes an important contribution to our understanding of social movements but that none is adequate on its own. In response he argues for a new approach which draws together key insights within the solid foundations of Pierre Bourdieu's social theory of practice. This new approach transcends the barriers which still often divide European and North American perspectives of social movements, and also those which divide recent approaches from the older 'collective behaviour' approach. The result is a theoretical framework which is uniquely equipped for the demands of modern social movement analysis. The clear and concise style of the text, as well as its neat summaries of key concepts and approaches, will make this book invaluable for undergraduate courses. It will also be an essential reference for researchers.

Contents
Introduction – Social unrest, movement culture and identity: the symbolic interactionists – Smelser's value-added approach – Rational actor theory – Resources, networks and organizations – Opportunities, cognition and biography – Repertoires, frames and cycles – New social movements – Social movements and the theory of practice: a new synthesis – References – Index.

c.192pp   0 335 20602 6 (Paperback)   0 335 20603 4 (Hardback)